Hon. Nathaniel P. Banks,
With the regards of the author

Gen. Banks, pp. 79, 90, 158.

CHARLES COWLEY.

VIEW OF LOWELL.

A

HISTORY OF LOWELL.

SECOND REVISED EDITION.

BY CHARLES COWLEY.

BOSTON:
LEE & SHEPARD.
LOWELL:
B. C. SARGEANT AND J. MERRILL & SON.
1868.

Press of Stone & Huse, Lowell.

PREFACE.

In an age so prolific in works of local history as ours, no apology need be offered for publishing this History of Lowell. Successors of the Pawtucket and Wamesit Indians,—heirs of the founders of American Manufactures,—contemporaries of the men of the "Legion of Honor," who went hence to defend the Nationality of America, and who, dying on the field of battle, have risen to enduring renown;—the people of Lowell are to-day in possession of a certain body of memories and traditions, not current elsewhere, but kept alive here by local associations, by the presence of historical objects, and by the local press.

Of these memories and traditions Lowell is justly proud. From them her people receive an educational stimulus not to be despised. She would no more part with these local reminiscences than Plymouth would part with her Pilgrim history, or than New York would forget those Knickerbocker memories, among which the genius of Irving is enshrined forever.

To gather and embalm all that seemed most valuable in this heritage of memories and traditions, has been the object of the present work, which covers the whole period from the discovery of the Merrimack River by De Monts, in 1605, to the year of Grace 1868.

The first edition, or rather the original germ, of this work, was published in 1856. With the aid of a mass of materials laboriously gathered during the last twelve years, I may hope that the value of the work has been greatly increased. The narrative has been thoroughly revised, and very much enlarged.

Several engravers of established reputation were employed to execute illustrative cuts. Many of these are well done: but some are so badly executed that, perhaps, an apology is due for their insertion in these pages; and others have been rejected altogether.

Materials were at hand for a much larger volume, or even for several volumes; but I have aimed to be concise,—considering Moses, who, in two lines, chronicled the creation of a world, (*pace* Colenso,) a much better model for the local annalist than he who filled several volumes with the burning of a Brunswick Theatre.

How far I have succeeded in the accomplishment of this self-imposed task, my readers must judge; and they will form the most charitable judgments, who best appreciate the great difficulties under which such a task must be prosecuted. If I have not wholly failed of my purpose, the work will possess attractions for all who are identified with Lowell, and perchance may descend to the Lowellians of the Future, and be read with interest hereafter, when he who wrote it shall have passed away.

THE AUTHOR.

March 4th, 1868.

HISTORY OF LOWELL.

CHAPTER I.

FROM THE DISCOVERY OF THE MERRIMACK TO THE INTRODUCTION OF MANUFACTURES.

Geology of the Merrimack—Discovery of the Merrimack—De Monts—Champlain—Concord River—Indian Rendezvous at Lowell—John Eliot—Gen. Gookin—Billerica—Chelmsford—Wamesit Reservation—Indians—Passaconaway—Wannalancet—Indian War—King William's War—Dracut—Purchase of Wamesit—Tewksbury—Convention in Dracut—Bunker Hill Incidents—Simeon Spaulding—Shay's Rebellion—Slavery—Pawtucket Canal—Bridge over the Merrimack—Middlesex Canal—Timber Trade.

HERODOTUS, with fine felicity, calls Egypt a gift from the Nile. In a similar sense, Lowell may be called a gift from the Merrimack. Her history, also, may be well begun with that noble artery of nature, the waters of which move the great wheels of her industry.

Long after America was upheaved from the bosom of the Atlantic, a chain of lakes occupied the valleys of the Merrimack and its tributaries, from the mountains to the sea. Proofs of this appear in the alluvial formation of these valleys, the shapes of their basins, their outlets, their different levels, and the stratified character of the soil. One of these lakes extended westward from Pawtucket Falls; and the limits of several others may be easily defined.* But long before the dawn of history, and probably long before man appeared on the earth, the attrition of the waters in the channels of these lakes, by widening and deepening their outlets, gradually diminished their depth, and at length left their basins dry.

* Potter's Manchester, p. 24; Fox's Dunstable, p. 8.

The draining of these lakes increased the volume of water which the Merrimack rolled down to the main.

The head of the Merrimack is at Franklin in New Hampshire, where the Winnepesawkee, the outlet of the lake of that name, unites with the Pemigewasset, an artery of the White Mountains. Like all the great rivers on the Atlantic slope, the Merrimack pursues a southerly course. But after following this course from Franklin to Tyngsborough, a distance of eighty miles, the Merrimack, unlike any other stream on the Atlantic, makes a detour to the north-east, and even runs a part of the way north-west. It is obviously unnatural that, after approaching within twenty miles of the head-waters of the Saugus, as the Merrimack does on entering Massachusetts, it should suddenly change its course, and pursue a circuitous route of more than forty miles to the sea. If the history of by-gone ages could be restored, we should probably find the Merrimack discharging its burden at Lynn, and not at Newburyport.

Changes like this, however, are not unfamiliar to geologists. Sometimes they have been caused by earthquakes, but more often, in these latitudes, by ice-gorges.* Whether this deflection in the course of the Merrimack was caused by subterranean convulsions, or by the formation in the old channel of an ice-blockade, cannot now be known ; but the fact of the change is unquestionable.

The discovery of the Merrimack took place under the auspices of Henry the Fourth, commonly called Henry the Great, whose reign forms one of the most brilliant eras in the annals of France. In 1603, Pierre Du Gua, Sieur de Monts, one of the ablest of the Huguenot chiefs, obtained a patent from this king, creating him Lieutenant-General and Vice-Admiral, and vesting in him the government of New France, which em-

---

* On earthquakes on the Merrimack, see Coffin's Newbury; on ice-floods, Hitchcock's Geology of Massachusetts, Part III.

braced all our Eastern and Middle States, together with the Dominion of Canada. On the seventh of March, 1604, De Monts sailed from Havre with an expedition for colonizing "Acadia," as his new dominions were called. He arrived on the sixth of April, and began at once the great work of exploration and settlement.* While talking with the Indians on the banks of the river St. Lawrence, in the ensuing summer, he was told by them that there was a beautiful river lying far to the south, which they called the Merrimack.† The following winter De Monts spent with his fellow-pioneers on the island of St. Croix, in Passamaquoddy Bay, amid hardships as severe as those which, sixteen years later, beset the Pilgrims at Plymouth.

On the eighteenth of June, 1605, in a bark of fifteen tons,—having with him the Sieur de Champlain, several other French gentlemen, twenty sailors, and an Indian with his squaw,—De Monts sailed from the St. Croix, and standing to the south examined the coast as far as Cape Cod. In the course of this cruise, on the seventeenth of July, 1605, he entered the bay on which the city of Newburyport has since arisen, and discovered the Merrimack at its mouth. The Sieur de Champlain, the faithful pilot of De Monts, and chronicler of his voyages, has left a notice of this discovery in a work which ranks among the most romantic in the literature of the sea. In closing this notice Champlain says: "Moreover, there is in this bay a river of considerable magnitude, which we have called Gua's River."‡

---

* Parkman's Pioneers of France in the New World.

† *Relationes des Jesuites*, 1604.

‡ *Plus y a en icelle bay une riviere qui est fort spaciuese, laqulle auons nomme la riviere du Gas* [*Gua*].—*Voyages en la Nouvelle France*, ed. 1632, p. 80 (Harvard University Library). In Potter's Manchester, and Chase's Haverhill, Captain Champlain himself is erroneously credited with the discovery of the Merrimack. The romantic career of Champlain, "the father of New France," is graphically sketched by Dr. Parkman, in his Pioneers of France in the New World. His works are soon to be published by the University of Lasalle.

Thus De Monts named the Merrimack from himself; but the compliment was not accepted. Regardless of the name with which it was baptized by its discoverer, the Merrimack clung, with poetic justice, to the name which it received from the Indians long before the flag of the Vice-Admiral floated over Newburyport Bay. The visit of Admiral De Monts, like that of Capt. John Smith in 1614, was attended with no result. Other renowned names were yet to be inscribed on the list of the visitors of the Merrimack. But its song was the song of Tennyson's brook:—

"For men may come and men may go,
But I roll on forever."

The King had stipulated, in his patent of New France, that De Monts should establish in Acadia the Roman Catholic creed, *("la foy catholique, apostolique et romaine;")* a singular condition indeed, considering that De Monts was a Protestant, and that Henry himself was only a "political Catholic." The expenses of the three expeditions which he sent to New France were ruinous to De Monts. Cabals were formed by his enemies; neither the loftiest motives nor the finest abilities could save him; and the tragic death of Henry by the dagger by Ravaillac, in 1610, completed his ruin as a public man. He died about the year 1620.*

In 1635, thirty years after the discovery of the Merrimack, the Concord, which the Indians called the Musketaquid, assumed a place in civilized history; the fame of its grassy meadows and of the fish that swarmed in its waters attracting settlers from England, who established themselves at Concord.‡

From a period too remote to be determined by either history or tradition, until after the great Indian Plague of 1617, Pawtucket Falls on the Merrimack, and Wamesit Falls on the

* See Haag's *Vies des Protestants Francais* (Boston Public Library).

‡ Thoreau's Week on the Concord and Merrimack Rivers; Reynold's Agricultural Survey of Middlesex County, in Transactions of Mass. Society for Promoting Agriculture, 1859; Shattuck's Concord.

Concord, were the sites of populous villages of Pawtucket or Pennacook Indians, who, indeed, remained, though with greatly diminished numbers, in the present territory of Lowell, forty years after the plague. Here, in spring-time, from all the circumjacent region, came thousands of the dusky sons and daughters of the forest, catching, with rude stratagem, their winter's store of fish. Here they sat in conclave round the council fire. Here they threaded the fantastic mazes of the dance. "Here was the war-whoop sounded, and the death-song sung; and when the tiger strife was over, here curled the smoke of peace."

The Pawtuckets, or Pennacooks, were among the most powerful tribes in New England, numbering, after the plague, several thousand souls. Their territory stretched almost from the Penobscot to the Connecticut, and included the whole of New Hampshire, a part of Massachusetts, and a part of Maine. At the head of this tribe, the first English settlers found the sagacious and wary Passaconaway, who, in 1644, after more than twenty years' observation of the progress of the English settlements, signed an agreement which is still preserved, renouncing his authority as an independent chief, and placing himself and his tribe under the colonial authorities.*

In 1647, the Rev. John Eliot, "the Apostle of the Indians," began a series of missionary visits to this place, which were continued by him till the villages of Wamesit and Pawtucket ceased to be. In 1656, Major-General Daniel Gookin was appointed Superintendent of all the Indians under the jurisdiction of the Colony, among whom were the Indians living here. Thus a sort of Indian Bureau was established, not unlike the Freedmen's Bureau of a later day. The Apostle Eliot and Judge Gookin won the entire confidence of the Indians, being about the only white men that came among them who did not come to rob them.

* I omit the details of the Indian history of Lowell, and refer the reader to my historical lecture on the "Memories of the Indians and Pioneers" of this region, published, in pamphlet form, in 1862.

In 1652, Captain Simon Willard and Captain Edward Johnson, under a commission from the colonial government, ascended the Merrimack in a boat, and surveyed the valley as far as Lake Winnepesawkee. A new impetus was given to the work of settlement, which, as early as 1653, reached the vicinity of Lowell. On the twenty-ninth of May, 1655, the General Court incorporated the town of Chelmsford, and also the town of Billerica.*

To secure the Indians from being dispossessed of their lands, on which they had erected substantial wigwams, made enclosures, and begun the business of agriculture, Eliot, in 1653, procured the passage of an act by the General Court, reserving a good part of the land on which Lowell now stands to the exclusive use of the Indians. The bounds of Chelmsford, and also of this Wamesit Indian Reservation, were modified and enlarged by the General Court in 1656 and in 1660. About 1665, a ditch, traces of which are still visible, was cut to mark the bounds of the Indian reservation; beginning on the bank of the Merrimack, above the Falls, and running thence southerly, easterly, and northerly, in a semi-circular line, including about twenty-five hundred acres, and terminating on the bank of the Merrimack, about a mile below the mouth of the Concord.

The year 1660 was signalized by an event claiming notice in this narrative, though it is uncertain whether it took place here or where Manchester now stands: the retirement of Passaconaway. Burdened with the weight of about four score years, this veteran chief gave a grand though rude banquet, which was attended by a vast concourse of chiefs, braves, and other Indians of every degree, together with a representation of the new race that was now claiming the ancient abode of the red man. Transferring his sachemship to his son, Wannalancet, the old chief made a farewell address, of which we

---

* Allen's Chelmsford; Myrick's Billerica; Barber's Historical Collections.

have the following report,—which is, perhaps, as trustworthy as the reports of speeches in the pictured pages of Livy:—

"I am now going the way of all the earth; I am ready to die, and not likely to see you ever met together any more. I will now leave this word of counsel with you: Take heed how you quarrel with the English. Harken to the last words of your father and friend. The white men are the sons of the morning. The Great Spirit is their father. His sun shines bright about them. Never make war with them. Sure as you light the fires, the breath of heaven will turn the flame upon you and destroy you."

The local sachem of this place during several succeeding years was Numphow, who was married to one of Passaconaway's daughters. But in 1669, Wannalancet and the Indians of Concord, New Hampshire, fearing an attack from the Mohawks, came down the Merrimack in canoes, took up their abode at Wamesit, and built a fort for their protection on the hill in Belvidere, ever since called Fort Hill, which they surrounded with palisades. The white settlers of the vicinity, participating in this dread of the Mohawks, shut themselves up in garrison houses.

In 1674, Gookin computed the Christian Indians then in Wamesit at fifteen families, or seventy-five souls, and the adherents of the old faith, or no-faith, at nearly two hundred more. At this time, the Indian magistrate, Numphow, the archetype of Judge Locke and Judge Crosby, held a monthly court, taking cognizance of petty offences, in a log cabin, near the Boott Canal. An Indian preacher, Samuel, imparted to his clansmen his own crude views of Christianity at weekly meetings in a log chapel near the west end of Appleton street. In May of each year came Eliot and Gookin, who held a court having jurisdiction of higher offences, and gave direction in all matters affecting the interests of the village. Numphow's cabin was Gookin's court-house, and Samuel's chapel was

Eliot's church. Wannalancet held his court as chief in a log cabin near Pawtucket Falls.

In 1675, came King Phillip's War, during which Wannalancet and our local Indians, faithful to the counsels of Passaconaway, either took part with the whites, or remained neutral. Their sufferings in consequence of this were most severe. Some of them were put to death by Phillip for exposing his designs; some of them were put to death by the colonists as Phillip's accomplices; some fell in battle in behalf of the whites; while others fell victims to the undiscriminating hatred of the low whites, whose passions, on the least provocation, broke out with hellish fury against the "praying Indians." In one instance, in 1676, when all the able-bodied Indians had fled to Canada, and when six or seven aged Indians, blind and lame, were left here in wigwams, too infirm to be removed, a party of scoundrels from Chelmsford came to Wamesit by night, set fire to these wigwams and burned all the invalids to death.* What is worse, so depraved was public sentiment during that period, these wanton and cowardly murderers were allowed to go unpunished. It was impossible to find a jury that would return a verdict of guilty against a white man who had killed an Indian, no matter under what circumstances of atrocity the murder had been committed.

During this war the white settlers in this region were gathered for protection in garrisons. Billerica escaped harm; but Chelmsford was twice visited by the partisans of Phillip, and several buildings were burned. Two sons of Samuel Varnum, living in what is now Dracut, were shot while crossing the Merrimack with their father in a boat.

In April, 1676, Captain Samuel Hunting and Lieutenant James Richardson, under orders from the Governor and Council, erected a fort at Pawtucket Falls, in which a garrison was

---

* See more of these atrocities in Cowley's Indian and Pioneer Memories; Gookin's Christian Indians in Transactions of the American Antiquarian Society, vol. 2; Oliver's Puritan Commonwealth; Willard Memoir.

placed, under command of Lieutenant Richardson. A month later, the garrison was reinforced, and Captain Thomas Henchman placed in command. This put an effectual check to the incursions of Phillip's party in this part of the colony.

When the war was over, and Wannalancet returned to Wamesit with the remains of his tribe, he found his corn fields in the hands of the whites, and he himself a stranger in the land of his fathers. By order of the General Court, he and his people were placed on Wickasauke Island, in charge of Colonel Jonathan Tyng of Dunstable. In 1686, Colonel Tyng, Major Henchman, and others, purchased of Wannalancet and his tribe all their remaining lands in this region, leaving them only their rights of hunting and fishing. At length, after passing through various vicissitudes, and doing numerous acts of kindness in return for the injuries which the colonists had inflicted on him, Wannalancet joined the St. Francis tribe in Canada, and ended his days among them.

During the nine years of King William's War, which followed the English Revolution of 1688, the people of all the towns of this region again took refuge in forts and fortified houses. The fort at Pawtucket Falls was occupied by a garrison under command of Major Henchman. But this did not entirely save them. On the first of August, 1692, a party of Indians, in league with the French in Canada, made a raid into Billerica, and killed eight of the inhabitants. On the fifth of August, 1695, a similar party made a raid into what is now Tewksbury, and killed fourteen of the people. A party of three hundred men, horse and foot, under Colonel Joseph Lynde, scoured all the neighboring country in vain, in search of the foe. From this officer, Lynde's Hill in Belvidere derives its name—he having fortified it, and for some time occupied it with his command.

In 1701, the town of Dracut was incorporated. It contained twenty-five families, and had previously formed a part of

Chelmsford.* It took its name from a parish in Wales, the original home of the Varnums.

Subsequent to the "Wamesit Purchase," made by Tyng and Henchman, already mentioned, the lands of the Indian Reservation were purchased in small parcels by various persons, who settled upon them as upon other lands in Chelmsford. But in 1725, when Samuel Pierce, who had his domicil on the Indian Reservation, was elected a member of the General Court, he was refused his seat, on the ground that he was not an inhabitant of Chelmsford. Thereupon the people of East Chelmsford, as Wamesit was then called, refused to pay taxes to Chelmsford; and to remedy this mischief, an act was passed annexing Wamesit to that town.

On the twenty-ninth of October, 1727, occurred the greatest earthquake ever known in this country. Walls and chimneys fell, and all the towns on the Merrimack suffered severely.

In 1734, the General Court incorporated the town of Tewksbury, the territory of which had previously belonged to Billerica. It took its name from the English parish of Tewksbury, on the Severn, in Gloucestershire, so famous in history as the scene of one of the bloodiest battles in the "Wars of the Roses." There the partisans of the House of York, under Edward the Fourth, and the partisans of the House of Lancaster, under the Amazonian Margaret, Queen of Henry the Sixth, encountered each other's battle-axes for the last time. There, after the battle, a Prince of Wales was barbarously murdered by two royal Dukes. There the glory of the royal House of Lancaster was eclipsed in blood.

In 1745, occurred the siege and capture of Louisburg. To the army which Sir William Pepperell led from Massachusetts against that renowned fortress, belonged young John Ford, and perhaps others, from what is now Lowell.

At the battle of Bunker Hill, two companies of Chelmsford men, one under Captain John Ford, the other under Captain

* Lowell Citizen and News, October, 1859.

Benjamin Walker, and one company composed largely of Dracut men, under Captain Peter Colburn, were present, and acquitted themselves with credit. There are two traditions connected with this event which must not be lost, notwithstanding the gigantic battles of the late Rebellion have thrown all the engagements of the Revolution into the shade. It is said that when the first man in Ford's company fell, his comrades, then for the first time under fire, were seized with panic; but thereupon one of Ford's officers began to sing Old Hundred in a firm voice, and this so reassured the men that they gave no further sign of panic. The other tradition of this battle is, that, just as the ammunition of the Americans was exhausted, and orders were given to retreat, a British officer mounted the breastworks, and, with a flourish of his sword, exclaimed, "Now, my boys, we have you." Hearing this, Captain Colburn of Dracut picked up a stone, about the size of a hen's egg, and, throwing it with all his might, hit the officer in the forehead, knocking him down backwards. The Captain and his men then hastily retreated with the rest of the American forces.

In November, 1776, committees from all the towns of this region met in convention at the house of Major Joseph Varnum in Dracut, and petitioned the colonial legislatures of Massachusetts and New Hampshire for a law to regulate prices, which had been fearfully enhanced by the Revolutionary War, then pending.* The proceedings of this convention show that its members participated in that ignorance of the principles of political economy, which was universal till the time of Adam Smith, and which is by no means dispelled in the days of John Stuart Mill.

This region has the honor of having contributed one of the most useful, though not one of the most brilliant, statesmen who served the American Colonies in their struggle for national independence—Simeon Spaulding of Chelmsford. He was a

*New Hampshire Historical Collections, vol. 2, pp. 58-68.

Colonel of Militia when the duties of the Militia, and the protection which it afforded, made that office one of real importance. From 1771 to 1775 he was a member of the General Court. From 1775 to 1778 he served in the Provincial Congress, and during one of these years was Chairman of the Committee of Public Safety. He was also a member of the Convention of 1779, which framed the State Constitution. He died in 1785.*

During Shay's Rebellion, in 1786, a body of Chelmsford Militia served under General Lincoln in the western counties; and "on the memorable thirtieth of January," as Allen writes, "performed a march of thirty miles, without refreshment, through deep snows, in a stormy and severely cold night; a march that would have done honor to the veteran soldiers of Hannibal or Napoleon."

The people of Chelmsford, from the earliest period of their local history, gave every encouragement to millers, lumbermen, mechanics, and traders, making grants of land, with temporary exemption from taxation, to such as would settle in their town. Accordingly, Chelmsford became distinguished for its saw-mills, grist-mills, and mechanics' shops of various kinds. Establishments of the same kind also arose in Billerica, Dracut and Tewksbury.

It is but fair, though far from flattering, to record the fact, that the mother towns of Lowell were among the last to abandon slavery.† Till near the beginning of the present century, negro slaves were kept on what is now the Moor farm, and also on what afterward became known as the Livermore place, where Phillip Gedney, a former British Consul at Demarara, then resided.

Toward the close of the last century, this region became the theatre of an active business in wood and lumber. The forests along the shores of the Merrimack, which had never

---

* Allen's Chelmsford; Lowell Courier, September 23—29, 1859.

† See Moore's Slavery in Massachusetts.

before rung with the sound of the woodman's axe, afforded an exhaustless supply of materials for rafts, which already commanded a good price at Newburyport and other towns on the sea-board. But the descent of the river at Pawtucket Falls was so precipitous,—the current so violent, and the channel so rocky,—that great difficulty was experienced in passing rafts down the rapids. A canal round the falls for the passage of boats, rafts and masts was first suggested for the convenience of the lumbermen, thirty years before any one dreamed of using the waters for the purpose of manufactures; though from about the time of the Revolution there had been a saw-mill below Pawtucket Falls, driven by the Merrimack. It was owned about this time by John Tyng of Tyngsborough, a Judge of the Court of Common Pleas.

In 1792, Dudley A. Tyng, William Coombs, and others, were incorporated as "The Proprietors of the Locks and Canals on Merrimack River."* They at once proceeded to open a canal, one and a half miles long, connecting Merrimack River above the falls with the Concord below. The level of the water in the lower end of the canal, a brief distance above the mouth of the Concord, was thirty-two feet lower than the level of the water at the upper end. The descent was accomplished by means of four sets of locks. The canal occupied less than five years in its construction, and cost fifty thousand dollars.

When the first boat passed down the canal in 1797, with the directors and other gentlemen on board, and hundreds of men, women and children as spectators on the banks, an incident occurred, of which Allen gives a very lively account. One side of the canal gave way; the water burst upon the the people, and the greatest confusion ensued. "Infants were separated from their mothers, children from their parents, wives from their husbands, young ladies from their gallants; and men, women, timber, and broken boards and planks, were seen promiscuously floating in the water." *Nantes—rari ap-*

* 7 Mass. Rep. p. 168.

parent in gurgite vasto. But no life was lost, and no serious injury incurred.

The stock of the Locks and Canals Company was divided into five hundred shares, owned by individuals in Middlesex and Essex Counties. But the dividends declared were never considerable; and the stock soon fell far below par in consequence of the successful competition of the Middlesex Canal with the business.

In the same year that the Locks and Canals Company were incorporated, Parker Varnum of Dracut and others were incorporated as "The Proprietors of the Middlesex Merrimack River Bridge," and the first bridge across the Merrimack was constructed by them at Pawtucket Falls. It was entirely of wood. Previous to this time, the only public conveyance over the Merrimack was by a toll ferry-boat. The Concord had been bridged nearly twenty years earlier.

In 1793, the Proprietors of the Middlesex Canal were incorporated. Mr. Weston, an eminent English engineer, was employed to survey the channel of the canal; and Loammi Baldwin of Woburn superintended its construction, and was the animating soul of the work. This canal began on the Merrimack, about a mile above Pawtucket Falls, extended south by east a distance of thirty-one miles, and terminated in Charlestown. It was completed in 1804, and cost seven hundred thousand dollars. It was twenty-four feet wide and four feet deep, and was fed by Concord River. In digging this canal, pine cones and charcoal were found, twelve feet below the surface, specimens of which were long exhibited in the Museum at Cambridge. The excavations made for this canal, and also those previously made for the Pawtucket Canal, disclosed unmistakable proofs that the channel of the Merrimack, in this vicinity, was once a considerable distance south and west of its present situation—that the Merrimack formerly ran by the southwest side of Fort Hill, instead of by the northeast side.

This Canal was the first in the United States that was opened for the transportation of passengers and merchandise; and some are still living who were often passengers in the neat little packet-boat, "Governor Sullivan," which plied between Boston and Lowell, through the waters of the Middlesex Canal, occupying nearly the whole day in the passage. Connecting Boston with the upper Merrimack, the channel of which was navigable the entire distance from Pawtucket Falls up to Concord, it formed an important artery for the lumber business, which had long been very extensive here, as well as for the new industries then in process of development. Vast quantities of timber grown around Winnepesawkee Lake, on the Merrimack and its branches, and on Massabesic Pond, and the produce of a great extent of fertile country, were transported to Boston by this canal.*

The first boat voyage from Boston, by the Middlesex Canal and the Merrimack River, to Concord, (N. H.), was made in the autumn of 1814. The first *steamboat* from Boston reached Concord in 1819. Had this canal been kept open until now, it is difficult to see why it might not still be profitably conducted. But its day has gone by, and its history may as well be ended here as hereafter.

As the competition of the Middlesex Canal ruinously reduced the value of the property of the Pawtucket Canal, so, in the retributive justice of years, other competition—the introduction of railroads—extinguished the value of the stock of the Middlesex Canal. A striking example of "the revenges of history." In 1853, navigation was discontinued in the canal, and soon afterward portions of its banks were levelled, and parts of the channel filled up. The income of the stock hardly averaged three and a half per cent.; and the proprietors, hopeless of any better dividends, disposed of all their saleable property, and abandoned their franchise, of which

* See Armory's Life of Governor Sullivan.

they had once been proud. On the third of October, 1859, the proprietors were declared, by a decree of the Supreme Judicial Court, to have forfeited all their franchises and privileges, by reason of non-feasance, non-user, misfeasance and neglect. Thus was the corporation forever extinguished.

CHAPTER II.

INTRODUCTION OF MANUFACTURES.

Modern Factory System—Inventors—Kay—Paul—Wyatt—Hargreaves—Highs—Arkwright—Peel — Crompton—Watt — Cartwright — Bell — Berthollet—Scheele—Chivalry of Industry—France—Manufactures in the United States—Beverly—Byfield—Samuel Slater — Moses Hale—War of 1812—Phineas Whiting—Josiah Fletcher—Oliver M. Whipple—Thomas Hurd—Winthrop Howe—Bridge over the Concord—Asahel Stearns—General Varnum.

The rise of the modern Factory System marks one of the grandest epochs in the progress of mankind. The arts of carding, spinning, weaving, bleaching, dyeing and printing cotton, woollen and linen fabrics, have been practiced from the remotest ages of history, and were practiced in pre-historic times. Scarcely a century has elapsed since these arts were pursued as mere domestic handicrafts. No progress of moment had been made in them, no new implements had been introduced, for a thousand years. But during the closing forty years of the last century, these arts were raised from a state of utter insignificance to a national and world-wide importance, and were developed into the most elaborate and mature system of industry the world has ever seen.

As the great inventions which wrought this wonderful change were achieved long before the building of Lowell, a rapid account of them will be all that the purposes of this history require. But they can hardly be passed unnoticed, for without them Lowell must have remained a border hamlet of an obscure town.

The first modern invention that led to any important improvement in manufacturing, was John Kay's fly-shuttle, patented in 1733, but strange to say, not introduced into this country for more than fifty years after it was first used in England.

In 1738, Lewis Paul obtained a patent for the first machinery for spinning,—invented, several years before, by John Wyatt. In 1740, manufacturing was commenced at Manchester, England. In 1748, Paul obtained a patent for the first cylinder carding-machine. In 1758, he obtained another patent for improved machinery for spinning.

In 1760, Robert Kay invented the drop-box, by which filling of different colors could be used in weaving with the fly-shuttle. In the same year, James Hargreaves constructed a carding-machine corresponding substantially with the carding-machines now in use. Two years later, Hargreaves obtained a patent for the spinning-jenney, which, however, seems to have been invented, in 1764, by Thomas Highs.

In 1769, Richard Arkwright obtained a patent for his spinning frame or throstle. Six years later, he obtained another patent for improvements in carding, drawing and spinning. In 1779, Robert Peel, father of the celebrated statesman, obtained a patent for improved machinery of the same kind. In the same year, Samuel Crompton combined the excellencies of Hargraves' jenny with Arkwright's throstle, in a new spinning-machine, which, from its hybrid nature, he called a mule.

These triumphs of inventive skill led to the substitution, first, of horse-power for hand-power, and then of water-power for horse-power. The year 1789 was signalized by the application of steam-power to manufacturing purposes, one of James Watt's engines being introduced in a factory in Manchester.

In 1785, the Rev. Samuel Cartwright took out his first patent for the power-loom. Other similar patents were afterward taken out by him and by others; but power-loom weaving realized only partial success until after the dressing-frame had been invented by Radcliff, Ross and Johnson in 1803; and 1806 is the accepted date of the successful introduction of the power-loom into Manchester in England.

In 1785, Thomas Bell obtained his patent for cylinder printing. Calico printing, however, had been introduced by the Claytons, twenty years before. In the same year, Berthollet first applied chlorine (then called dephlogisticated muriatic acid) to bleaching. But Scheele, a Swedish chemist, had discovered the properties of chlorine in destroying vegetable colors, ten years prior to its application by Berthollet in France.

Thus, as an able writer says, "while Burke was lamenting the fall of chivalry, while Hastings was extending the British Empire in the East, and while Pitt was initiating his retrograde policy, men of that class which was destined to reap the most benefit from the transformation, were inaugurating the industrial system, destined to succeed the first, utilize the second, and destroy the third. From the weaver's cottage at Blackburn, and from the barber's shop at Preston, went forth powers as pregnant with consequences to Britain [and to the world] as ever issued from the Parliament-House at Westminster, or the Council-Chamber in Bengal."*

Other nations followed. In France, the genius of Napoleon introduced the Cotton Manufacture, including yarns, cloths, and prints. "Before the Empire, the art of spinning cotton was not known in France; and cotton clothes were imported from abroad."†

These inventions of the mechanical genius of Europe soon found their way to the United States. The first machinery for carding and spinning cotton put in operation in this country, was started at Beverly, in Massachusetts, in 1787, and was driven by horse-power. Other cotton factories were soon

* Westminster Review, April, 1861.

† Napoleon the Third's *Napoleonic Ideas*, p. 69.

PAWTUCKET FALLS AND BRIDGE.

afterward established in Connecticut, Rhode Island, New York, Pennsylvania, Delaware and New Jersey. But the year 1793—the same year in which Eli Whitney gave to the world his invaluable legacy of the Cotton Gin—is the generally accepted date of the Cotton Manufacture in the United States, since it was during that year that Samuel Slater—"the father of the Cotton Manufacture in America"—started his first cotton factory, with Arkwright machinery, driven by water-power, at Pawtucket in Rhode Island. By a singular coincidence of dates, in the same year, the first factory in this country, for carding and spinning *wool* by machinery, was started at Byfield in Massachusetts.

At the commencement of the present century, the cotton and woollen factories of Great Britain were counted by hundreds: and, perhaps, a dozen such factories had been started in the United States.*

This rapid survey of the rise of modern manufactures brings us to the starting of the first carding machine in the region of Lowell. It was in 1801 that Moses Hale, whose father had long before started a fulling mill in Dracut, established his carding mill on River Meadow Brook,—the first enterprise of the kind in Middlesex County. This mill still stands, between Hale's Mills and Whipple's Mills, and was one of the mills which for many years were run by the late Joshua Mather, a native of Preston, the town of Richard Arkwright, the great inventor and systematizer of cotton-spinning machinery in England. A saw-mill was also started about the same time by Mr. Hale, on the same stream.

In 1805, the bridge built across Merrimack River at Pawtucket Falls in 1792, was demolished, and a new bridge, with stone piers and abutments, constructed in its place, at a cost exceeding fourteen thousand dollars. This bridge is still

*See Batchelder's valuable little book on the Cotton Manufacture; Bains' History of the Cotton Manufacture in Great Britain; Bishop's History of American Manufactures; White's Memoir of Samuel Slater, etc.

standing, though essential improvements have been made in it from time to time. It was made free in 1860.

The year 1812 brought the second war between the United States and Great Britain, when British cruisers swept our commerce from the seas. Until then, most of our manufactured goods had been imported from England. Domestic manufactures there were comparatively none, except such domestic fabrics as were spun upon the spinning-wheel, and woven upon the hand-loom, by the dames of the rural districts. No sooner was importation stopped by the war, than imported fabrics commanded famine prices. Public attention was irresistibly attracted, and a powerful impetus given, to American manufactures. Large investments of capital were made; and mills started up all over the Union, but more especially in Massachusetts. Such of them as were started here, were driven by Concord River power. No "wizard of mechanism" had yet laid his hand on the lordly Merrimack, and put it on duty, like a chained convict or a galley slave.

In 1813, twenty-six years after the first attempt in the United States to manufacture cotton by machinery was made at Beverly, Captain Phineas Whiting and Major Josiah Fletcher erected a wooden cotton-mill on the present site of the Middlesex Company's mills, at an outlay of about three thousand dollars, and carried on the business with some success. John Golding entered upon a similar enterprise near by, about the same time, but failed.

The year 1815 is associated with the tradition of the most disastrous gale that had swept New England since the famous gale of 1635, when the tide rose twenty feet perpendicularly in Narragansett Bay. It was particularly severe in the town of Chelmsford, then including Lowell. It "spread the ruin round," like a devastating fire. Not less than fifty thousand cords of standing timber, besides several houses, were destroyed,—the trees being torn up by the roots, and the houses removed from their foundations.

The saw-mill and grist-mill of the Messrs. Bowers, at Pawtucket Falls, were started in 1816. About the same time, another grist-mill was started by Nathan Tyler, where the Middlesex Company's Mill No. 3 now stands. At the junction of the Concord and Merrimack rivers, stood the saw-mill of Captain John Ford. There is a tradition, not very well authenticated, that Captain Ford once killed an Indian by pitching him into the wheel-pit of this saw-mill; the Indian being on the watch for a chance to take the life of the captain, who had killed one of his brothers during a former war.

In 1818, Moses Hale started the powder-mills on Concord River, with forty pestles. Mr. Oliver M. Whipple and Mr. William Tileston of Boston engaged in the business with Mr. Hale in 1819. In 1821, Whipple's Canal was opened by them. In the same year, Moses Hale disposed of his interest in the business to David Hale, who retained his connection with it till 1827, when he in turn sold out to his partners, and became editor of the New York *Journal of Commerce*. Mr. Tileston retired in 1829, and Mr. Whipple remained as sole proprietor till 1855, when the manufacture of powder was discontinued in Lowell. The business was enlarged from time to time, and was in its zenith during the Mexican War. Nearly a million pounds of powder were manufactured here during a single year of that contest. Mr. Whipple amassed a handsome fortune by the manufacture of this "destructive element." When Mr. Whipple first came to Lowell, in 1818, his whole capital was but six hundred dollars. His subsequent success in his business operations entitles him to a high place among those who, without the aid of inherited wealth, make their own fortunes, and conquor their own position in the world.

In 1818, Thomas Hurd removed to East Chelmsford (as we must still call Lowell), and purchased the cotton mill, started five years before, by Whiting & Fletcher. He converted it into a woollen mill, and ran sixteen hand-looms for the manufacture of satinets. He also built a larger brick mill for the manufacture of the same class of goods. Mr. Hurd's mill was destroyed by fire, and rebuilt in 1826. About this time, being in want of additional power, he built the Middlesex Canal, conveying water from Pawtucket Canal to his satinet mills. Mr. Hurd was the first man in this country who manufactured satinet by water-power, having had a mill at Stoneham before he came to Lowell. He continued to run these works until the great re-action of trade in 1828, when he became bankrupt, and the property, in 1830, passed into the hands of the Middlesex Company.

About the time of Mr. Hurd's appearance here, Winthrop Howe started a mill for the manufacture of flannels at Wamesit Falls in Belvidere. Mr. Howe continued to manufacture flannels by hand-looms till 1827, when he sold his mill to Harrison G. Howe, who introduced power-looms in lieu of hand-looms, and continued the business till 1831, when he sold it to John Nesmith and others.

The bridge built across the Concord near its mouth in 1774, was demolished in 1819, and its place supplied by a superior structure. The bridge on East Merrimack Street, connecting Belvidere with the main part of the city, stands near the site of the bridge of 1819, the last-named bridge having been several times renewed.

The dam across Concord River at Massic Falls, where Richmond's Batting Mills now stand, was constructed about this time, and a Forging Mill established, by Messrs. Fisher & Ames. Their works were considerably extended in 1823, and continued by them till 1836, when they sold their privilege to Perez O. Richmond.

While new men were thus coming to this place, an old and distinguished resident—Asahel Stearns—removed elsewhere. He was the pioneer lawyer of this vicinity, and has scarcely had a superior among all his successors. He was born at Lunenburg, June 17, 1774, and graduated at Harvard in 1797. He was educated for the bar, admitted to practice about 1800, and married the same year. He opened an office near Pawtucket Falls, where he practiced law till 1817. He was for several years District Attorney; Member of Congress in 1815–17; and in the latter year was appointed Professor of Law at Harvard, which position in 1829 he resigned. He published, in 1824, a work of much celebrity on the Law of Real Actions, and was a Commissioner with Judge Jackson and Mr. Pickering to revise the Statutes of the Commonwealth. He died at Cambridge, February 5, 1839, in the sixty-fifth year of his age. He was a learned and skillful lawyer, a zealous advocate, a gentleman of suavity, integrity and kindness.

Within a few years after the removal of Mr. Stearns, occurred the death of the most distinguished man of the Merrimack Valley—Major-General Varnum of Dracut. Born in 1751, Joseph B. Varnum had accomplished the "three score years and ten" which the Psalmist allots to man, when, in 1821, he received that summons which no child of mortality can ever disobey. The record of his life shows him to have been continually in office; and the traditions that have survived him represent him as a man of extraordinary native powers, highly developed, not so much by books as by contact with men and events. He was a Captain of Militia at the age of eighteen, through the Revolution, and until 1787, when he became a Colonel. In 1802, he was made Brigadier-General, and three years later Major-General, which rank he retained till his death. From 1780 to 1795, he was an active member of the Massachusetts Legislature. As President of the Senate, he presided at the trial of Judge Prescott, and had a rough "passage" with Daniel Webster, who was Prescott's counsel. He was a member of the Convention which framed the State Constitution in 1780, and of the Convention which revised it in 1820. From 1795 to 1817, he was a member of Congress; for four of these years he was Speaker of the House, and for one year he was President *pro tempore* of the Senate. The traveller from Lowell on the Methuen road often turns aside, in passing through Dracut, to read his epitaph on the head-stone which stands where his ashes repose.

CHAPTER III.

THE FIRST MANUFACTURING CORPORATION.

The Waltham Company—The Lowell Family—Judge Lowell—John Lowell—Francis C. Lowell—Patrick T. Jackson—Nathan Appleton—Introduction of the Power-Loom—Paul Moody—Death of Francis C. Lowell—John Lowell, Junior.

ONE of the most interesting events connected with the early history of the Cotton Manufacture in America, was the introduction of the power-loom, in 1814, at Waltham. The chief actor in this enterprise was FRANCIS CABOT LOWELL, from whom our city was so appropriately named. Among the others were Patrick Tracy Jackson, Nathan Appleton, and Paul Moody, who afterward became the fathers of Lowell, and introduced here "the Waltham system," in all its details of factory machinery, factory boarding-houses, and wages paid monthly in cash. Some account of these men and of this Waltham enterprise must therefore be given before we proceed to the building of the mills at Lowell.

The Lowells are among the most distinguished families in America, and are the descendants of Percival Lowell, who emigrated from Cleaveland, near Bristol, in England, and settled in Newbury in 1639. The first member of this family who achieved any particular distinction was the Hon. John Lowell, father of Francis Cabot Lowell, and son of the Rev. John Lowell, the first minister of Newburyport. He was a leading member of the Provincial Assembly in 1776, and of the Convention which framed the Constitution of Massachusetts in 1780. He was the principal champion of the movement for the abolition of slavery in this State in 1783,—an active and influential member of the Continental Congress,—Judge of the Court of Appeals in Admiralty, appointed by Congress,—and the first Judge of the District Court of Massachusetts, by appointment of President Washington.

Judge Lowell died in 1802. His sons all rose to distinction. One of them, John Lowell, always refused to accept public office, but wielded a controlling influence in the Federal party for more than twenty years,—held the highest rank in the profession of the Law,—was one of the founders of the Massachusetts General Hospital, the Boston Athenæum, the Boston Savings Bank, the Hospital Life Insurance Company, and other institutions for the public good, and died of apoplexy in 1840, at the age of seventy years.

Francis Cabot Lowell, another son of the distinguished Judge Lowell, was born in Newburyport, April 7th, 1774, and graduated at Harvard in 1783. He engaged in mercantile business, with good success, in Boston. His friend and associate, Patrick Tracy Jackson, was also born in Newburyport, in 1780, and was the son of the Hon. Jonathan Jackson, who was a member of the Continental Congress in 1782, and filled other distinguished positions in State and Nation. As Marshal of the District of Massachusetts, by appointment of President Washington, the father of Mr. Jackson served the monitions, etc., issued by the father of Mr. Lowell, as Judge of the District Court.

Nathan Appleton was one year senior to Mr. Jackson, and five years junior to Mr. Lowell, having been born in 1779, at New Ipswich in New Hampshire. In 1794, he engaged in commercial pursuits, at Boston, with his brother, Samuel Appleton, whose partner he became as soon as he attained his majority, in 1800. In the next year, business called him to Europe. While in France, he met Napoleon Bonaparte, then firmly seated in the Consular Chair, and preparing to ascend the Imperial Throne,—his star burning brightly in the zenith, — his brow radiant with the glory of Marengo. In 1810, Appleton's business again called him to Europe. In 1811, at Edinburgh, he met his Boston friend, Francis Cabot Lowell; and the meeting, as we shall see, proved prolific of results.

The restraints imposed on commerce, which finally culminated in the war of 1812, led Mr. Lowell to close his business as a merchant; and in 1810, on account of the feebleness of his health, he visited England with his family, and spent two years in that country and in Scotland. While there, his mind became deeply impressed with the importance of manufacturing industry as a source of national wealth; and he took pains to make himself master of all the information that was obtainable, touching the machinery and processes that had been introduced by the manufacturers of Great Britain, with a view to their introduction into the United States. It was while full of these plans that he met Mr. Appleton at Edinburgh, as already stated. Mr. Appleton entered readily into his designs, urged him to go on with them, and promised coöperation.

In 1813, Lowell returned to Boston, with a fixed idea that the Cotton Manufacture, then monopolized by Great Britain, could be successfully introduced here. He saw and admitted that the advantages of cheap labor, abundant capital, superior skill, and established reputation, were all on the side of the English. But the raw cotton could be procured cheaper here; water-power was more abundant than in England; and he thought that the superior intelligence and enterprise of the American population would ensure the success of the Cotton Manufacture in these States, in spite of the competition of all Europe.

Mr. Lowell communicated these ideas to his brother-in-law and fellow-townsman, Patrick Tracy Jackson, whose business had been suspended by the war then flagrant between Great Britain and the United States. Jackson eagerly enlisted in the enterprise, and was not discouraged by difficulties which would have thwarted a less resolute man. The result was, the incorporation of Messrs. Lowell, Jackson, Appleton and others as the Boston Manufacturing Company, with a capital of one hundred thousand dollars, followed by the purchase of water-power at Waltham, and the successful starting of the power-loom in 1814.*

The Waltham power-loom, in so far as it differed from the power-loom previously introduced in Great Britain, was the sole product of Mr. Lowell's genius; and his success is the more remarkable from the fact that he had no model to go by, but only his own recollections of his observations in Europe, aided by imperfect drawings, brought with him on his return.

Being in want of a practical mechanic, Mr. Lowell and his associates secured Paul Moody, whose mechanical skill was well known, and whose success fully justified the choice. Mr. Moody was born in Amesbury in 1777, and had been for some time engaged in the manufacturing business in that town, in connection with Mr. Ezra Worthen. His aid was invaluable in the starting of the first mill at Waltham, though he did not remove to reside there till 1814.

The original design of Messrs. Lowell and Jackson was only to start a weaving-mill, and to buy their yarn of others. No such establishment as a mill where raw cotton was manufactured into finished cloth, without going through different hands, and forming two distinct businesses, was then dreamed of. The practice was to run spinning-mills and weaving-mills as separate establishments. But as soon as their loom was completed, they found it expedient to spin their own yarn, rather than to buy it of others. They accordingly fitted up a mill with seventeen hundred spindles, at Waltham.

Their sizing-machine they constructed by improving upon Horrock's dressing-machine, patented in England. Mr. Lowell and Mr. Moody both had a hand in the invention of their double-speeder for spinning. The mathematical scholarship of Mr. Lowell was as indispensable to its success as the mechan-

---

* The first *broad* power-loom was constructed and started in 1817, at Goshen, Conn., by Lewis M. Norton, who obtained the idea of it from the Edinburgh Encyclopædia. Mr. Norton, however, realized poor success in the manufacture of broadcloth. See his Letter to Samuel Lawrence, Lowell *Courier*, April 22, 1843.

ical ingenuity of Mr. Moody. The peculiar invention of Mr. Moody was the filling-throstle. The machines invented or improved by these ingenious men were substantially the same as those now in use, though subsequent inventions have still further improved and perfected them.

The enterprise proved a splendid success; the capital stock of the Company was increased, first to four hundred thousand, and afterward to six hundred thousand dollars, and the business extended as far as the water-power of Waltham and Watertown would permit. The original suggestion and most of the chief plans were made by Mr. Lowell, who was the informing soul of the whole proceeding; and when the enterprise was fairly started, the general management of it was committed to Mr. Jackson.

While cotton cloth was selling at thirty-three cents per yard, Mr. Lowell, fired with the presentiment of what his plans would accomplish, predicted to a friend, that "within fifty years, cotton cloth would be sold for four-pence a yard." The prediction was called "visionary" then; but it has long since been realized. Our far-sighted adventurers were frequently advised, by meddlesome outsiders and gossiping Mrs. Grundys, that they would soon overdo their new business. No sooner did one mill send forth its cloth, than all agreed that it would be the last. The markets would be glutted. Goods would lie by, and rot in the warehouses. Bankruptcy, ruin, pauperism, would ensue. But our adventurers kept right on, paying no attention to the Mrs. Grundys. True, they saw not all the future, nor "half the wonders that would be;" but they remained firm in the conviction that by improved machinery they could compete successfully with England in all the markets of the globe; and experience has proved that this conviction was not without foundation.

The peace of 1815 proved ruinous to many of our manufacturers, whose business had been greatly inflated by the war. In 1816, a new tariff was to be made; and Mr. Lowell visited

Washington, to impress upon members of Congress the importance, the prospects and the dangers of the Cotton Manufacture, and the policy of shielding it from foreign competition by legislative protection. Constitutional objections have often, in more recent times, been urged against the protective system. No objection of this kind was then heard of. The New England States were too exclusively engaged in commerce to listen to him; but the Middle States favored the new plan. The States of the West were divided; the South, as usual, held the balance of power; and Mr. Lowell's appeal to the interests of the Southern planters prevailed. The famous minimum duty of 6¼ cents per square yard on imported cotton fabrics was proposed by Mr. Lowell, recommended by Mr. Lowndes, advocated by Mr. Calhoun, and incorporated into the tariff of 1816.

In this way, American Manufactures were protected from British competition, and nursed into a vigorous life. It is to this provision of law, says Mr. Everett, that "New England owes that branch of industry which has made her amends for the diminution of her foreign trade; which has kept her prosperous under the exhausting drain of her population to the West; which has brought a market for his agricultural produce to the farmer's door; and which, while it has conferred these blessings on this part of the country, has been productive of good, and nothing but good, to every portion of it."

The whole credit of this policy is due to Mr. Lowell. But he did not live to witness the realization of his plans. "Man proposes, but God disposes." He died in Boston, September 2d, 1817, at the age of forty-three; and committed to others the completion of his vast designs. Like his brother, the eminent lawyer, he shunned public office; but he contributed more than a thousand of the common herd of hum-drum statesmen to the advancement of national industry and well-being. As Mr. Everett eloquently says: "In the great Temple of Nature,—whose foundations are the earth,—whose pillars are the eternal hills,—whose roof is the star-lit sky,—whose organ tones are the whispering breeze and the sounding storm,—whose architect is God,—there is no ministry more sacred than that of the INTELLIGENT MECHANIC."*

His son, John Lowell, was worthy of his sire. Wandering amid the ruins of Thebes, and feeling the approaches of death, by his last will, "penned with a tired hand on the top of a palace of the Pharaohs," he made a princely bequest of $240,000 to found the Lowell Institute at Boston.

CHAPTER IV.

MANUFACTURING HISTORY OF LOWELL.

Purchase of Pawtucket Canal—First Visit—Merrimack Company—Reconstruction of the Canal—Kirk Boott—Ezra Worthen—Paul Moody—Warren Colburn—Calico Printing—John D. Prince—Management of the Merrimack Company—Re-organization of the Locks and Canals Company—James B. Francis—Hamilton Company—Samuel Batchelder—Management of the Hamilton—Appleton Company—Lowell Company—Proposed Reform in Sales—Middlesex Company—Ruin and Re-organization—Suffolk Company—Tremont—Lawrence—Bleachery—Boott Company—Belvidere Company—Perez O. Richmond—Massachusetts Company—Dismissal of Operatives—Men of whom more might have been made—Whitney Mills—Machine Shop—Prescott Company—Miscellaneous Manufacturers and Mechanics—Increased Productivity in the Future.

In 1821, Messrs. Appleton and Jackson, elated with the splendid success of their establishment at Waltham, were looking about for water-power for operations on a more gigantic scale. In September, 1821, they examined the water-fall at Souhegan, but found it insufficient. In returning, they passed the Nashua River, but they were not aware of the existence of the fall which the Nashua Company have since improved;

* See Edward Everett's Memoir of John Lowell; Robert C. Winthrop's Memoir of Nathan Appleton; John A. Lowell's Memoir of Patrick T. Jackson; Nathan Appleton's Introduction of the Power-Loom and Origin of Lowell, etc.

neither were they aware of the existence of the water-power of the Pawtucket Canal. Shortly afterwards, Mr. Moody, while on a visit to Amesbury, mentioned to Ezra Worthen that the company at Waltham were in quest of water-power. Mr. Worthen had been familiar with Pawtucket Falls from his boyhood, and very naturally replied, "Why don't they buy up Pawtucket Canal? That will give them all the power of Merrimack River. They can put up as many mills as they please there, and never want for water."

On returning to Waltham, Mr. Moody went out of his way to look at the canal, and Mr. Worthen accompanied him. Arriving at Waltham, they related to Mr. Jackson a description of the place, and Mr. Worthen chalked out upon the floor a map of Merrimack River, including both Pawtucket Falls and the Canal. Mr. Jackson listened eagerly to their story, and was soon convinced that a large manufacturing town could here be built up. The great idea of possessing himself of the whole power of Merrimack River filled his mind; and with characteristic sagacity, he at once put himself in communication with Thomas M. Clark, of Newburyport, the Agent of the Pawtucket Canal Company, and secured the refusal of most of the shares of the stock of that Company at less than par.

Mr. Appleton and Kirk Boott entered eagerly into the enterprise with Mr. Jackson, and, through the agency of Mr. Clark and others, all the stock of the Canal Company was purchased, and some of the lands needed for using the water-power. But the wisest men cannot foresee everything. Four farms, containing about four hundred acres, covering what is now the most densely peopled portion of Lowell, were bought at from one to two hundred dollars per acre; and most of the lands thus purchased were afterward sold at from twelve cents to a dollar per foot. But there was a great deal more land which the founders of Lowell then overlooked; and when these lands were wanted, the proprietors were shrewd enough to fix their own prices, and at a pretty high figure too.

The value of land was of course suddenly largely enhanced. For example:—Nine undivided tenths of the Moses Cheever farm were bought in 1821 for eighteen hundred dollars; and the owner of the other one-tenth had agreed to convey the same for two hundred dollars. Before he had conveyed it, however, he died, suddenly, insolvent; and the one-tenth was sold by order of court. But such had been the increase in its value, that the Locks and Canals Company paid upward of three thousand dollars for seven and a half-tenths of it; and the remaining two and a half-tenths were sold, one year afterward, for upward of five thousand dollars.*

In November, 1821, Nathan Appleton, Patrick T. Jackson, Kirk Boott, Warren Dutton, Paul Moody, and John W. Boott, made a visit to the canal, perambulated the ground, and scanned the capabilities of the place; and the remark was made that some of them might live to see the place contain twenty thousand inhabitants. Nathan Appleton did, indeed, live to see it contain nearly forty thousand. Here, in the vicinity of Boston, was a river, with a water-shed of four thousand square miles, delivering its volume of water over a fall of thirty feet. Evidently, the Manchester of America was to be here.

On the fifth of February, 1822, these gentlemen and others were incorporated as the Merrimack Manufacturing Company, with Warren Dutton as President. Their capital, at first, was $600,000; but this capital has been four times increased, and is now $2,500,000. The first business of the new company was to erect the dam across the Merrimack at Pawtucket Falls, widen and deepen Pawtucket Canal, renew the locks, and open a lateral canal from the main canal to the river, on the margin of which their mills were to stand. Five hundred men were employed in digging and blasting, and six thousand pounds of powder were used. The canal, as reconstructed, is sixty feet

---

* Miles's Lowell as it Was and as it Is.

wide, and eight feet deep, and capable of supplying fifty mills. It has three sets of locks.

In deepening this canal, ledges were uncovered, which showed indisputable marks of the attrition of water. Many cavities were found in the ledge, such as are usual where there are water-falls, worn by stones kept in motion by the water. Some of these cavities measured a foot or more in diameter, and two feet in depth. Here had once been the channel of the Merrimack.

The first mill of the company was completed, and the first wheel started, September 1st, 1823. The first return of cloth was made in the following November. The bricks used in building the mills of this and the succeeding manufacturing corporations, were boated chiefly from Bedford and Merrimack, in New Hampshire.

The first Treasurer and Agent was Kirk Boott. He was born in Boston in 1791, and received an academic education at the famous Rugby School in England. He entered Harvard College, but never graduated. His tastes being military, a commission was purchased for him; and he served five years as an officer in the British Army. He fought under Wellington in the Peninsular War, and commanded a detachment of troops at the siege of San Sebastian, in 1813. His courage was perfectly bullet-proof. When the wars of Napoleon ended with his captivity at St. Helena, Boott resigned his commission, and, in 1817, returned to Boston. Through the intimacy that arose between him and Mr. Jackson, while the latter was agent of the mills at Waltham, he was employed as the company's agent. He established himself here in the spring of 1822, took charge of the mills, and infused into the whole place much of his own determined spirit and unconquerable will. He became, by the general consent of all, *the man* of the place, so that for fifteen years the history of Lowell was little more than the biography of Kirk Boott.

Ezra Worthen removed here at the same time with Mr. Boott, and his services as superintendent were of inestimable value. Like Mr. Lowell, Mr. Worthen was not permitted to see even "the beginning of the end" of his plans. He died June 18th, 1824.

Mr. Moody also removed here from Waltham, in 1823, and took the charge of the company's machine shop. This shop was completed in 1825, and cost one hundred and fifty thousand dollars. He remained in this position during a period of eight years, when his labors were terminated by death, July 5th, 1831. Born and bred a mechanic, Mr. Moody was none the less a gentleman. Skill in mechanism was his forte; but his general capacity was large; and when he died, all felt that one of the ablest citizens, and one of the most estimable men, had fallen.

The place left vacant by Mr. Worthen, in 1824, was subsequently filled by Warren Colburn, the distinguished author of a series of popular school-books on Arithmetic. Mr. Colburn was born in Dedham in 1793, and graduated at Harvard University in 1820, at the ripe age of twenty-seven years. He was distinguished while at college for his assiduous devotion to the mathematics. After graduating, he engaged as a school-teacher in Boston, and while thus employed prepared those works on Arithmetic which have forever intimately associated his name with that science. Prior to Mr. Worthen's decease, Mr. Colburn had acquired some experience in charge of the mills at Waltham. His abilities were such as amply enabled him to fill Mr. Worthen's place. "He readily perceived and appreciated the peculiar character of a manufacturing community in New England, and projected at once a scheme of lecturing, adapted to popular improvement."* He actually delivered in Lowell several courses of the best Lyceum Lectures, several years before any popular Lyceums were organized at all. He

* See Edson's excellent Memoir of Warren Colburn, in Barnard's American Journal of Education, September, 1856.

died September 13th, 1833. Though he filled no higher offices than those of factory superintendent, church warden, school committee, college committee, lyceum lecturer and writer of school-books, Mr. Colburn was nevertheless one of the great men of America. Here he will be especially remembered for his efforts, in connection with Rev. Dr. Edson, to build up, upon a permanent basis, that complete system of public schools, which is the pride of the place.

The successors of Mr. Colburn as Superintendents of the Merrimack Mills have been, from 1833 to 1848, John Clark; in 1848, Emory Washburn, afterward Governor of the Commonwealth; in 1849, Edmund Le Breton; from 1850 to 1866, Isaac Hinckley, who was succeeded by John C. Palfrey.

The founders of the Merrrimack Company had from the first contemplated the introduction of calico-printing. "I was of opinion," says Appleton, "that the time had arrived, when the manufacture and printing of calicos might be successfully introduced into this country."* And although calicos were probably printed at Taunton and Dover before they were at Lowell, the attempt was first begun here, under Allan Pollock. The printing business, however, was not perfected to any considerable degree until 1826, when the late John D. Prince, senior, resigned his position at Manchester in England to take the Superintendency of the Merrimack Print Works. Here he remained till 1855, when Henry W. Burrows succeeded him. The skill of Mr. Prince, assisted by Dr. Samuel L. Dana as chemist, won for the Merrimack Prints an unequalled renown in all parts of the globe. On his retirement, the Company gave him an annuity of $2,000 per annum. He did not, however, live long to enjoy it, but died suddenly, January 5th, 1860, at the age of eighty years, leaving to us, and to the Lowellians of the future, the grateful memory of a fine old English gentlemen,—"one of the real old stock,"—

* Origin of Lowell, p. 17.

who dispensed to his friends a baronial hospitality, and to the poor a charity that was as liberal as his own resources.

The Merrimack Company have divided upon an average a dividend of thirteen per cent. on their stock. For many years, fabrics bearing their imperial name have commanded a cent a yard more than the fabrics of other companies equal in cost and equal in intrinsic quality. Such a result can only be ascribed to the consummate ability of the Company's managers. Voltaire said, he knew many merchants in Amsterdam, of more penetration and administrative ability than Ximenes, Mazarin or Richelieu. So may we say, that the men whose sagacity achieved such remarkable success in the business of manufacturing, were men of far higher calibre than those who have generally presided over the Executive Departments at Washington.

During the late War, however, the Merrimack Company showed great "lack of sagacity and forethought"*—in stopping their mills—in dismissing their operatives—in discontinuing the purchase of cotton—and in selling their fabrics at a slight advance on their peace prices, and at less than the actual cost of similar fabrics at the time of sale. Had they not committed this stupendous blunder, they might have realized many millions of dollars during the War. But instead of boldly running, as companies elsewhere did, they took counsel of their fears, and their spacious mills stood on the bank

"As idle as a painted ship upon a painted ocean."

The blunders of this company were naturally copied by others—the younger companies being accustomed to "dress" on the Merrimack. In this instance, the blunders of the older company were not only copied, but exaggerated and intensified to a fatal degree. The other cotton companies actually sold out their cotton, and several of them made abortive experiments in other branches of manufactures, by which they incurred

*Report of the Committee of the Proprietors, 1863.

MERRIMACK MILL, NO 6.

losses, direct and indirect, exceeding the amount of their entire capital. It is but fair to add, that most of these abortive experiments were made in opposition to the judgment of the local agents.

The Merrimack have five mills and print works, with 100,000 spindles, and 2,450 looms. When all are in operation, they employ 1,700 females and 700 males. Their weekly consumption of cotton is 80,000 pounds, and their return of cloth 450,000 yards. They print 500,000 yards per week of Prints, No. 30 to 37, and Chintzes.

In 1825, the old Locks and Canals Company of 1792 was reēstablished as a separate corporation. The Merrimack Company, at the time of their incorporation, owned the original charter of the Locks and Canals Company, the entire water-power of Merrimack River, and the lands abutting thereon. The Proprietors of the Locks and Canals were now reorganized, with an amendment to their charter, allowing them to purchase, hold, sell or lease land and water-power, to the amount of $600,000. The Merrimack Company conveyed to the Locks and Canals Company all their water-power and all their lands; and then so much of it as was required for their own purposes, was reconveyed to the Merrimack Company. By this arrangement, the Merrimack Company was placed upon the same basis as other manufacturing companies more recently established. The Locks and Canals Company had other objects to pursue. The affairs of this company, in addition to those of the Merrimack, were placed in the master hand of Kirk Boott. On the death of Mr. Boott, in 1837, Joseph Tilden became Agent for one year, when Patrick T. Jackson succeeded him. Mr. Jackson was succeeded for a short time by William Boott. In 1845, James B. Francis was appointed Agent, and in this position, which he has ever since retained, he has earned the distinction of the best water-engineer in the United States. He had been eleven years engineer of this company, when the duties of Agent were superadded to his duties as engineer. At first,

5

he was associated with that excellent engineer, George W. Whistler, father of James Whistler, the gifted artist.

For twenty years, the business of this company was, to furnish land and water-power, and build mills and machinery for the various manufacturing companies successively organized in Lowell. After all the mill-powers were disposed of, another re-organization took place. The standard adopted for a mill-power was the power required to run the second mill built at Waltham, which contained 3584 spindles,—or the right to draw twenty-five cubic feet of water per second, on a fall of thirty feet, being about sixty horse power.* This company have never engaged in manufacturing operations. They kept in operation two machine shops, a foundry, and a saw-mill, until 1845, when the Lowell Machine Shop was incorporated to take the charge of this business. They constructed all the mill-canals to supply the various companies with water-power, and erected most of the mills, and the boarding-houses attached to them, together with most of the machinery which they severally contain. They employed constantly from five to twelve hundred men, and built two hundred and fifty thousand dollars worth of machinery per annum. The stock was long the best of which Lowell could boast, being worth thrice, and even four times its par value. Their present business is to superintend the use of the water-power, which is leased by them to the several companies. Their stock is held by these companies in the same proportion in which they hold the water-power.

The first sale of water-power was to the Hamilton Manufacturing Company, incorporated in 1825, with a capital of $600,000, afterward increased to $1,200,000. The first Agent of this Company was Samuel Batchelder. It was under his skillful management that the power-loom was here first applied to twilled and fancy goods, and that cotton drills were first manufactured. Mr. Batchelder was born at Jaffrey, in New Hampshire, in 1784, five years before the first cotton mill was started

* Appleton's Origin of Lowell, p. 28.

in America. He assisted in starting one of the first cotton mills in his native State, in 1807. On quitting the Hamilton, he assisted in establishing the York Mills at Saco, Maine, of which he has been for many years Treasurer, as well as of the Everett Mills at Lawrence. With his remarkable business habits, he has always combined the love of books; and his work on the Cotton Manufacture is one of the most valuable contributions yet made to the literature of that prolific theme. Mr. Batchelder was followed in the Agency of the Hamilton, in 1831, by the late John Avery, to whom in 1864 Oliver H. Moulton succeeded.

Following the example of the Merrimack, the Hamilton Company established Print Works, of which the late William Spencer was Superintendent till his death, September 27th, 1862. William Hunter was then appointed Superintendent, and to him in 1863 succeeded William Harley.

The management of the Hamilton during the War was particularly unfortunate. Not only were the mistakes of the Merrimack repeated here; but—what was worse—when the War was drawing to a close, the Hamilton threw out a large portion of their cotton machinery, and put in a lot with which to manufacture woollen goods, and purchased a large stock of fine wool, paying for this machinery and wool the ruinous prices which the War had entailed. Thus, they superadded to their losses by the War, a new category of losses caused by the collapse of prices on the return of peace.

The Hamilton have five mills and print works, with 51,268 spindles and 1,348 looms, requiring the labor of 850 females and 425 males. Their weekly consumption of cotton is 50,000 pounds, and of clean wool 10,000. Their weekly product is 235,000 yards of Delaines, Flannels, Prints, Ticks, Sheetings, and Shirtings, No. 10 to No. 53. The number of yards printed per week is 120,000, and the number dyed is 6,000.

In 1828, the Appleton Company was incorporated, with a capital of $600,000. John Avery was their Agent till 1831, when George Motley succeeded him. It was in the mills of this company that Uriah A. Boyden's famous turbine water-wheels were first used with success.* Though the managers of the Appleton, during the late War, shared, for a time, the delusion that the country would have "peace in sixty days," and under that delusion sold their cotton, and allowed their mills to stand idle, they acquired, quicker than many others, a true view of the national situation ; and the management of this company, when tested by its results during a period of nearly forty years, must be pronounced successful in an eminent degree.

The Appleton have three mills, with 20,608 spindles, and 717 looms. They employ, when running to their full capacity, 400 females and 120 males. Their weekly consumption of cotton is 50,000 pounds, and their weekly return of cloth is 130,000 yards of Sheetings and Shirtings, Nos. 14 and 20.

In 1828, the Lowell Manufacturing Company was incorporated, with a capital of $900,000, since increased to $2,000,000. In starting their jacquard looms they employed Claudius Wilson, one of the most ingenious and useful mechanics that has ever appeared in Lowell, who emigrated from Scotland to enter this company's service. This company's mills were the first in the world where power-looms were introduced for weaving woollen carpets. These looms were invented by E. B. Bigelow, and rank among the most wonderful triumphs of mechanical genius the world has ever witnessed. Alexander Wright was Agent of this Company till his death in 1852, when Samuel Fay succeeded him.

In 1859, a discussion arose among the stockholders touching the mode of selling their products. An attempt was made to make the selling agents personally interested in augmenting their sales, and enhancing the income from the company's

---

* Francis' Lowell Hydraulic Experiments.

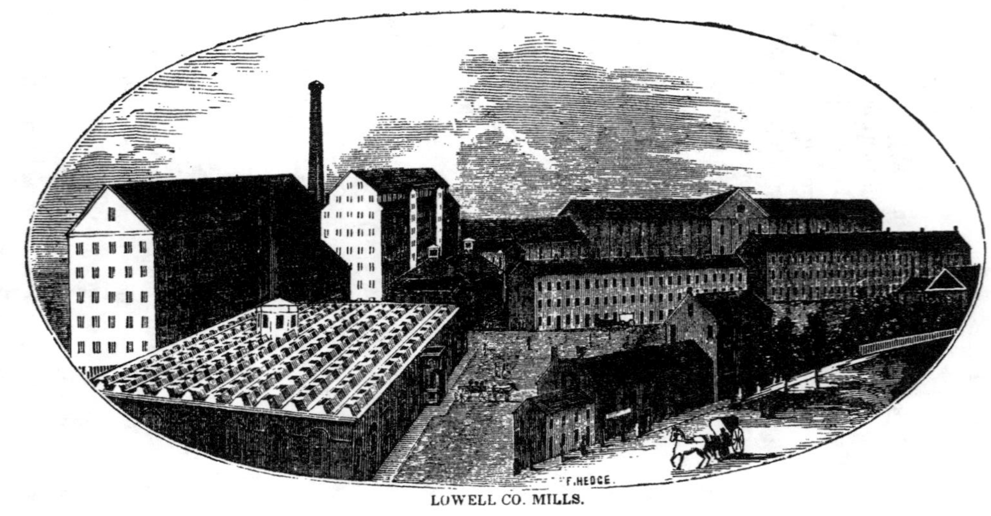

LOWELL CO. MILLS.

stock.* This change has been successfully made by the Middlesex, but has not yet been adopted by the Lowell.

The Lowell have one carpet mill, one worsted mill, and one cotton mill. The number of spindles run is 12,500 on worsted and wool, and 2,816 on cotton. They employ 1,000 females and 450 males, and consume 4,000 pounds of cotton, and 63,-000 of clean wool, per week. Their productive power is 35,-000 yards of Carpets, 13,000 of Sheetings, and 4,500 of Stuffed Goods, per week. They have 432 looms, of which 258 weave Carpets, 124 Cottons, and 50 Stuffed Goods.

In 1830, Samuel Lawrence, William W. Stone, and others were incorporated as the Middlesex Company, with a capital of $500,000,—afterward increased to $1,000,000, but subsequently reduced to $750,000,—and engaged in the manufacture of broadcloths, cassimeres, etc. James Cook was the Agent of this Company's mills for fifteen years. He was succeeded, in 1845, by Nelson Palmer,—in 1846, by Samuel Lawrence,—and in 1848, by Oliver H. Perry, who retained the Agency for three years. In 1851, William T. Mann became Agent, but was succeeded, in 1852, by Joshua Humphrey, who remained in charge six years. In January, 1858, James Cook was recalled. Nine months later, Oliver H. Perry was recalled.

The mismanagement of the Middlesex Company's affairs during many years was astonishing. The entire capital of the Company was lost through the mistakes and irregularities of Samuel Lawrence, William W. Stone and their associates. In 1858, the Company was reorganized, with new managers and a new subscription of stock. Five hundred shares, of the par value of one hundred dollars each, formed the capital with which the Middlesex Company took their "new departure" in

---

* Report of Dr. Ayer, Peter Lawson and H. J. Adams, the Committee of the Proprietors, 1859.

5*

the voyage of life.* This capital has since been increased to $750,000.

Until now, all our manufacturing companies had sold their products through commission-houses in Boston and New York, whose compensation was determined by the gross amount of sales—not by the amount of profits. The wisdom of this policy had been often questioned by sagacious stockholders, without, however, leading to any change. The Middlesex Company now adopted a different mode of selling their products, making their sales through their Treasurer, whose compensation depended mainly upon the profits realized by the Company. By this arrangement, the business of selling was kept directly under the Company's control, and the interests of the selling agent made identical with those of the Company. Since their reorganization, they have been remarkably successful,—their per centage of profits exceeding those of any other company in Lowell.

The Middlesex have three mills and dye-houses, with fifty sets of cards, consuming 25,000 pounds of wool per week. They run 16,400 spindles, 240 broad and 22 narrow looms. They employ 452 males and 320 females, producing Broadcloths, Doeskins, Cassimeres and Shawls.

The Suffolk Manufacturing Company was incorporated in 1831, with $600,000 capital. Robert Means was their Agent until 1842, when John Wright succeeded him. They have two mills.

An ill-advised experiment in the manufacture of cassimeres was made by the Suffolk, during the War, but it aborted, leaving them depleted of their capital. When in full operation, they run 21,432 spindles, and 815 looms,—employ 410 females and 205 males,—consume 30,000 pounds of cotton per week,

* Dr. Ayer and Gen. Butler bought largely of this stock, and their investments yielded them splendid returns. Those who think Gen. Butler's fortune was derived solely from the plunder of Louisiana and Virginia, should look into the Company's books, and learn their mistake.

—and make 125,000 yards, per week, of Corset Jeans, Sheetings, and Shirtings, Nos. 14 to 22.

The Proprietors of the Tremont Mills were incorporated in 1831. Their capital is $600,000, and they have two mills. Their Agents have been, from 1831 to 1834, Israel Whitney; from 1834 to 1837, John Aiken; from 1837 to 1859, Charles L. Tilden; and since 1859, Charles F. Battles.

The experiment in cassimeres which was made by the Suffolk, was repeated by the Tremont, both having the same Treasurer—Henry V. Ward. The same disasters followed, and here too cassimeres were discarded. The productive capacity of the Tremont is about equal to that of the Suffolk,—viz: 20,960 spindles, and 764 looms, run by 500 females and 120 males. The weekly consumption of cotton, when in full operation, is 37,000 pounds, and the weekly return of cloth 135,000 yards of Sheetings and Shirtings, Nos. 14 to 20, and Flannels.

The Lawrence Manufacturing Company were incorporated in 1831. Their capital is $1,500,000; and they have five mills and dye-houses. William Austin was their Agent till 1837, when John Aiken was transferred from the Tremont Mills. In 1849, Mr. Aiken was succeeded by William S. Southworth, who remained till 1865, when William F. Salmon succeeded him.

The Lawrence had the same Treasurer during the War as the Suffolk and Tremont; but instead of experimenting in cassimeres, the Lawrence engaged in hosiery, incurring, directly and indirectly, a loss of half a million dollars. The Lawrence have 60,432 spindles, 1,564 looms, and 163 knitting machines, requiring the labor of 1,350 females and 350 males. Their weekly consumption of cotton, when all their machinery is running, is 110,000 pounds, and 2,000 of wool. Their fabrics are Shirtings, Sheetings, Printing Cloth, Cotton and Merino Hosiery.

In 1831, the Suffolk and Western Canals were cut, to supply the Suffolk, Tremont and Lawrence with water-power.

The Lowell Bleachery was incorporated in 1832, with a capital of $50,000, since increased to $300,000. Jonathan Derby was in charge the first year. From 1833 to 1835, Joseph Hoyt was in charge. Then succeeded Charles T. Appleton, who retained the Agency till 1846, when Charles A. Babcock succeeded him. The present Agent, Frank P. Appleton, succeeded Mr. Babcock, in 1853.

The Bleachery establishment consists of four mills and dye-houses, employing 360 males and 40 females. They dye 15,000,000 yards, and bleach 8,000,000 yards, of cloth per annum.

The Boott Cotton Mills were incorporated in 1835, with a capital of $1,200,000, and commenced operations in 1836. Benjamin F. French had charge of these mills till 1845, when Linus Child succeeded him. In 1862, William A. Burke was transferred from the Machine Shop to succeed Mr. Child. When Mr. Burke came, the stock of the Boott had fallen forty per cent. below par, and was paying no dividends. Since then an extensive policy of reconstruction has been pursued; the stock has risen to par, and has paid good dividends.

The Boott have five mills, with 71,324 spindles and 1,878 looms, employing 1,020 females and 290 males. Their weekly consumption of cotton is 100,000 pounds, and their weekly return of cloth 350,000 yards of No. 14 Drillings, Sheetings, Shirtings and Printing Cloth, No. 30 to No. 40.

In 1832, W. B. Park, of Boston, purchased the flannel mill near Wamesit Falls, in Belvidere, of John Nesmith, who, as we have previously seen, had purchased these premises of Harrison G. Howe. Mr. Park divided most of the lands adjoining into convenient lots and sold them at an enhanced price to a number of individual purchasers. Without observing too rigid an adherence to the order of chronology, we will here give the remaining history of these mills. In 1834, Eliphalet Barber, Walter Farnsworth, and George Hill, of Boston, purchased these mills of Mr. Park, and carried on the business until 1851, as the Belvidere Flannel Manufacturing Company. They also extended their business by the purchase of the stone mill, which had before been owned by the Whitney Mills. In 1851; Charles Stott and Walter Farnsworth bought out the company's interest, and carried on these mills on their own account; but their business was soon impeded by fire. The stone mill was burned in 1851, and the old flannel mill in the year following. In 1853, under the old charter granted to W. B. Park in 1834, the Belvidere Woollen Manufacturing Company was reorganized,—Messrs. Stott and Farnsworth conveying one-third of their interest to the new company. The large brick mill, at Wamesit Falls, was built the same year. Another large mill at Whipple's Mills was built in 1862. The capital of this company—originally only $50,000—is now $200,000. Charles Stott has been Agent since 1835.

It was in 1836 that Perez O. Richmond, who had for two years previously been engaged in manufacturing batting, near Wamesit Falls, established himself at Massic Falls, where he experienced distinguished success in that business. When he began manufacturing operations in Lowell in 1834, he borrowed six hundred dollars from a friend, with which he bought and started a few carding machines. When he died in 1854, he left an estate worth over one hundred and twenty-five thousand dollars, above all his liabilities.

The Massachusetts Cotton Mills—the youngest of the great corporations now existing in Lowell—were incorporated in 1839, with a capital of $1,200,000, which was afterward increased by the absorption of the Prescott Company to $1,800,000. The Agents of this Company have been, from 1839 to 1849, Homer Bartlett; from 1849 to 1856, Joseph White; and since 1856, Frank F. Battles. The Superintendents of the Prescott Mills, (a part of the same Company's establishment,) have been, from 1845 to 1849, Homer Bartlett; from 1849 to 1856, Frank F. Battles; and since 1856, William Brown.

The Massachusetts have six mills, with 67,872 spindles and 1,887 looms, employing 1,300 females and 400 males. They consume 180,000 pounds of cotton, and make 540,000 yards of cloth, per week; their fabrics being Sheetings, Shirtings and Drillings, No. 12 to No. 22.

In 1839, John Nesmith and others were incorporated as the Whitney Mills, and for several years they manufactured blankets in the stone mill near Wamesit Falls. But the business proved a failure, and they sold their machinery to Joseph W. Mansur and John D. Sturtevant. The blanket manufacture finally found a grave in the Tariff of 1846. That Tariff, the result of the financial charlatanry of Robert J. Walker, President Polk's Secretary of the Treasury, raised the duty on all imported wools to thirty per cent., while it reduced the duty on imported flannels and blankets to twenty-five and twenty per cent.

It was in 1839 that Charles P. Talbot & Co. commenced the business of manufacturing dye-stuffs and chemicals in Lowell and Billerica. This business, small in its beginning, has gradually swelled to the amount of $500,000 per annum. A flannel mill has also been started by the Messrs. Talbot, at Billerica, with eight sets of cards.

In 1845,—the year of the second reorganization of the Proprietors of the Locks and Canals,—the Lowell Machine Shop was incorporated, with a capital of $600,000. William A. Burke, who had previously been Agent of the Manchester (N. H.) Machine Shop, was the first Agent, and was succeeded in 1862 by Mertoun C. Bryant. Mr. Bryant dying soon afterward, Andrew Moody succeeded him.

The War, which brought death and ruin to so many others, was improved by this company to the utmost advantage; and since the War, they have realized a hundred thousand dollars in a single year.

The establishment of this company consists of four shops, a smithy and foundry, employing 800 men;—3,000 tons of cast iron, 400 tons of wrought iron and 35 tons of steel are consumed annually, in the manufacture of Cotton and Paper Machinery, Locomotives, Water-Wheels, Machinists' Tools, and Mill-work.

A machine for bending ship timber is now in process of construction here, the weight of which will exceed 200 tons.

While the Machine Shop was getting under way as an independent corporation, the Prescott Manufacturing Company, incorporated in 1844, with a capital of $800,000, was consolidated with the Massachusetts; the change being made with a view to economy.

Having now traced in outline the origin and progress of all the great corporations of Lowell, we may here insert a statistical summary of the most salient facts touching their productive capacity.

Capital stock of the corporations	$13,650,000
Number of mills	47, and dye-houses, etc.
Number of spindles	429,474
Number of looms	12,117
Female operatives	8,890
Male operatives	4,672
Yards of cotton cloth produced per week	2,248,000
Pounds of cotton consumed per week	646,000
Yards dyed and printed per annum	45,002,000
Tons anthracite coal consumed per annum	35,100
Bushels charcoal consumed per annum	20,000
Gallons oil consumed per annum	97,650
Pounds starch consumed per annum	2,190,000
Water-power	nearly 10,000 horse-powers.
Steam-power	32 engines—4,375 horse-powers.
Wages of females, clear of board, per week	$3.50 to $3.75
Wages of males, clear of board, per day	$1.00 to $2.00
Medium produce of a loom, No. 14 yarn, yards per day	45
Medium produce of a loom, No. 30 yarn, yards per day	30
Average per spindle per day	1¼

In 1829, one mill was burned down, and, in 1853, another. Both these mills belonged to the Merrimack Company; and although fires have been frequent, no other mills of the great corporations have been lost by that devouring element. This comparative exemption from the ravages of fire has been secured by the most efficient system of watching, which has been practiced here from the first. The corporations also have an elaborate system of "sprinklers," which enables them, in an instant, to wet down the whole or any part of a room, or of all their rooms, so that fires are arrested at once. This admirable machinery of sprinklers, however, was not introduced until after the establishment of the reservoir on Lynde's Hill, in 1850. A system of mutual insurance against fire was also adopted by the corporations about the same time; but so perfect are their facilities for preventing and suppressing fires, the cost of their insurance has been less than a tenth of one per cent. on the value of the property insured.

In connection with those corporations that stopped their mills more or less during the War, the question may be asked,—How would the great men who founded the factory system of Lowell regard this ruthless dismissal of hundreds and thousands of operatives, dependent on their day's wages for their day's bread? The founders of Lowell were far in advance of their times. How mindful they were of the well-being of their operatives! With what thoughtful care did they establish, at their own cost, their admirable system of boarding-houses, with the most efficient moral police, and with every provision for religious worship! To them the condition of their operatives was a matter of the highest interest.* Not so to their successors. The impartial historian cannot ignore the fact, painful as it is, that nine of the great corporations of Lowell, under a mistaken belief that they could not run their mills to a profit during the War, unanimously, in cold blood, dismissed ten thousand operatives, penniless, into the streets!

This crime, this worse than crime, this *blunder*, entailed its own punishment,—as all crimes do by the immutable law of God. When these companies resumed operations, their former skilled operatives were dispersed, and could no more be recalled

* Appleton's Origin of Lowell, p. 15.

than the Ten Lost Tribes of Israel. Their places were poorly filled by the less skilled operatives whom the companies now had to employ. So serious was this blunder, that the smallest of the companies would have done wisely, had they sacrificed a hundred thousand dollars, rather than thus lose their accustomed help.

During the last forty years, a great variety of mechanical talent has been developed by the corporations of Lowell. But strange to say, no method has been devised to retain in the service of the companies the talent thus developed, by opening to its possessors a wider field of action. Accordingly, when an overseer, or employé of any grade, has so mastered his business as to be fitted to fill the higher positions,—so often filled by men wholly ignorant of manufacturing processes,—his almost only hope of advancement lies in quitting the companies' employ.

Among the men heretofore employed in the mills, who found no adequate sphere on the corporations, and who have risen to higher theatres of action outside of the Lowell mills, the first names that occur are Phineas Adams, Sylvanus Adams, W. L. Ainsworth, D. M. Ayer, Jefferson Bancroft, Joseph Battles, E. B. Bigelow, Ezekiel Blake, Cornelius Blanchard, Francis A. Calvert, Josiah G. Coburn, John L. Cheney, Joshua Converse, D. D. Crombie, A. G. Cumnock, E. S. Davis, Orlando Davis, George Draper, Oliver Ellis, Franklin Forbes, William Hunter, Daniel Hussey, L. W. Jaquith, G. H. Jones, Peter Lawson, Pliny Lawton, George Lund, Foster Nowell, George K. Paul, Hannibal Powers, T. L. Randlett, E. A. Straw, Royal Southwick, Charles P. Talbot, Thomas Talbot, Rufus Whittier, Claudius Wilson, Hubbard Willson, Walter Wright, S. J. Wetherell, Lothrop Wetherell, and John Yeaton; and many others might readily be recalled.

Synchroniously with the building of the factories and boarding-houses of the corporations, a large number of small private establishments were started in various parts of Lowell, by machinists, blacksmiths, house-builders, carpenters, dyers, carriage and harness makers, artificers of tools, and all sorts of workers in wood and in iron,—in short, by all classes of mechanics and artisans who could in any way contribute to the building and beautifying of an inland town. Many of these congregated near Wamesit Falls, in Belvidere. There too were subsequently started the manufacturing establishments of James O. Patterson, John D. Sturtevant, Aaron Cowley, Roger Lang, James Siner, Samuel C. Shapleigh, Moses A. Johnson, and others. Most of these establishments have long since disappeared from Belvidere—the manufacturers finding a more desirable theatre at Whipple's Mills, and the miscellaneous classes of mechanics establishing themselves at Mechanics' Mills in the westerly part of Lowell. This region of Mechanics' Mills,—built up largely by William Livingston and Sidney Spaulding,—has been the focus of most of the lumber business done in Lowell since 1846. No water-power is used there; but planing mills, saw-mills, and other works are run by steam.

It was long the policy of the corporations to discourage any manufacturing enterprize that was not incorporated. This policy was based partly on a love of methodicity and an unreasoning attachment to incorporated forms of industry, and partly on the selfish desire to have the whole body of the people of Lowell subject to their sway. But notwithstanding this discouragement, many independent hives of manufacturing industry have been started from time to time; and some of them have realised remarkable success.

In 1846, Oliver M. Whipple gathered, in the southerly part of Lowell, that group of industrial establishments ever since called Whipple's Mills, which are supplied by the water-power of Concord River, estimated at five hundred horse-powers. In his long and active career, Mr. Whipple has rendered many valuable services to the public. Some of these have already been forgotten, and the memory of most of the rest will probably perish with the generation now in being. But whatever else may be forgotten, this will not be forgotten,—that when all the water-power of the Merrimack had been monopolized by great corporations, he laid hold on the water-power of the Concord, and held it, with a firm hand, for the use, chiefly, of independent manufacturers. For nearly twenty years, he continued to let land, buildings and water-power, on the most liberal terms, to every man of merit that would embark in any manufacturing adventure. As the region of Whipple's Mills becomes more thickly peopled, the magnitude of the service thus rendered by Mr. Whipple will more and more appear; and Lowell, when she calls the roll of her benefactors, can never omit his name.

Among the first establishments at Whipple's Mills were Smith & Meadowcroft's bolt factory, Thomas Barr's print shop, Aaron Cowley's carpet factory, Sylvester Crosby's bobbin shop, and C. H. Crowther's dye house. Afterward came Roger Lang, James Siner, and George Naylor, carpet manufacturers; Carroll & Thompson, dyers; Charles R. Littler, calico printer; the Lowell Wire Fence Company; John Cowley, woollen manufacturer; John Sugden, Richard Rhodes, and James Dugdale, worsted spinners, and a multitude more.

During the late War, portions of the water-power of the Concord, at Whipple's Mills, were purchased and applied by the Belvidere Woollen Manufacturing Company, Luther W. Faulkner & Son, Charles A. Stott, and others. The *residuum* of this water-power passed, for a time, into the hands of Ephraim B. Patch, who sold it, in 1865, to the Wamesit Power Company, which was incorporated the same year, with a capital of $150,000. By this company, water-power is still leased to private manufacturers, as in former years by Mr. Whipple.

During the two lustrums between 1845 and 1855, the number of spindles run by the great corporations of Lowell, was exactly doubled. Only 200,000 spindles were in operation in 1845. The spaces between the mills were then built up, and other extensions made, and, in 1855, the number of spindles running was 400,000, with 12,000 looms.

In 1860, Moses A. Johnson and others established a mill at Wamesit Falls, for the manufacture of cattle's hair into various forms of felted goods. The use for which this fabric was originally designed, was the sheathing of the copper of ships; but it has since been applied extensively to a great variety of uses—such as underlaying carpets, roofing, packing, etc. In 1866, this business was removed to Pawtucket Falls. In 1867, the Lowell Felting Mills were incorporated, with a capital of $100,000, and with Moses A. Johnson as Agent.

Outside of the great corporations, there is no establishment in Lowell, involving near so much capital, as the Laboratory of Dr. James C. Ayer & Co., established in 1843, and now employing one hundred males and fifty females. The advertising disbursements of this firm exceed $140,000 annually. Five and a half million copies of Ayer's Almanac, printed by steam at their establishment, are annually distributed, *gratis*, in English, French, Dutch, German, Norwegian, Spanish, Portuguese, and Chinese. About 325,000 pounds of drugs, of the value of $850,000,—220,000 gallons of spirit, of the value of $550,000, and 460,000, pounds of sugar, costing about $98,000,—are annually expended here. About $1,500,000 bottles, 185,000 pill boxes, 425,000 square feet of packing boxes, and 112,000 square feet of card board, are also used. The paper and printing ink consumed annually amount in value to $75,000. The products of this mammoth laboratory are sent to every part of the globe, at an expense of $48,000 a year for freight, and $2,800 for postage,—150 letters on an average being sent out every day.

The principal manufacturing and mechanical establishments in Lowell, not already mentioned, are as follows;

American Bolt Company, Bolts.
Thomas Atherton & Co., Machinists.
Sager Ashworth, Files.
Milton Aldrich, Hand Screws.
A. H. & J. H. Abbott, Carriages.

J. W. Bennett & Co., Metallic Roofing.
Artemas L. Brooks, Saw Mill and Planing Mill.
D. C. Brown, Reeds, Loom Harnesses, etc.
S. L. Buckman, Harnesses.
James A. Brabrook, Harnesses.
T. F. Burgess & Co., Iron Machinery.
H. R. Barker, Gas and Steam Pipes, etc.
Ephraim Brown, Money Drawers, etc.
Blodgett, Reed & Pease, Stone Cutters, etc.
S. R. Brackett, Worsted Yarns.
George L. Cady, Belt Hooks, etc.
George Crosby, Extension Tables, etc.
Coburn, Wing & Co., Shuttles.
John H, Coburn, Shuttles.
Coburn & Park, Stone Quarries.
Cutter & Walker, Shoulder Braces.
Samuel Convers, Carriages.
Cole & Nichols, Foundry.
Elbridge G. Cook, Tannery.
Carter & Roland, Wool Washers.
Charles H. Crowther, Dyeing.
Alfred H. Chase, Fancy Cloths.
Weare Clifford, Dyeing.
Asahel Davis, Dovetailing Machines, etc.
Luke C. Dodge, Babbeting Metal, etc.
Davis & Melindy, Planing Mill.
Alfred Drake, Card Combs.
James Dugdale, Woollen Yarns.
Dobbins & Crawford, Steam Boilers.
Eagle Braid Mills, Braid.
Willis G. Eaton, Currier,
N. B. Favor & Son, Doors, Sashes and Blinds.
William Fiske, Coverlets.
L. W. Faulkner & Son, Woollens.
George W. Field, Machinist.
Fuller & Read, Wood Turners.
Josiah Gates & Sons, Hose, Belts, etc.
Joseph Green, Mats and Rugs.
Hart & Colson, Furniture.
Hill Manufacturing Company, Suspenders.
Howe & Goodhue, Card Clothing.
John Holt, Press-dyed Flannels.

Andrew J. Hiscox & Co., Files.
Howes & Burnham, Lumber.
George W. Harris, Loom Harnesses, etc.
Henry A. Hildreth, Wire Worker.
B. S. Hale & Son, Insulated Wire.
H. B. & G. F. Hill, Carriages.
Eliphalet Hills, Wood Turner.
Hubbard & Blake, Patent Leather.
J. S. Jaques & Co., Shuttles.
Joel Jenkins, Carriages.
Keyes and Sugden, Worsted Yarns,
Richard Kitson, Cotton Machinery.
D. S. Kimball, Furniture.
J. A. Knowles, Jr., Scales.
Wm. Kelley, Doors, Sashes and Blinds.
Benjamin Lawrence, Machinist.
Lowell Arms Company, Fire Arms.
Lowell Card Company, Card Clothing.
Daniel Lovejoy, Machine Knives.
David Lane, Woollen Machinery.
Livingston, Carter & Co., Flannels, etc.
William E. Livingston, Grist Mill, etc.
John McDonald, Carpets.
John Mather, Carpets.
William & Luke McFarlin, Ice.
J. V. Meigs, Patent Guns.
Norcross & Saunders, Lumber.
George Naylor, Carpets.
Parsons & Gibby, Copperstamps, etc.
F. S. Perkins, Iron Machinery.
Parker & Cheney, Bobbins.
M. C. Pratt, Doors, Sashes and Blinds.
Isaac Place, Doors, Sashes and Blinds.
J. G. Peabody, Doors, Sashes and Blinds.
John Pettengill, Cisterns, etc.
J. M. Peabody, Set Screws.
John N. Pierce, Machinist.
George Ripley & Co., Batting.
Robinson & Nourbourn, Machinists.
Runals, Clough & Co., Granite Workers.
Charles B. Richmond, Paper.
Joseph Robinson & Co., Acids and Charcoal.

Amos Sanborn & Co., Silver Ware.
Samuel Smith, Set Screws.
Charles A. Stott, Flannels.
A. C. Sawyer, Harnesses, etc.
Hamilton Sawyer, Machinist.
Solon Stevens, Reeds, Loom Harnesses, etc.
Styles, Rogers & Co., Grist Mill.
B. F. & J. Stevens, Machinists.
Taylor Chemical Company, Chemicals.
Upton & Blake, Shoulder Braces.
U. S. Bunting Co., Bunting. D. W. C. Farrington, Agent.
William Walker & Co.. Woollens.
Woods, Sherwood & Co., Wireworkers.
H. & A. Whitney, Lumber.
S. H. Wright, Machinist.
Edward F. Watson, Bobbins.
Phineas Whiting & Co., Belts.
Charles H. Western, Patterns, etc.
H. H. Wilder & Co., Brass Foundry.
S. N. Wood, Grist Mill.
White & Plaisted, Saw Mill.
White & Chase, Flocks.

There are also various manufacturing establishments in the circumjacent towns, which can hardly be ignored in connection with the manufacturing history of Lowell. Among these are the following:

Billerica.

C. P. Talbot & Co., Flannels, Dye Stuffs and Chemicals.
J. R. Faulkner & Co., Flannels.
Hill & Proctor, Machinery.
Robert Prince & Co., Soap.
Thomas Patten, Furniture.

Chelmsford.

Eagle Mills, Woollens. Isaac Farrington, Treasurer.
Christopher Roby & Co., Swords, Edge Tools, etc.
Baldwin Company, Worsted. Peter Anderson, Agent.
Silver & Gay, Woollen Machinery, Tools, etc.
Chelmsford Foundry. W. H. B. Wightman, Treasurer.
George T. Sheldon, Hosiery.

Merrimack Hosiery Company. G. T. Sheldon, Treasurer.
Warren C. Hamblet, Grist Mill.

DRACUT.

Merrimack Mills, Woollens. Edward Barrows, Agent.
George Ripley & Co., Paper.

TEWKSBURY.

Fosters & Co., Furniture.
J. F. Huntington, Peat.

TYNGSBOROUGH.

Nathaniel Brinley, Lumber and Boxes.

WESTFORD.

Abbot Worsted Co., Worsteds. J. W. Abbot, Treasurer.
Charles G. Sargent, Machinery.

The water-power of the Merrimack has been increased by the superaddition of reservoirs near its sources, which cover a hundred and fifteen square miles. It now amounts to the enormous volume of four thousand cubic feet per second for all the hours during which the mills are run, or nearly ten thousand horse-powers; and the whole of this has been applied. The Merrimack alone use the whole fall of thirty-three feet. To the other companies, the water is delivered from two levels. The Hamilton, Appleton, Lowell, Suffolk, Tremont and Machine Shop draw from the upper level, under a fall of somewhat more than thirteen feet; while the Middlesex, Lawrence, Boott and Massachusetts draw from the lower level, under a fall of something more than seventeen feet.

Within less than a mile below the settled portion of the city, are Hunt's Falls, where the Merrimack River, reinforced by the Concord, makes another descent of ten feet. No part of this water-power has yet been applied to manufacturing purposes; though the utilization of the whole of it is only a question of time. Here are the means to increase the productive power of Lowell by more than thirty per cent. At present, however, the cost of the dam, canal, etc., which would be required in applying this power, would probably exceed the value of the power that would be obtained.

Besides Hunt's Falls, the superaddition of steam-power to the water-power, and the invention of contrivances to diminish the friction of the machinery and enable it to be run with less power, will lead to considerable further increase of our productivity as a manufacturing city. Moreover, the experiments of Bonelli foreshadow many probable future improvements in manufactures, from the application of electricity to various process, especially to the weaving. We are very far yet from the point of culmination. Before the present century expires, Lowell is destined to contain seventy-five thousand inhabitants. Nor will her progress end even there. When the men of our times are all gathered to their fathers, she bids fair to renew her youth, and to march, with firm step, toward the goal of that ideal perfection, which is forever approached, but never attained.

CHAPTER V.

GENERAL HISTORY OF LOWELL. 1820—1835.

East Chelmsford in 1820—*The Journal*—Local Militia—Orators of Independence-Day—James Dugdale—Central Bridge—Mechanics' Association—Lowell a Town—Postmasters—William Livingston—Odd Fellows—Ephraim K. Avery—Sarah Maria Cornell—Boston and Lowell Railroad—Judge Livermore—Police Court—*The Advertiser*—Francis A. Calvert—Gen. Jackson—Henry Clay—Col. Crockett—George Thompson—Michael Chevalier—Steamboat on the Merrimack—Mechanics' Hall *The Courier*—Local Scenery.

In 1820, the village of East Chelmsford, together with Belvidere and Centralville, contained about two hundred and fifty inhabitants. Whipple's Powder Mills were then in operation, and Howe's Flannel Mill. Several saw-mills and grist-mills also contributed to the life of the place. Hurd's Mill, now at Whipple's Mills, then stood in the present Middlesex Company's yard. Ira Frye's Tavern stood where the American House now stands, and furnished "provender for man and beast." At Massic Falls stood a blacksmith's shop; and there were a few other such establishments as country villages usually afford. Scattered about, were a few substantial dwelling-houses,—of which the Livermore House in Belvidere was the most conspicuous—and about a dozen farm-houses, cottages, etc.

The operations of the Merrimack Company attracted a numerous and daily increasing population; and the gables of a hundred new houses shortly pierced the sky. In 1822, a regular line of stages was established between East Chelmsford and Boston. Previous to this, business men, like Mr. Whipple and Mr. Hurd, had often paid five dollars for the conveyance of a single letter from Boston.

In 1824, a weekly paper called the *Chelmsford Courier*, was established in Middlesex Village, and became, at once, the organ of the rising community. It was published by William Baldwin, and edited by Bernard Whitman. In a short time, it passed into the hands of E. W. Reinhart, who changed its name first to *Chelmsford Phœnix*, and afterward to *Merrimack Journal*. He also removed it to what is now Lowell. In November, 1825, John S. C. Knowlton purchased the paper of Mr. Reinhart, and after the incorporation of the town, changed its name to the *Lowell Journal*.

On July 4th, 1825, was organized the Mechanic Phalanx, the first Company of Militia in Lowell. Four other companies of Militia were afterward organized here: the City Guards, in 1841; the Watson Light Guard, in 1851; the Lawrence Cadets, in 1855. The Phalanx and the Guards still live; but the two last companies passed away during the War, giving place to the Putnam Guards and the Sargeant Light Guards.

In 1825, the anniversary of American Independence was celebrated here with appropriate ceremonies. The principal events of the day were an oration by the Rev. Bernard Whitman, of Chelmsford, the first editor of the paper now called the Lowell *Journal*, and a public dinner at the Stone House near Pawtucket Falls, then just erected by Captain Phineas Fletcher, and now the elegant private residence of Dr. James C. Ayer. The successors of Mr. Whitman in the line of Fourth-of-July oratory have been as follows:—In 1826, Samuel B. Walcott; in 1828, Elisha Bartlett; in 1829, Dr. Israel Hildreth; in 1830, Edward Everett; in 1831, John P. Robinson; in 1832, Rev. Thomas J. Greenwood; in 1834, Thomas Hopkinson; in 1835, Rev. E. W. Freeman and others; in 1836, Rev. Dr. Blanchard; in 1841, Rev. Thomas F. Norris and John C. Park; in 1847, Rev. John Moore; in 1848, Dr. Bartlett, again; in 1851, Rev. Joseph H. Towne; in 1852, Rev. Matthew Hale Smith; in 1853, Jonathan Kimball; in 1855, Augustus Woodbury; in 1860, Dr. Charles A. Phelps; in 1861, George S. Boutwell and others; in 1865, Alexander H. Bullock; in 1867, Judge Thomas Russell, and others.

Another event occurred about 1825, of more importance than a Fourth-of-July oration—viz., the arrival of James Dugdale, an ingenious mechanic from Lancashire, who became overseer of a spinning-room on the Merrimack, where he introduced the English "dead spindle," and revolutionized the mode of spinning coarse yarns.

In 1825, the Central Bridge Corporation was incorporated. The only mode of crossing Merrimack River at this point until now, had been by what was called "Bradley's Ferry." This ferry was purchased by the Central Bridge Company, for one thousand dollars. The bridge was so far completed during this and the following season that tolls for foot-passers and carriages were received early in December, 1826. The tolls for foot-passers were abolished in 1843. The bridge itself was rebuilt in 1844; and covered in 1849. The original cost of the bridge was twenty-one thousand dollars; the cost of rebuilding was nine thousand; and the cost of covering four thousand. In 1855, the bridge was laid out by the City Council as a public highway,—a foolish act, which involved the city in most tedious and expensive litigation,* and for which the proprietors of the bridge recovered over $26,000, as damages, costs, etc. The present bridge was built in 1862 at a cost of nearly $34,000,—an outlay of money scarcely less reckless than the seizure of the old bridge.

In 1825, the Middlesex Mechanics' Association was incorporated to minister, by a library of books, now nearly 10,000 volumes, by public lectures, by occasional fairs, and various other means, to the intellectual needs of the people. This was only two years subsequent to the founding of the famous Mechanics' Institute in London—the first of a most useful class of popular institutions, originating in the genius of Dr. Birkbeck, and helped into existence by Lord Brougham. Thus Lowell followed the lead of London with a more rapid step than many of the great English towns.

One hundred years had now elapsed since the Wamesit Indian territory was annexed to the town of Chelmsford. The time had come for a separation; and the inhabitants of East Chelmsford petitioned to be incorporated as a town, and that that town be called Merrimack. Mr. Boott suggested the name of Derby, probably on account of his family associations with that place, which was also in the immediate vicinity of one of the earliest English seats of the Cotton Manufacture. The influence of Mr. Appleton finally caused the name of Lowell to be adopted, out of respect to his associate in the Waltham Company, Francis Cabot Lowell.†

At the inauguration of the Lowell Institute at Boston, December 31st, 1839, Edward Everett delivered a biographical discourse on John Lowell, its founder, and paid a well-merited tribute to that founder's father, from whom was named our City of Spindles. "Pyramids and mausoleums," says the

* See 4 Gray's Reports, p. 474.

† The ancient form of this name was Loule, afterward Lowle. It, perhaps, had the same origin as Lovell.

orator, "may crumble to the earth, and brass and marble mingle with the dust they cover; but the pure and well-deserved renown, which is thus incorporated with the busy life of an intelligent people, will be remembered, till the long lapse of ages and the vicissitudes of fortune shall reduce all of America to oblivion and decay!"

The municipal independence of Lowell began on the first day of March, 1826. The population of the new-born town was about two thousand.

The first post-master was Jonathan C. Morrill, who had been appointed postmaster at East Chelmsford in 1823. The post-office was located at the corner of Central and William Streets. Captain William Wyman succeeded Mr. Morrill in 1829, when the post-office was removed to the site of the present City Hall. As successive administrations came into power at Washington, different post-masters, of different party affiliations, were appointed. Mr. Wyman was succeeded by Eliphalet Case, who removed the office from the City Hall to Middle Street; Mr. Case by Jacob Robbins; Mr. Robbins by S. S. Seavy; Mr. Seavy by Alfred Gilman; Mr. Gilman by T. P. Goodhue; Mr. Goodhue by F. A. Hildreth, who removed the office to its present location, and who was succeeded in 1861 by John A. Goodwin, the present incumbent.

The years 1827 and 1828 were marked by great depression in the commercial and manufacturing circles of the country. Lowell was enveloped in the common cloud. Mr. Hurd, the satinet manfacturer, became bankrupt; but the two corporations—the Merrimack and the Hamilton—kept on in the even tenor of their way, too strong to be crushed.

In spite of all this, however, Lowell still advanced, augmenting her population at the rate of one thousand souls, and her valuation-table many thousand dollars, every year. The business facilities of the place were much increased in 1828 by the establishment of the Lowell Bank, with a capital of two hundred thousand dollars.

In 1828, William Kittredge brought one ton of coal to Lowell in a baggage wagon. It was the first coal ever seen here, and was considered a sufficient supply for the Lowell market for a year. When the first coal fire was started, in the law office of Samuel H. Mann, more than a hundred incredulous persons called to satisfy themselves whether the "black rocks" would actually burn.

In 1829, the Lowell Institution for Savings was incorporated. In the same year, William Livingston established himself in the coal and wood trade. For a quarter of a century, Mr. Livingston was one of the most active, most enterprising and most public-spirited men in Lowell. Much of the western portion of the city was built up by his instrumentality. His efforts to save Lowell from the oppressive monopoly of her railroad business by a single company, mark him as a man far ahead of his time. If the men of business here had sustained those efforts, as an enlightened sense of self-interest dictated, Lowell would now have two competing railroad routes to Boston; and, with cheap freight and a prompt transmission of merchandise, her progress would be vastly accelerated. In politics, Mr. Livingston was a Democrat of the old school, and his principles brought him into antagonism with all attempts to establish monopolies, and with all political and incorporated "rings." He was always active in politics as in every other sphere of human activity. In 1836 and 1837, he was a member of the State Senate. He died in Florida, whither he had gone to escape the rigors of our northern clime, of consumption, March 17th, 1855; and his place in the business and other circles of Lowell has not yet been filled.

It is from 1829 that Odd Fellowship dates its existence in Lowell, Merrimack Lodge having been instituted during that year. This Lodge was the last of this order in the State, that succumbed to the opposition which all secret societies at one time encountered in Massachusetts. But in 1836 it ceased to exist. It was re-organized in 1839, and has continued ever since. Four other Lodges were afterward formed, two of which still live—Mechanics', instituted in 1842, and Oberlin, instituted in 1843. Two Encampments were also instituted here, one of which—Monomake, established in 1843—has survived to the present time.

In July, 1830, an acquaintance was formed between two persons in Lowell, whose names are destined to be associated forever, being cemented by the triple bond of adultery, abortion and murder. One of them was Ephraim K. Avery, Pastor of the First Methodist Episcopal Church, now in Hurd street; the other was Sarah Maria Cornell, a member of the same church, a fair but frail factory girl, employed on the Hamilton Corporation. The reverend hypocrite made frequent calls at the Hamilton counting-room for interviews with his paramour; * and then it was—

> "The golden hours on angel wings
> Flew o'er him and his dearie."

Little did either of them dream that the amorous dalliances in which they then indulged, would culminate, in a few fleeting months, in one of the most appalling tragedies in the annals of New England. Others besides Avery enjoyed the favors of Miss Cornell, who was finally expelled from his church for criminality and lying. In 1832, Avery removed to Bristol, Rhode Island. Miss Cornell followed, and took up her abode where she could communicate with him by personal interviews, as well as by letter.

On the night of the twentieth of December, 1832, loud cries and groans were heard in Tiverton, a few miles from Bristol; but the bloody tragedy then and there enacted, was not discovered until the following morning. The dead body of Miss Cornell was then found suspended by the neck in a stack yard fence, near the spot where such terrible cries had been heard

* This statement is inconsistent with the narrative of Avery, published with the report of his trial, by Richard Hildreth and B. F. Hallett; but I had it from the late Ithamar W. Beard, who was employed in the Hamilton counting-room at the time, and who, unlike Avery, had no motive to lie.

on the evening before. There was indisputable evidence that prior to the murder Miss Cornell had undergone the manipulations of an abortionist. By a remarkable coincidence, the day following that on which Miss Cornell was thus put out of the way, had been assigned by the Presiding Elder for the trial of Mr. Avery, before an ecclesiastical court, on a charge of adultery committed with Miss Cornell, in the preceding August, at a camp meeting at Thompson, in Connecticut.

Avery was soon afterward arrested at his hiding-place at Rindge, in New Hampshire, and carried to Newport, where, on the sixth of May, 1833, he was arraigned for trial. He was the first clergyman in the United States that was ever tried on an indictment for murder; and his case was one of the most remarkable in the annals of crime. His trial continued for twenty-eight consecutive days. He was defended by the celebrated Jeremiah Mason and Richard K. Randolph, and was finally acquitted. A Committee of the New England Conference reported, and the Conference unblushingly resolved, that Avery was not only innocent of the murder, but that he was also innocent of adultery with Miss Cornell. But the time had gone by when the convictions of mankind could be controlled by the decree of an ecclesiastical conclave. Avery having had the impudence to preach to his old society in Lowell, shortly after the murder, a party of gentlemen, not altogether blind to all moral distinctions, prepared to bear him from the town on a rail. But before their preparations were completed, Avery fled. His pursuers gave expression to their resentment by hanging him in effigy.

In 1830, the Town Hall was built, and the Fire Department established. Our population had then increased to six thousand four hundred and seventy-seven souls; the principal streets of the present city had been laid out; and the once rural hamlet had begun to wear a decidedly urban aspect.

It was in 1830, that Patrick T. Jackson undertook the Cyclopean work of the Boston and Lowell Railroad. The line for a macadamized road had already been surveyed, when this road was projected; and it was a part of the original plan to have the cars drawn by horses. But just "in the nick of time," the intelligence of Mr. Stephenson's brilliant success in his experiment with locomotive steam-engines on the Liverpool and Manchester Railroad, reached the ever-open ears of Mr. Jackson, and convinced him that a similar road might be established here also. He corresponded with the best inventors and mechanics of England, availed himself of their valuable suggestions, and in five years the work was successfully completed.

As a matter of course, all the incorrigible fogies of the country pronounced the project of a railroad with cars propelled by steam, to be radical, wild and visionary. Many a Mrs. Grundy indulged liberally in ridicule at both Mr. Jackson and his "castle-in-the-air" railroad. The stockholders complained of the repeated and enormous assessments which he imposed upon them, without any prospect, as those timid creatures thought, of any future dividends. Probably no other man then living in Massachusetts could have sustained himself against an opposition so powerful and so various. But the iron mind of that truly great man,—true to itself as the needle to the pole,—overcame every obstacle, and pressed right onward to the goal.

How much the actual cost of this railroad exceeeded all previous calculations, one fact will sufficiently indicate. In 1831, a Committee of Stockholders estimated the whole cost at four hundred and fifty thousand dollars; but out of the exuberant liberality of their generous hearts, they advised that six hundred thousand dollars be raised for that work; so that Mr. Jackson might have means "enough and to spare." But when, in 1835, the road had been completed, the actual cost was found to have been eighteen hundred thousand dollars! or three times the cost of the Middlesex Canal, and three times the cost estimated in 1831!

This has often been represented as the first railroad started on this continent. But the Boston and Quincy Railroad was the first that carried freight—using horse-power. It was built in 1827. The first passenger road was the Baltimore and Ohio, opened with horse-power for fifteen miles in 1830. Locomotives were first used in 1831 on the Mohawk and Hudson Railroad, and in 1832 on the Baltimore and Ohio, and on the South Carolina Railroad. The Boston and Providence, Boston and Worcester, Boston and Lowell Railroads, were each open in 1835.

In cutting through the mica slate and gneiss rock near the Northern depot, to lay the track of this railroad, remarkable intrusions of trap rock were uncovered, severing and disturbing the general strata. Similar seams of trap rock were afterward disclosed when the cut was made through the ledge on Fletcher street. Phenomena like these are always of interest to geologists.

In 1831, the Railroad Bank was established, with a capital of six hundred thousand dollars.

On the fifteenth of September, 1832, occurred the death of the distinguished Judge Livermore. Edward St. Loe Livermore was the son of the Hon. Samuel Livermore, and was born at Londonderry (N. H.) in 1761. In 1783, he commenced the practice of law at Concord, and was Solicitor for Rockingham County from 1791 to 1793. From 1797 to 1799, he was a Judge of the Superior Court of New Hampshire. He was elected Representative in Congress from the old Essex North District in 1807, and reëlected in 1809. He removed to what is now Belvidere about 1816, purchasing the estate of Phillip Gedney, on which he resided till his death. The Livermore estate then passed into the hands of John Nesmith, another native of Londonderry, and of the same sinewy Scotch-Irish stock, which has given to the United States so many distinguished men—Presidents Jackson, Polk, Buchanan, and Johnson, Generals McClellan, Grant, Sherman, Butler and Mc-

Dowell, not to mention James Gordon Bennett and Horace Greeley.

In 1833, the Police Court was established—being the first local court established here, since Major General Daniel Gookin played the part of judge, assisted by the Apostle Eliot and the Christian Indian Chiefs. The first Justice of the new court was Joseph Locke.

The bounds of the city were extended in 1834, by the annexation of Belvidere;* and the same year gave birth to the Lowell *Advertiser*. After running for some time under the editorship of B. E. Hale, the *Advertiser* passed into the hands of Eliphalet Case. In the list of Mr. Case's successors are found the names of N. P. Banks, H. H. Weld, J. G. Abbott, I. W. Beard, William Butterfield, Henry E. and Samuel C. Baldwin, Fisher A. Hildreth, Robbins Dinsmore, and J. J. Maguire. The *Advertiser* always supported the Democracy; but the Democracy never supported the *Advertiser*; and in 1864 it collapsed.

In 1833 the Lowell Irish Benevolent Society was established. Their charitable disbursements amount to fifteen hundred dollars per annum. In 1843, this society was incorporatad by the Legislature.

In 1833, Francis A. Calvert began in Lowell that career of mechanical invention, which has given to the world the burring-machine, the comber, and the cotton-willow. The first worsted-spinning machinery in Lowell was built and started by him. As the final product of his genius, the world is yet promised a percussive steam-engine, though this *chef d'œuvre* remains thus far imperfect. His ingenious brother, William W. Calvert, came to Lowell in 1825, and remained for twenty years. He died in 1847, at Panama.

On the 26th of June, 1833, Andrew Jackson, President of the United States, made a visit to Lowell, accompanied by

* The beautiful faubourg of Belvidere received its name originally as a term of reproach, on account of the lawless scenes then frequently witnessed there.

Martin Van Buren, then Vice President, Judge Woodbury, and other members of the Cabinet. A brief address of welcome was made by Joshua Swan, Chairman of the Board of Selectmen; to which the President made an appropriate response. He then proceeded through the principal streets, where triumphal arches had been erected and decorated artistically with flags and flowers. He was escorted by the Selectmen, the Committee of Arrangements, (of which Kirk Boott was Chairman), a regiment of militia, a cavalcade of two hundred citizens, six hundred school children, and over twenty-five hundred factory girls. Clothed in white, these Lowell factory girls looked like "livered angels." They walked four deep, and their beauty and their elegance of dress were greatly admired. The procession passed in review before the President, with drums beating, cannon booming, banners flying, handkerchiefs waving, and nine times nine hearty cheers of welcome. The old hero could hardly have been more moved amid the din of battle at New Orleans, than by the exhilerating spectacle here presented. He seemed to enter Lowell, as Scipio entered Rome after the defeat of Hannibal, or as Napoleon entered Paris after the treaty of Campo Formio. The procession over, the President visited the Merrimack Company's mills, and saw some of the works put in operation by the girls in their gala attire. On his return to the hotel, he was visited by a young lady, who requested the privilege of kissing the father of her country. It was a startling request; but Jackson submitted with becoming resignation.

It is interesting to observe how a spectacle like this impressed the imagination of the distinguished French statesman, Chevalier, now Minister of Finance to Napoleon the Third:—

"If these scenes were to find a painter, they would be admired at a distance, not less than the triumphs and sacrificial pomps which the ancients have left us delineated in marble and brass; for they are not mere grotesques after the manner of Rembrandt—they belong to history, they partake of the grand; they are the episodes of a wondrous epic which will bequeath a lasting memory to posterity, that of the coming of democracy."

Four months after Jackson's departure, October 25th, 1833, Henry Clay visited Lowell, was shown through the mills and schools, and treated with all the attention due to so distinguished a guest. Luther Lawrence was Chairman of the Committee of Arrangements, Kirk Boott having declined. Remembering how Clay had advocated the declaration of war against England in 1812,—how he had made his country the cat's-paw of Napoleon,—and how, on Napoleon's downfall, he had patched up a hasty peace, without securing one of the objects for which war had been declared,—Mr. Boott utterly refused to assist in any honors to Mr. Clay.

In the evening, Mr. Clay addressed the citizens in the Town Hall, which was illuminated with candles; and though Kirk Boott was not there, the hall was filled to its utmost capacity. Never, probably, has an orator faced a more enthusiastic audience. Never was an audience moved by a more impassioned orator.

Nineteen years rolled away; the twenty-fifth of October came round again: but the sleep that knows no waking had fallen on Henry Clay; and all that was mortal of his great compeer, Daniel Webster, lay in the chamber at Marshfield attired for the tomb!

In May, 1834, the famous comic statesman, Colonel David Crockett, visited Lowell, and was hospitably entertained at the Stone House, near Pawtucket Falls. He visited the factories; and at the Middlesex Mills, Samuel Lawrence presented him with a suit of broadcloth. He met the young men of Lowell, by their request, at supper, and made a shrewd, sensible speech, full of Crockettisms and fun.*

A few months after Crockett, came George Thompson, Member of Parliament and Abolitionist, who, as many a village politician verily believed, was sent on his campaign in the United States by the British Government, and had his pockets loaded with British gold, for the express purpose of breaking

*Crockett's Life of Himself, p. 217.

up our glorious Union. On October 5th, 1834, he spoke in the Town Hall, where "gentlemen of property and standing" banded together and mobbed him as an emissary of the devil. A brick which was thrown at him through the window, and which failed to hit him, was long preserved as a sacred relic by the late H. L. C. Newton, one of Thompson's most ardent friends.

It was in 1834 that M. Chevalier, the French political economist, already mentioned, was sent to this country by M. Thiers, Minister of the Interior to Louis Phillippi, for the purpose of inspecting the public works of the United States. His impressions touching the characteristics of our social organization and the workings of our political institutions, were published in letters to the *Journal des Debats,* and afterward as a separate work. These letters attracted great attention at the time. In a letter from Lowell, he says:

> "Unlike the cities of Europe, which were built by some demi-god, son of Jupiter, or by some hero of the seige of Troy, or by an inspiration of the genius of a Cæser or an Alexander, or by the assistance of some holy monk, attracting crowds by his miracles, or by the caprice of some great king, like Louis XIV. or Frederick, or by an edict of Peter the Great, it (Lowell) is neither a pious foundation, a refuge of the persecuted, nor a military post. It is a *speculation of the merchants of Boston.* The same spirit of enterprise which the last year suggested to them to send a cargo of ice to Calcutta, that Lord William Bentinck and the Nabobs of the India Company might drink their wine cool, has led them to build a city, wholly at their expense, with all the edificies required by an advanced civilization, for the purpose of manufacturing cotton cloths and printed calicoes. They have succeeded, as they usually do, in their speculations." *

Foreseeing that the Merrimack Valley and indeed all New England would become to Boston what Lancashire was to Liverpool, M. Chevalier continues:

> "The inhabitants possess in the highest degree a genius for mechanics. They are patient, skillful, full of invention;—they must increase in manufactures. It is in fact already done, and Lowell is a little Manchester."

So pleased was M. Chevalier with the factories and factory girls of Lowell, that, more than thirty years later, in 1866, when a member of the Commission charged with the organiza-

* Letters from the United States, p. 131.

tion of the Exposition of 1867, he wrote to Senator Sumner, invoking his efforts to have a group of these girls sent to Paris, with their looms, so that they might be seen in Paris, at work, as they are seen in Lowell.

In 1835, Joel Stone of Lowell and J. P. Simpson of Boston built the steamboat "Herald," and placed her upon the Merrimack to ply twice a day between Lowell and Nashua. But owing to the shortness of the distance, the inconvenience of the landing-places, and the necessity for shiftings of the passengers and baggage, this enterprise proved a failure, even before the railroad was opened between the two termini. It was, however, continued by Joseph Bradley until after the opening of the railroad, when the boat was taken to Newburyport, and sold for service elsewhere.

In the same year that the "Herald" began her trips, the Nashua and Lowell Railroad Company was incorporated, with a capital of $600,000. The Lowell Almshouse dates from the same year.

The Hall of the Middlesex Mechanics' Association was also erected in 1835, chiefly by contributions from the various manufacturing companies of Lowell. In this hall hang full-length paintings of George Washington, Kirk Boott, Patrick T. Jackson, Abbott Lawrence, Nathan Appleton, and John A. Lowell. There, too, are half-length portraits of Daniel Webster and Elisha Huntington, with busts of Abraham Lincoln and George Peabody.

On the sixth of January, 1835, first appeared the Lowell *Courier*, the oldest daily newspaper now existing in Middlesex County. For ten years it was published tri-weekly only, but became a daily in 1845. Its publishers were Leonard Huntress and Daniel H. Knowlton, and it was printed in the office of the *Mercury*—a weekly paper started in 1829, and afterward consolidated with the *Courier*. In the February following, the *Journal* also was consolidated with the *Courier*. In the editorial roll of the *Journal*, and of the *Courier*, during the last forty years, we find the names of John S. C. Knowlton, John R. Adams, John L. Sheafe, Edward C. Purdy, John S. Sleeper, H. H. Weld, John P. Robinson, Seth Ames, Charles H. Locke, Daniel H. Knowlton, Leonard Huntress, Thomas Hopkinson, Elisha Bartlett, Elisha Huntington, Elisha Fuller, Albert Locke, Robbins Dinsmore, William O. Bartlett, Daniel S. Richardson, William Schouler, William S. Robinson, James Atkinson, Leander R. Streeter, John H. Warland, Charles Cowley, John A. Goodwin, Benjamin W. Ball, Samuel N. Merrill, Homer A. Cooke, Zina E. Stone and George A. Marden.

In this list are many of the ablest men that have ever resided in Lowell. Under their management this paper was often quoted as authority by other journals in New England. But the gravitation of all things toward Boston, with the immense and inevitable superiority of the papers of that city, has arrested the growth of the *Courier*, and of many other papers within equal proximity to "the Hub." What with steam-railroads, horse-railroads, telegraphs and the habit of traveling, Lowell is now, practically, as near to Boston as Charlestown was in the first days of the *Courier*. It is time that counts now. Space is extinguished.

By this time, the fame of Lowell as a theatre of the Cotton Manufacture had extended throughout Christendom. The solid Englishman, the impressible Frenchman, the phlegmatic Dutchman, thought the tour of the United States incomplete until he had visited Lowell. It was not enough to visit New York and New Orleans, traverse the prairies, climb the Alleghanies, and listen to the thunder of Niagara. He must come to the City of Spindles, and enter the great temples of the "Divinity of Labor," each more spacious than the Temple of Jeddo, the Mosque of St. Sophia, or the Cathedral of Milan; and hear from the legions of priests and priestesses "the Gospel according to Poor Richard's Almanac."

Through these visitors, Lowell first awoke to the singular beauty of her own natural scenery. The whole valley of the

Merrimack is noted for its picturesqueness; but from the mountains to the main, there is no lovelier scene than that which meets the eye when from the summit of Christian Hill, we look down upon Lowell, and survey the varied landscape unrolled like a beautiful map before us. The spacious natural amphitheatre surrounded by hills, — the sky-blue rivers, — the long lines of mills,—the labyrinth of brick and masonry, —the obeliscal chimnies curtaining the heavens with smoke,— the spires of churches, belfries of factories, and gables o houses,—the radiant cross of St. Patrick's pointing away from earth,—the forests in the background, and the noble blue mountains of Monadnock, Wachusett and Watatic in the distance,—all combine to form a scene that must be pleasing to every eye that has been quickened to the beauties of art and nature.

CHAPTER VI.

CHURCH HISTORY OF LOWELL.

St. Anne's—First Baptist—First Congregational—St. Paul's—First Universalist—Unitarian—Appleton Street Congregational—Worthen Street Baptist—St. Patrick's—Freewill Baptist—Second Universalist—Third Baptist —John Street Congregational—Worthen Street Methodist—St. Peter's—Ministry-at-Large—Kirk Street Congregational—High Street Congregational—St. Mary's—Third Universalist—Central Methodist—Lee Street Unitarian—Prescott Street Wesleyan—Methodist Protestant Church—St. John's.

St. Anne's Church was the first edifice that was dedicated to religious worship in the present territory of Lowell, since the erection of that modest log chapel in which the Rev. John Eliot and his Indian assistant, Samuel, preached to the copper-colored Christians of Wamesit, two centuries ago.

The founders of the Merrimack Corporation made early provision for religious worship among their operatives. "In December, 1822," says Appleton, "Messrs. Jackson and Boott were appointed a committee to build a suitable church; and in April, 1824, it was voted that it should be built of stone, not to exceed a cost of nine thousand dollars." The Episcopal form of service was adopted, because Mr. Boott was an Episcopalian, and naturally desired to bring into "the Church" as many as possible of the people then flocking to East Chelmsford, some of whom had drank of one dilution of Christianity, some of another, and some of none at all. The church was organized, February 24th, 1824, and was called originally "The Merrimack Religious Society."

The first public religious services were conducted by the Rev. Theodore Edson, on Sunday, March 7th, 1824, in the Merrimack Company's School House, which was opened to pupils the same year. The church edifice and the parsonage adjoining were erected in 1825. It is a substantial edifice, built of dark stone, with Gothic doors and arched windows, and shaded by forest trees. The cost of the edifice, including subsequent additions, was about $16,000. It was consecrated by Bishop Griswold, March 16th, 1825.* The Rev. Dr. Edson, the first and only rector of this church, bids fair to celebrate the Jubilee of St. Anne's, in 1874.

In the tower of St. Anne's is a chime of eleven bells, mounted in 1857, weighing nearly ten thousand pounds and costing over $4,000. Their sonorous tones would be better appreciated had they been placed higher.

> "Amid these peaceful scenes their sound
> Has soothed the wretched—cheered the poor;
> In them has Love a solace found,
> And Hope a friend sincere and sure."

On the eighth of February, 1826, the First Baptist Church was organized. The church edifice—one of the largest in Lowell—was built the same year, the land being given to the society by Mr. Thomas Hurd, the satinet manufacturer mentioned in a former chapter. The edifice, which cost over $10,000, was dedicated November 15th, 1826, when the Rev. John Cookson was installed as pastor. He was dismissed August 5th, 1827, and was succeeded, June 4th, 1828, by the Rev. Enoch W. Freeman, who remained until his mysterious death, September 22nd, 1835. Rev. Joseph W. Eaton was ordained pastor of this church, February 24th, 1836, and dismissed February 1st, 1837. Rev. Joseph Ballard was installed December 25th, 1837, and dismissed September 1st, 1845. Rev. Daniel C. Eddy was ordained, January 29th, 1846, and dismissed after a longer pastorate than any of his predecessors, at the close of 1856. Dr. Eddy was Speaker of the Massachusetts House of Representatives in 1855, and Chaplain of the Senate in 1856. Rev. William H. Alden was installed June 14th, 1857, and dismissed in April, 1864. Rev. William E. Stanton was ordained November 2nd, 1865.

The First Congregational Church was organized June 6th, 1826. The church edifice was built in 1827, on land given

* See the St. Anne's Church case, 14 Gray, pp. 586-613; and Edson's Thirtieth Anniversary Sermon.

by the Locks and Canals Company, and cost, with improvements, some $13,000. The first pastor, Rev. George C. Beckwith, was ordained July 18th, 1827, and dismissed March 18th, 1829. Rev. Amos Blanchard, D. D., was ordained December 5th, 1829, and dismissed May 21st, 1845, when he became pastor of the Kirk Street church. Rev. Willard Child was installed pastor, October 1st, 1845, and dismissed January 31st, 1855. Rev. J. L. Jenkins was ordained October 17th, 1855, and dismissed in April, 1862. Rev. George N. Webber was installed in October, 1862, and dismissed April 1st, 1867. Rev. Horace James, the present pastor, succeeded him.

The Hurd Street Methodist Episcopal Church dates from 1826. The edifice is the largest Protestant church in Lowell; it was erected in 1839, at an expense of $18,500. It being the custom of the denomination to make frequent changes in the location of their clergy, the pastors of this church have been numerous, and their terms of service brief. Rev. Benjamin Griffin was pastor in 1826; A. D. Merrill in 1827; B. F. Lambert in 1828; A. D. Sargeant in 1829; E. K. Avery in 1830 and 1831; George Pickering in 1832; A. D. Merrill, for the second time, in 1833 and 1834; Ira M. Bidwell in 1835; Orange Scott in 1836; E. M. Stickney in 1837 and 1838; Orange Scott, again, in 1839 and 1840; Schuyler Hoes in 1841 and 1842; W. H. Hatch in 1843 and 1844; Abel Stevens in 1845; C. K. True in 1846 and 1847; A. A. Willets in 1848; John H. Twombly in 1849 and 1850; G. F. Cox in 1851 and 1852; L. D. Barrows in 1853 and 1854; D. E. Chapin 1855; George M. Steele in 1856 and 1857; H. M. Loud in 1858 and 1859; William R. Clark in 1860 and 1861; Daniel Dorchester in 1862 and 1863; Samuel F. Upham in 1864, 1865 and 1866. In 1865, Rev. Mr. Upham was Chaplain of the Massachusetts House of Representatives. He was succeeded by Rev. S. F. Jones, in 1867.

In July, 1827, a society was organized under the name of the First Universalist Church. In the following year, they erected their church on Chapel street, but removed it in 1837 to Central street. The edifice cost $16,000. The first pastor settled over this church was the Rev. Eliphalet Case, who officiated here from 1828 to 1830, but afterward abandoned the ministry to become a reformer, a politician, a post-master, a journalist, and a rum-seller. The next four pastors were Calvin Gardner, from 1830 to 1833; Thomas B. Thayer, from 1833 to 1845; E. G. Brooks, in 1845; and Uriah Clark, from 1846 to 1850, when he began to develope "Free Love" proclivities. Rev. T. B. Thayer was again settled here in 1851, and remained till October, 1857. He was much beloved by his people, and the regrets which attended his departure, were intensified by a painful accident shortly afterward, which involved the fracture and almost loss of a leg, with the additional affliction of a newspaper war with some of his own surgeons. In 1859, Rev. J. J. Twiss succeeded Dr. Thayer.

At the time of the organization of this society, the lords of the loom, under the monarchy of Kirk Boott, exercised arbitrary power, not only over the acts and votes, but also over the thoughts and even over the charities of those in their employ. To cherish the hope that the loving-kindness of the Father will attend the whole family of man through the life to come, was enough to put any man under a cloud. For contributing toward the erection of this church, and for advocating the principles of Gen. Jackson, Mr. (now Rev.) T. J. Greenwood was dismissed from his place as an overseer on the Merrimack Corporation by the direct order of Mr. Boott. Such an act of bigotry would hardly occur now. We have made some progress during the forty years of Lowell. By the way, it was in Mr. Greenwood's room, that Nathaniel P. Banks began his career as a "bobbin-boy," ere yet he aspired to become a lawyer, legislator, governor, major-general, etc.

The South Congregational (Unitarian) Church was organized November 7th, 1830. The edifice cost $32,000, and was dedicated December 25th, 1832. Rev. William Barry was pastor of this church from 1830 to 1835; Henry A. Miles, D. D., from 1836 to 1853; Theodore Tibbetts, in 1855 and 1856; Frederick Hinckley, from 1856 to 1864. Rev. Charles Grinnell was ordained pastor February 19th, 1867.

The Appleton Street (Orthodox) Congregational Church dates from December 2nd, 1830. The edifice, which cost $9,000, was erected in 1831. The succession of pastors has been—William Twining from 1831 to 1835; U. C. Burnap, from 1837 to 1852; George Darling, from 1852 to 1855; John P. Cleaveland, D. D., from 1855 to 1862, when he became Chaplain of the Thirtieth Regiment, in the Department of the Gulf; J. E. Rankin, from 1863 to 1865. Rev. A. P. Foster was ordained October 3rd, 1866.

The Worthen Street Baptist Church was organized in 1831. The edifice known as St. Mary's Church was built for this society. The present edifice was built in 1838, costing $8,000. The pastors have been—James Barnaby, from 1832 to 1835; Lemuel Porter, from 1835 to 1851; J. W. Smith, from 1851 to 1853; D. D. Winn, from 1853 to 1855; T. D. Worrall, of memory like Uriah Clark, from 1855 to 1857; J. W. Bonham, from 1857 to 1860; George F. Warren, from 1860 to 1867.

The digging of the canals and the building of the mills early attracted the sons of "the Emerald Isle" to Lowell. Different clergymen of their faith attended them here, secured for the time such places as were obtainable, and offered "the clean sacrifice for the quick and dead." In 1831, a church was erected called St. Patrick's, which was replaced in 1854 by the splendid edifice which now bears that name, the cost of which was about $75,000. This building is 186 feet long by 106 wide. The height of the body of the church is 61 feet from the floor. The architecture is of the Gothic style of the thirteenth century. Bishop Fitzpatrick of Boston, assisted by Bishop O'Riley of Hartford, consecrated this church, October 29th, 1854. The pastors of St. Patrick's have been—Revs. John Mahoney, Peter Connelly, James T. McDermott, Henry J. Tucker, and John O'Brien. Among the many assistants that have officiated here, was Rev. Timothy O'Brien, who died in 1855, and to whose memory an elegant monument was erected in St. Patrick's Church-yard.

In 1833, a free church of the Christian denomination was organized under the ministry of Rev. Timothy Cole. Successful for some years, the experiment finally failed; and Cole's church, after passing through the hands of the Methodists, became first a dance-hall, and afterward the armory of the Jackson Musketeers, an Irish military company, whose muskets were taken from them by Gov. Gardner. Having mentioned the Jackson Musketeers, it is but fair to say that when the late war broke out in 1861, they forgot and forgave the Know Nothing fanaticism of 1855, and, rushing to arms among the first, illustrated on many a bloody field how bravely the sons of Ireland die for their adopted homes.

The Freewill Baptist Church was organized in 1834. The proprietors were incorporated in 1836. The spacious edifice on Merrimack street, opposite Central street, was erected in

1837, at a cost of $20,000, which was largely contributed by the factory girls. There preached the somewhat famous Elder Thurston, now no more; an honest man, and popular as a preacher, but incapable of managing important matters of business, such as he was foolishly encouraged to undertake, in connection with this church. Through his incapacity, more than ten thousand dollars was lost, in the course of six years, and a tremendous panic ensued. He was denounced as a thief, and indicted and convicted of cheating; but the Supreme Court set the verdict aside, and the prosecution of the elder was stopped.

Then arose controversies about the church property,* which was under more than fifty attachments at once. These suits ended adversely to the society; and on July 29th, 1846, the deacons were forcibly ejected from the church by Joseph Butterfield, a Deputy Sheriff, on an execution issued upon a judgment belonging to Benjamin F. Butler, Thomas Hopkinson, and Tappan Wentworth, who personally assisted in ousting the deacons.

That comedy might follow tragedy, the new proprietors, Benjamin F. Butler and Fisher A. Hildreth, converted the church into a museum and theatre. After being used thus for nine years, once struck by lightning, and three times burned, in 1856, this ill-starred edifice was fitted up for a dance-hall, a bowling alley, lawyers' offices, a newspaper office, an exchange, etc.

Attempts have been made to use one part of it as a lecture-hall, but without success; though the famous Lola Montez, the discarded mistress of the late king of Bavaria, delivered her lecture on Beautiful Women here. Nor have the attempts to use this edifice as a caucus-hall been any more successful. The last attempt of the kind was made in 1860. On that memorable occasion, Theodore H. Sweetser began a speech; but just as he was capping his first climax, a gentleman who

*8 Metcalf, 301; 2 Cushing, 597; 4 Cushing, 302.

disapproved of his remarks, suddenly turned off the gas, and "brought down the house" in the wildest merriment and confusion.

The strategical manœuverings by which this edifice was transferred from the ecclesiastical proprietors to their lay successors, were none too creditable to the consciences of the manipulators. But perhaps they did not fully realize the scandalousness of their proceedings, and failed to hear the still, small voice of conscience in following the more clamorous calls of avarice and ambition.

More than twenty years have now elapsed since the perversion of this edifice into a museum. Let us hope that before another twenty years have rolled by, this church—the monument of the piety of the factory girls of Lowell—will be restored to its original purposes, and reconsecrated to the worship of the everliving God.

In 1853, another edifice was built on Paige street, costing $16,700, now occupied by this church. The pastors of this church have been—Revs. Nathaniel Thurston, Jonathan Woodman, Silas Curtis, A. K. Moulton, J. B. Davis, Darwin Mott, (a wolf in sheep's clothing, who finally ran away with another man's wife,) George W. Bean, and J. B. Drew.

The Second Universalist Church was gathered in 1836, and the house erected in 1837, at a cost of $20,000. The pastors of this church have been—Z. Thompson, from 1837 to 1839; Abel C. Thomas, from 1839 to 1842; A. A. Miner, D. D., from 1842 to 1848; L. J. Fletcher, who became involved in his domestic relations, and remained but a few months; L. B. Mason, from 1848 to 1849; I. D. Williamson, from 1849 to 1850; N. M. Gaylord, from 1850 to 1853. John S. Dennis, Charles Cravens and Charles H. Dutton were then settled here for a few months each. In 1859, Rev. L. J. Fletcher again became pastor, having, since his former settlement, run a varied career as preacher, play-writer, actor, gold-miner, school-master, lawyer, politician, judge of insolvency, etc. His second pastorate continued three years, and was eminently successful. Rev. F. E. Hicks succeeded Mr. Fletcher, but soon died, and was succeeded in 1866 by Rev. John G. Adams.

On July 4th, 1836, the Lowell Sabbath School Union was organized, by the pastors of the several evangelical churches, and the superintendents and teachers of the various Sunday Schools connected therewith.

The John Street (Orthodox) Congregational Church was organized May 9th, 1839. Their edifice was built the same year, at a cost of $20,000, and dedicated January 24th, 1840. Rev. Stedman W. Hanks, the first pastor, was ordained March 20th, 1840, and dismissed February 3rd, 1853. He was succeeded by Rev. Eden B. Foster, D. D., who resigned his charge in 1861, but resumed his ministrations here in 1866. During his absence, Rev. Joseph W. Backus, was pastor.

In 1840, the Third Baptist Church was organized. In 1846, the edifice now occupied by the Central Methodist Church, was built for this society, costing about $14,000. After battling for life for nearly twenty years, under the pastorates of Revs.

John G. Naylor, Ira Person, John Duncan, Sereno Howe, John Duer, and John Hubbard, this church was disbanded in 1861.

The mention of the Rev. Sereno Howe renders it proper to say, that during his seven years' residence in Lowell, from 1849 to 1856, his private life was irreproachable. That he afterward became addicted to licentious indulgencies, in Abington, may, in charity, be attributed to constitutional infirmities, against which he may have struggled long and bravely, but in vain.

> "What's done we partly may compute,
> But know not what's resisted."

The Worthen Street Methodist Episcopal Church was organized October 2nd, 1841, and the edifice erected in 1842, at a cost of $8,800. The succession of pastors has been—Revs. A. D. Sargeant, A. D. Merrill, J. S. Springer, Isaac A. Savage, Charles Adams, I. J. P. Collyer, M. A. Howe, J. W. Dadmun,

William H. Hatch, A. D. Sargeant, (again), L. R. Thayer, William H. Hatch, (again), and J. O. Peck, one of the gayest Lotharios that ever flourished in the Lowell pulpit. Rev. George Whittaker succeeded Mr. Peck in 1867.

St Peter's Roman Catholic Church was gathered on Christmas Day, 1841, and the edifice built the same year, costing $22,000. Rev. James Conway, the first pastor of St. Peter's, was succeeded in March, 1847, by Rev. Peter Crudden.

In 1843, the Lowell Missionary Society established a Ministry-at-Large after the style of that established in Boston by the Rev. Dr. Tuckerman. Rev. Horatio Wood has officiated in this ministry since 1844. He has also labored assiduously and successfully in Free Evening Schools, Sunday Mission Schools, etc.

The Kirk Street Congregational Church dates from 1845, and the edifice from 1846. The cost of the land, edifice, organ, etc., was $22,000. Rev. Amos Blanchard, D. D., has been pastor of this church ever since its organization.

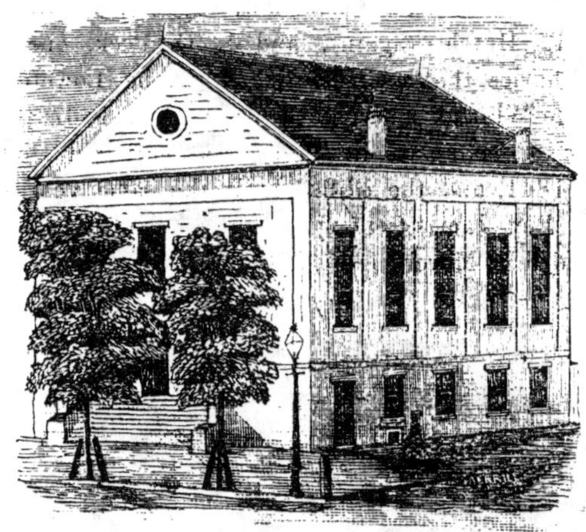

In the substantial elements of parochial strength, this church is one of the strongest in Lowell. Yet four lines suffice for its history—it having had no changes in its pastorate, no heresy, no schism, no scamps, no scandal. "Happy are the people whose annals are barren."

The High Street Congregational Church was organized in 1846. Their edifice, which cost $12,500, was built by St. Luke's Church, an Episcopal society which was formed in 1842, and which perished in 1844, under Rev. A. D. McCoy. The pastors have been—Rev. Timothy Atkinson, from 1846 to 1847; Rev. Joseph H. Towne, from 1848 to 1853; and Rev. O. T. Lamphier, from 1855 to 1856. Rev. Owen Street, the present pastor, was installed September 17th, 1857.

St. Mary's Roman Catholic Church was originally built for the Baptists, but was ill located for any Protestant sect. After passing through various vicissitudes, in 1846, it was purchased by the late Rev. James T. McDermott, and consecrated March 7th, 1847. Father McDermott's independence of mind involved him in a controversy with his Diocesan, the late Bishop Fitzpatrick; and for years this church has been closed. This is much to be regretted; for in Lowell, as in all the centres of population, the Roman Catholic Church has a great body of the poor and laboring classes in her communion; and as Brownson remarks, "the country is more indebted than it is aware of, to the Catholic priesthood, for their labors among this portion of our population."*

In 1843, the Third Universalist Church was organized, and the edifice now known as Barrister's Hall built for its use. But after a languid existence under Revs. H. G Smith, John Moore, H. G. Smith, (again), and L. J. Fletcher, it was dissolved. The two last pastors of this church were not in full fellowship with their denomination, but preached independently as ecclesiastical guerrillas.

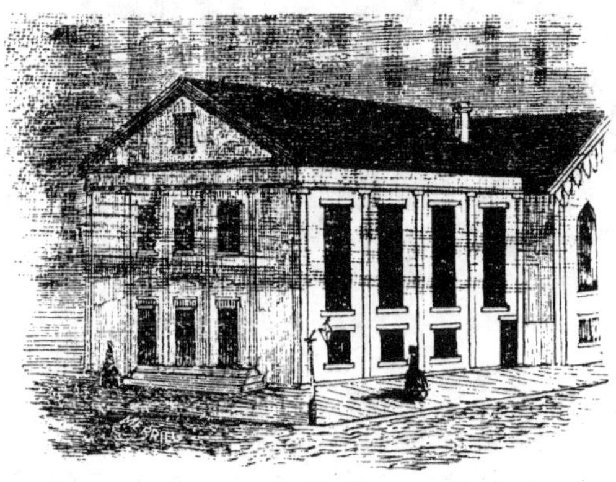

The Central Methodist Church occupied this edifice, after the collapse of the Universalist society, until 1861, when they secured the building of the Third Baptist Church, then defunct. This Central Methodist society was gathered in 1854. The pastors have been—Revs. William S. Studley,

*Father O'Brien estimates the number of Roman Catholics in Lowell to be fifteen thousand.

Isaac S. Cushman, Isaac J. P. Collyer, Chester Field, Lorenzo R. Thayer and J. H. Mansfield. Rev. Andrew McKeown succeeded Mr. Mansfield in 1865, and remained two years. He was succeeded in 1867 by Rev. William C. High.

In 1850, a picturesque stone edifice, of Gothic style, with stained windows, was erected on Lee street, at a cost of $20,000. It was designed for a Unitarian society, organized in 1846, which occupied it until 1861, whose pastors were Revs. M. A. H. Niles, William Barry, Augustus Woodbury, J. K. Karcher, John B. Willard, and William C. Tenney.

Since 1864 it has been occupied by a society of Spiritualists.

The wooden edifice on Prescott street containing Leonard Worcester's clothes-making establishment, has an ecclesiastical history that must not be lost. It was the first church erected by the Episcopal Methodists in Lowell, and was built in 1827. It stood originally at the corner of Elm and Central streets. It is from this church or chapel that Chapel Hill derives its name. On the completion of the Hurd street church in 1839, this edifice was closed. But on the organization of the Wesleyan Methodists as a separate denomination, this church passed into their hands. In 1843, it was removed to Prescott Street. Here successively preached Revs. E. S. Potter, James Hardy, Merritt Bates, William H. Brewster,* and Daniel Foster, who became Chaplain of the Massachusetts House of Representatives in 1857, and subsequently Chaplain of the Thirty-Third Regiment of Massachusetts Volunteers, and who was killed in battle at Fort Harrison, September 30th, 1864, while in command of a company of the Thirty-Seventh Colored Troops.

If Captain Foster was the last, Mr. Hardy was the most popular in this succession of pastors. He began his ministry here in 1846, and flourished brilliantly for a time, selecting the best sermons of the ablest English divines, and palming them off as his own—his too credulous people admiring and wondering at his ability and versatility.

"And still he talked, and still the wonder grew,
That one small head could carry all he knew."

Mr. Hardy, however, proved anything but a good shepherd He developed tendencies toward practical Mormonism and Free Love. He not only had one wife too many, but he was discovered in a *liason* with one of the ladies of his choir, and his pastorate was brought to an abrupt termination. He subsequently "took a degree" in a New York penitentiary for bigamy, and died ingloriously.

On July 5th, 1855, the stone edifice on Merrimack street erected by the late William Wyman, was dedicated as a Methodist Protestant Church. There preached Revs. William Marks, Richard H. Dorr, Robert Crossley, and others,

---

* Mr. Brewster had previously been pastor of a second Wesleyan society, which long occupied the edifice on Lowell street, where Rev. Timothy Cole formerly preached.

both clerical and lay, not the least of whom was Captain Wyman himself. But after a few years the enterprise aborted; and the edifice passed into the hands of the Second Adventists, a society formed here as early as 1842.

St. John's Episcopal church was erected in 1861, and consecrated by Bishop Eastburn, July 16th, 1863. Rev. Charles W. Homer, who had previously been assistant minister at St. Anne's, was the first rector. On November 22nd, 1862, he resigned, and was succeeded in 1863, by Rev. Cornelius B. Smith, to whom in 1866 succeeded Rev. Charles L. Hutchins. In this edifice is a Memorial Window to the late Elisha Huntington.

Besides the churches herein chronicled, others have been formed at various times, which acquired no permanent foothold, but experienced all varieties of fortune, and passed into the limbo of oblivion, leaving no discernable footprints on the ever-changing sands of time.

The number of churches now "in commission" here is eighteen. The population of Lowell is about forty thousand. If, then, we assume each church to have, upon an average, six hundred attendants, we shall have, in the aggregate, ten thousand eight hundred church-goers; and if to this we add twenty-two hundred who are reached through the Ministry-at-Large, the Mission Schools, etc., we shall still have twenty-seven thousand souls unprovided with stated religious instruction.

CHAPTER VII.

SCHOOL HISTORY OF LOWELL.

District Schools—High School—Edson—Washington—Bartlett—Adams—Franklin—Moody—Green—Mann—Colburn—Varnum—Intermediate—Evening—Carney Medals—Superintendence, etc.

Before the manufacturing companies began their operations here, the eastern school district of Chelmsford contained two common district schools, one near the pound on the old Chelmsford road, and the other near Pawtucket Falls. In 1824, the Merrimack Company, at their own expense, established a school for the children of their operatives, and placed it under the supervision of Rev. Theodore Edson, their minister. This school—the germ of the present Bartlett Sehool—was kept in the lower story of the building then occupied by the Merrimack Religious Society. Colburn's "First Lessons," and his "Sequel" were introduced here, though much denounced and opposed by those who did not understand them. In the following year, the opposition to Colburn's books abated, the school being then in charge of Joel Lewis, who had been a pupil of Colburn, and understood the use of his books.

In 1826, the new-born town of Lowell was divided into six school districts; and one thousand dollars was appropriated for the support of schools during that year. The school for the first district was that which the Merrimack Company had founded; that for the second district stood near where the Hospital now stands; that for the third, near the Pound; that for the fourth, near Hale's Mills; that for the fifth—the germ of the present Edson School—near the site of the Free Chapel; that for the sixth, near the south corner of Central and Hurd streets. As population multiplied, other schools were opened, but the number of districts remained unchanged until 1832, when the district system terminated.

The first School Committee consisted of Theodore Edson, Warren Colburn, Samuel Batchelder, John O. Green, and Elisha Huntington. Their report was read in the town meeting in March, 1827, and recorded in the town book. The appropriate custom of reading school committees' reports in town meeting is now universal in Massachusetts. Concord, which claims the honor of leading in this custom, did not adopt it until 1830, four years after it had been introduced in Lowell.*

In the management of these schools, the School Committee, for some years, encountered many difficulties, through the fierce antagonisms of interest and feeling which arose between the old settlers and the operatives in the mills. The old prejudice against Colburn's books soon revived with unwonted fury, especially in the third district, which was the smallest and the most troublesome in the town. In the winter of 1826–7, a teacher—Perley Morse—was employed by the Prudential Committee, who joined in the opposition to Colburn's books, and whom the School Committee refused to approve; but the Prudential Committee, contrary to law, backed by the people, sustained him in his school. The excitement reached its crisis at the town meeting in March, 1828. The report of the School Committee had no sooner been read, than, by vote of the meeting, it was *laid under the table*, and a motion was made that the Committee be laid under the table too. Neither Colburn, nor Edson, nor any of their associates were then re-elected; but a new Committee was chosen, perfectly supple and subservient to popular caprice.

The operation of the complex machinery of the District system was attended with constant friction; and on the third of September, 1832, a town meeting was held to determine

---

*Edson's Colburn School Address, p. 12. Mr. Boutwell's statement on the sixty-first page of his last report as Secretary of the Board of Education, requires correction. For the roll of School Committee-men, see the Appendix to the Regulations of the School Committee, 1867. See also Merrill's school sketches in Lowell *Courier*, December, 1859.

whether the town would authorize a loan of $20,000 to defray the expense of buying land and building two large school houses, with the view of consolidating all the public schools of the town in two large schools, and thus superseding the District system altogether. The whole body of corporation influence, with Kirk Boott to wield it at his imperial will, was brought to bear against the proposed reform; and not a few of the old settlers also clung with fond tenacity to their "*deestrict*" schools. So formidable was this opposition, that, although the local clergy and all the most intelligent friends of education strongly favored the innovation, only one man was found with courage enough to advocate it in town meeting. Single handed and alone, Theodore Edson met Kirk Boott and his allies breast to breast; not hesitating

> "To beard the lion in his den,
> The Douglass in his hall."

During a protracted and tumultuous debate, Edson held his ground unflinchingly, and finally carried his point by twelve majority. Chafing under their defeat, the adherents of the old system called another town meeting on the nineteenth of the same month, when another debate ensued, more tumultuous and more decisive than the last. Two new champions — John P. Robinson and Luther Lawrence — entered the list with Boott; but Edson stood alone as before, and when the vote was taken, carried his point by thirty-eight majority, — convincing his opponents that it would be folly to renew the fight.

The part played by Dr. Edson in this contest was never forgiven by Boott, who even withdrew from the church in which the Doctor officiated. For a time, none of the corporation nabobs would have anything to do with the schools thus erected contrary to their sovereign will and pleasure. It was only when Henry Clay came to Lowell that their High Mightinesses were graciously pleased to let the light of their countenances shine for a moment on the benighted little Hottentots that filled the North and South Grammar Schools.

To detail in full the history of all the schools would be tedious; but the principal schools must not be passed unnoticed; for, as Edward Everett observes, "the dedication of a new first-class school house is at all times an event of far greater importance to the welfare of the community than many of the occurrences which at the time attract much more of the public attention, and fill a larger space in the pages of history."

In December, 1831, the Lowell High School was opened ununder Thomas M. Clark, now Bishop of Rhode Island, as principal teacher. One of his classes contained four boys whose subsequent history may well excite pride in their teacher, if so unsanctified a feeling ever obtains access to the episcopal breast. These boys were Benjamin F. Butler, whose exploits have been recorded with fond exaggeration by Parton; Gustavus V. Fox, the energetic Assistant Secretary of the Navy during the War; E. A. Straw, the efficient Agent of the Amoskeag Mills at Manchester; and George L. Balcom, of Claremont, one of the wealthiest and most successful men in New Hampshire.

The present High School House was erected in 1840, and reconstructed in 1867. Mr. Clark was succeeded in September, 1833, by Nicholas Hoppin; in August, 1834, by William Hall; in May, 1835, by Franklin Forbes; in August 1836, by Moody Currier; in April, 1841, by Nehemiah Cleaveland; in July, 1842, by Mr. Forbes (again;) and in July, 1845, by Charles C. Chase, who has ever since ably and worthily sustained himself at the head of the Lowell corps of teachers.

On February 18th, 1833, the South Grammar School-House was opened, and two schools were united and placed in it. One was the school of what had been the fifth district, which, since November 5th, 1827, had been taught by Joshua Merrill. The school thus formed was the same that afterward took the name of the Edson School. Joshua Merrill had charge of it until October, 1845,* when Perley Balch succeeded him.

* In 1841 and 1842, Mr. Merrill had for his assistant Theodore H. Sweetser, who has since acquired notoriety by his success at the Bar.

In 1856, this edifice was reconstructed, and the Washington School consolidated with the Edson. This Washington School was founded March 24th, 1834, kept for four years in the North School-House, and then removed to the South School-House. Its principals were Nathaniel D. Healey from 1834 to 1835; Samuel S. Dutton and Isaac Whittier in 1835; John Butterfield from 1835 to 1840; Jonathan Kimball from 1840 to 1851; Albert T. Young from 1851 to 1853; P. W. Robertson from 1853 to 1856.

In May, 1833, the North Grammar School-House was completed, and the school, which, until then, had occupied the Merrimack Company's school-house, was moved into the upper part of it, and has continued to occupy it ever since. The principals of this school have been—Joel Lewis from 1825 to 1826; Alfred V. Bassett from 1826 to 1829; Walter Abbott from 1829 to 1830; Reuben Hills from 1830 to 1835; Jacob Graves from 1835 to 1841; G. O. Fairbanks from 1841 to 1842; O. C. Wright from 1842 to 1843; Jacob Graves from 1843 to 1847; and J. P. Fisk from 1847 to 1856, when the edifice was reconstructed and Samuel Bement became principal. Originally known as the Merrimack School, on being removed in 1833 it took the name of the North Grammar School, which it retained till 1850, when the School Committee named it the Hancock School. On the reconstruction of the building in 1856, this school received the name of the Bartlett School, in honor of Dr. Bartlett, the first Mayor of Lowell. At the same time, the Adams School, was consolidated with the Bartlett. The Adams was opened in 1836 in the lower part of the North Grammar School-House. Its first principal was Otis H. Morrill, to whom Samuel Bement succeeded in 1851.

The City Charter of 1836 provided that the School Committee should consist of six persons specially chosen, in addition to the Mayor and Aldermen; but in 1856 the Charter was amended, and the Aldermen detached from the School Committee, the number of which was increased to twelve, besides the Mayor and the President of the Common Council.

The Franklin Grammar School dates from the winter of 1839, when Rufus Adams opened a school near where the Franklin now stands. George Spaulding taught here from 1840 to 1844, when Nelson H. Morse succeeded him. The present edifice was erected in 1845, and remodeled in 1863. In 1848, Mr. Morse was succeeded first by Ephraim Brown, and afterward by Ephraim W. Young. In 1849, Amos B. Heywood was placed in charge of this school.

On January 8th, 1841, the Moody Grammar School was opened under Seth Pooler, who had been an assistant in the High School since 1838, and who continued principal of the Moody School until 1856, when Joseph Peabody succeeded him.

A few months subsequent to the opening of the Moody School, the Green School was opened. Samuel C. Pratt was principal from 1841 to 1843; Aaron Walker, Junior, from 1843 to 1845; Charles Morrill from 1845 to 1866, when he was chosen Superintendent of Schools. Charles A. Chase succeeded him.

On January 8th, 1844, the Mann Grammar School-House was opened. The school itself had existed as a public school ever since 1835, when the arrangement for comprehending the Irish schools in the public school system of Lowell was first effected by the School Committee and Rev. James Connolly,* the Roman Catholic priest. In 1839 another school was consolidated with it which had previously been in charge of Daniel

* See Reports of the School Committee, 1836 and 1844; Mrs. Mann's Life of Horace Mann, p. 262; New Englander, April, 1848. This arrangement was that the teachers of the Irish children's schools should be Roman Catholics. They were, however, to be subject to examination, and their schools to visitation by the School Committee, in the same manner as other teachers and schools. In a few years, however, the jealousies which rendered this arrangement advisable, subsided, and differences of creed ceased to be recognized in any form in connection with the public schools.

McIllroy. The principals of the present Mann School have been—Patrick Collins, from 1835 to 1838; Daniel McIllroy, from 1838 to 1841; James Egan, from 1841 to 1843; Michael Flynn, from 1843 to 1844; George W. Shattuck, from 1844 to 1853. P. W. Roberston and Albert T. Young were then each in charge for a few months; but before the close of 1853, Samuel A. Chase was appointed principal, and has remained here ever since.

On December 13th, 1848, the Colburn School was opened, when Dr. Edson delivered an address, full of interesting reminiscences of the early school history of Lowell. Aaron Walker, Junior, was principal from 1848 until 1864, when Fidelia O. Dodge succeeded him.

On the annexation of the faubourg of Centralville in 1851, the Varnum School was opened. A. W. Boardman was principal during the two first years, and was succeeded by D. P. Galloupe. Originally kept in the old Academy Building, in 1857, it was removed into the spacious edifice which it now occupies.

In 1851, the School Committee established Intermediate Schools to meet the wants of a numerous class of Irish pupils, too large to be placed to the Primaries, and too backward to be admitted to the Grammar Schools. But in ten years the necessity which called these schools into being, was no longer felt, and they were consolidated with the Grammar Schools.

In 1857, two free Evening Schools which had previously been conducted by the Lowell Missionary Association, were, by vote of the School Committee, comprehended within the public school system of Lowell. In 1859, there were six public evening schools—three for boys and three for girls—under the supervision of the School Committee.* They had two sessions per week and imparted instruction to about five hundred pupils. If any schools should be public and free, surely the *evening schools* of the industrious uninstructed poor

* Report of School Committee, 1859, pp. 28–31.

should be public and free. Yet these have been suffered to languish and die; and the Missionary Society has resumed the work which properly belonged to the city.

In 1858, Mr. James G. Carney presented one hundred dollars to the city, upon the condition that the interest thereof shall annually be appropriated to the procuring of six silver medals, to be distributed to the six best scholars in the High School, forever,—three in the girls' department and three in boys' department. The liberal donation was accepted, and the faith of the city pledged to the just discharge of the trust.* Such was the origin of the Carney Medals, which will continue to be striven for by the pupils of the High School when the dust of unnumbered centuries shall cover the grave of their founder.

In 1859, the experiment of a Superintendent of Public Schools was first tried in Lowell, George W. Shattuck being appointed to that office. But toward the close of the year a popular clamor was raised, and the office abolished. It was revived in 1864, when Abner J. Phipps was made Superintendent. The credit of the revival of this useful and necessary office is largely due to the School Committee. Mr. Phipps was succeeded in 1866 by Charles Morrill.

In 1863, John F. McEvoy, John H. McAlvin and others founded the Lowell High School Association. Annual levees are held by this society, whereat the lives, adventures, songs, services, speeches, hair-breadth escapes and deeds of valor by flood and field of the past pupils of the High School, are commemorated with becoming enthusiasm.

The public educational system of Lowell now consists of one high school, eight grammar schools, and forty-seven primaries, which would probably not suffer by comparison with the schools of other cities in New England.

---

* See Carney Medal Documents, appended to the Report of the School Committee of 1859.

CHAPTER VIII.

GENERAL HISTORY OF LOWELL. 1835—1850.

Marriage and Death of Enoch W. Freeman—Hannah Kinney—Her Trial for Murder—Elias Howe—James C. Ayer—Financial Revulsion—Lowell becomes a City—Death of Kirk Boott—Market House—Courts in Lowell—Death of Luther Lawrence—Wendell Phillips—Lowell Hospital—The Commons—Museum—*The Offering*—Death of Sheriff Varnum—Death of President Harrison—The Cemetery—*Vox Populi*—Charles Dickens—William Graves—President Tyler—Webster Incidents—City Library—Elisha Fuller—Henry F. Durant—Medical Society—Dr. Miles' Book—Newspaper Libels—John G. Whittier—Merrimack River Fisheries—Judge Locke—Judge Crosby—President Polk—Death of Patrick T. Jackson—Northern Canal—Abraham Lincoln—Death of President Taylor—Battle of Suffolk Bridge—Father Mathew—Reservoir on Lynde's Hill.

"The Minister's Wooing" had deeply exercised the ladies of the First Baptist Church, long before that subject employed the pen of Mrs. Harriet Beecher Stowe. Church Committees, *Ex Parte* Councils and Mutual Councils were again and again appointed to consider the scandals growing out of the courtship of Rev. Enoch W. Freeman and Hannah Hanson.* Mr. Freeman was, of course, sustained; but there was still an undercurrent of discontent in the church, on account of his connection with this remarkable woman. She was a native of Lisbon, in Maine, was the cousin of Mr. Freeman, and had had some tender correspondence with him in early life. In January, 1822, she was married to Ward Witham, at her father's house in Portland. Four children were the fruit of this marriage, which proved anything but a happy one. In February, 1832, the Supreme Judicial Court, sitting at Boston, granted her a decree of divorce from the bond of matrimony, on account of the criminality of Witham. A correspondence between Mr. Freeman and her soon afterward commenced, which culminated in their marriage, September 23rd, 1834. For six months they boarded with Mrs. Charlotte Butler,

* Life of Mrs. Kinney, by Herself.

whose son Benjamin—the future pro-consul of New Orleans—was at that time intended for the Baptist ministry. As Pope sighed

"How sweet an Ovid was in Murray lost,"

so may others lament that a Boanerges of the pulpit was spoiled in Butler. In March, 1835, Mr. and Mrs. Freeman made a visit to the father of Mr. Freeman, in Maine. During that visit, the elder Freeman suddenly died, exhibiting the same symptoms which were afterward observed in the case of his son.

Mrs. Freeman continued to be the subject of scandal after her marriage, on account of her supposed intimacy with George T. Kinney of Boston, who had assisted her in obtaining her divorce, and to whom she was said to have been engaged. It was said that Kinney was a frequent visitor at Mr. Freeman's house, and that he was there on the morning of Sunday, September 20th, 1835. On that day, after morning service, Mr. Freeman became suddenly ill, and experienced repeated vomitings. He, however, returned to his pulpit, and commenced the afternoon services, but was unable to proceed, and returned to his house. He continued to grow worse, suffering intense pain internally, until five o'clock on the morning of the following Tuesday, when death released him from his sufferings. He was thirty-seven years of age, and had been married exactly one year. He was a most uxorious husband, and on his death-bed requested that all his wife's children by Witham should adopt his surname. If he really died by poison administered by his wife, his last words to her—"Never feel alone; I shall always be with you"—must have come home with terrible emphasis to her depraved soul.

Just as he closed his eyes in death, he was asked whether he had any advice to leave to his church. He replied, "Tell them to be humble, faithful, zealous and united in love." A *post mortem* examination showed his stomach to have been highly inflamed, but the contents were not subjected to a chemical analysis—no suspicion being then entertained that the death was caused by poison. Mrs. Freeman appeared to be deeply affected by her bereavement. One week subsequently, she was confined. She remained for some time in Lowell, keeping a milliner's shop on Merrimack street. She afterward removed to Boston, from whence she sent a weeping willow to be planted by the monument erected over Mr. Freeman's grave. On November 26th, 1836, she was married to George T. Kinney, a man five years younger than herself—a drunkard, a *roué* and a gambler. On August 10th, 1840, Kinney died in a manner similar to Mr. Freeman; and a coroner's jury found that his death was caused by poison administered by his wife.

Long before the death of Kinney, suspicions had been entertained in Lowell that there had been foul play with Mr. Freeman—that his wife had been guilty of the "deep damnation of his taking off." In consequence of these suspicions, one week subsequent to the death of Kinney, Mr. Freeman's remains were exhumed in the Middlesex street burying-ground and found to be in a remarkable state of preservation. Many a subject has been used to illustrate anatomical lectures, which was more decomposed than the body of Mr. Freeman.

Immediately after Kinney's funeral, Mrs. Kinney made a visit to some of his friends in Thetford, Vermont. There she was arrested and taken back to Boston to stand her trial for murder. On her way thither she stopped at Lowell, arriving here on Sunday afternoon, August 30th. After a few moments' delay, at the American House, she again left in the stage for Boston, in the custody of an officer. Just as the stage was leaving, the congregation to whom Mr. Freeman had ministered, and among whom she had once moved in all the dignity of a pastor's wife, poured along the streets at the close of their afternoon services. With what emotion they gazed on the weeping prisoner, and with what agony she met their gaze, it is easier to imagine than describe.

The trial of Mrs. Kinney for the murder of Kinney began December 21st, 1840, and closed on Christmas Day. The defence was conducted by Franklin Dexter and George T. Curtis. Although she was acquitted by the jury, there have always been persons among those who knew her, who have persisted in believing that she was guilty,—that she poisoned two husbands and one husband's father,—in short, that she was an American Lucretia Borgia. But while the deaths of the three supposed victims are most easily explained upon the hypothesis of poison, the total absence of motive on the part of the accused, envelopes each case in the gravest doubt.

In 1835, Central Village contained about forty dwelling houses. Central Village Academy was incorporated and enjoyed a flourishing existence for some years.

It was in 1835 that Elias Howe, Junior—then a boy of sixteen—came to Lowell. He remained here two years, employed in building cotton machinery. While here, he probably became acquainted with the experiments which John A. Bradshaw was then making with the sewing machine. Nine years later, he invented the famous Lock-Stitch Sewing Machine, for which he obtained a patent in 1846. Little, however, did he appreciate the value of his invention; for he offered to sell his patent for the sum of five hundred dollars—a patent from which he afterward realized half a million dollars in a single year! He died October 3rd, 1867, at Brooklyn.

Among the crowds that took up their abode here synchroniously with Mr. Howe, was a slender youth of seventeen summers, who now stands the foremost of those who have achieved wealth and fame in the manufacture of patent medicines. James C. Ayer was born in Groton, Connecticut, May 5th, 1818, exactly six months earlier than his friend and fellow-citizen, Gen. Butler. His first experiences here were in the family of his uncle, James Cook, and in the High School. As the ardent boy walked occasionally through the Middlesex mills, (of which his uncle was then Agent,) and saw the stockholders and directors in all their pride and pretention, he doubtless hoped that the time would come when he too would be a stockholder and a director. What was then a dream of fancy has long since been realized as a fact.

After quitting the High School, and studying for a short time in the Westford Academy, young Ayer entered the apothecary shop of Jacob Robbins, where he devoted much of his attention to chemistry. In 1843, he commenced the manufacture of medicines for popular use. The result of his enterprise is the mammoth laboratory of which an account has already been given.* The first machine for making pills was invented by him. In recognition of his acquisitions in chemistry and kindred sciences, in 1860, the University of Pennsylvania, in Philadelphia, conferred on him the degree of Doctor of Medicine. Similarity of tastes and opinions on various points brought him into contact with Horace Greeley; and for some years past, Dr. Ayer has been the largest stockholder in the *New York Tribune.*

The people of Lowell participated with their fellow citizens all over New England in the mania which arose prior to 1835, first, respecting the lands in Maine, and afterward spreading till it inflated the prices of land in all the principal cities and towns of New England. Visionary schemes were projected, castles in the air erected, and the wildest expectations cherished that large fortunes were to be made as quickly as by the seal of Solomon or the lamp of Aladdin. This splendid bubble, bursting in 1837, left all its dupes in the gulf of penury. When the commercial history of this country shall be written, it will be found to present a constant series of alternate periods of wild speculation, and periods of bankruptcy. When business has been good, credits have been extended too far; and a general reaction has ensued. But the elastic spirit of the people and their recuperative energy have always saved the country from protracted periods of depression.

---

* *Ante* p. 64.

In 1835, discussion began as to the expediency of procuring a city charter; and a strong party in favor of a charter was soon formed. On the seventeenth of February, 1836, a town meeting was held, Joseph W. Mansur presiding, when Luther Lawrence, Chairman of a Committee previously appointed to consider the subject of a city government, made a report. In view of "the number of our inhabitants,—their dissimilar habits, manners and pursuits,—the rapid and progressive increase of our population,—the variety of interest and the constant changes which are taking place,"—the committee recommend that the Legislature be petitioned to grant a charter to make the town a city. "The principal defects in the operation" of the town government are stated by the Committee to be "the want of executive power, and the loose and irresponsible manner in which money for municipal purposes is granted and expended." *

A Committee, of which Luther Lawrence was Chairman, was appointed to draft a Charter. They reported at an adjourned meeting, on the twenty-seventh of the same month. On the eleventh of April, the Charter was formally adopted, in town meeting, by a vote of 961 yeas against 328 nays.

The population of Lowell was then 17,633. Benjamin Floyd, the author of the ten first Lowell Directories, wildly predicted that in ten years from that time, Lowell would contain 64,000 inhabitants; and in twenty years, 256,000!

In 1836, the Lowell Dispensary was incorporated. This association provides medicines and medical services free of charge to the poor.

As illustrating the Puritanic spirit of young Lowell, Chevalier records the fact, that in 1836 a man was fined by the municipal authorities for exercising the trade of *common fiddler;* he was treated as if he had outraged the public morals.

On the eleventh of April, 1837, the hand that had so long and so ably guided the affairs of Lowell was suddenly with-

* Town Records, vol. 1, p. 304.

drawn:—Kirk Boott dropped dead from his chaise in the street. A chronic disease of the spine, contracted "on the tented field," was doubtless the cause of his sudden demise. As Agent of the Merrimack, and of the Locks and Canals, and as a citizen, participating in every local enterprise, he had been the great propelling power of Lowell ever since the building of the city began. Many a crisis has since arisen when the counsel and influence of another Boott would have been received with grateful enthusiasm. We have sighed, and sighed again, "O, for the Coming Man!" But the Coming Man has never come; and of Kirk Boott we may truly say—"We ne'er shall look upon his like again."

In May, 1837, all the banks in the United States suspended specie payments. Their paper depreciated on an average twelve per cent. The commerce and industry of the country, so long suspended upon the Dædalian wings of paper money, were prostrated. But through the judicious management of the corporations, Lowell suffered little from the general paralysis.

In 1837, the city government committed its first great blunder—in building the Market House. It is the fixed habit of the people to have their meat brought by butchers to their doors. To expect to change their habits by merely building a market house, was grossly absurd. Of course the experiment failed.

In the same year, the Legislature established an annual term of the Supreme Judicial Court, and a term of the Common Pleas, at Lowell. A county jail, on the modern plan of separate cells, was erected in 1838, and in the same year, the Nashua and Lowell Railroad was opened for travel and the transportation of freight.

On the seventeeth of April, 1839, Luther Lawrence, the second in the succession of our Mayors, was suddenly killed, by falling a distance of seventeen feet, into a wheel-pit in one of the Middlesex mills, and fracturing his skull. He was the son of Samuel Lawrence, a major of the Revolution, and the oldest brother of Abbott, Amos, William and Samuel Lawrence, who were all intimately associated with the manufacturing interests of Lowell. He was born at Groton, September 28th, 1778, and graduated at Harvard in 1801. He studied law with Timothy Bigelow, whose sister he afterward married. He commenced practice in Groton, where he soon gathered round him a host of valuable clients. He repeatedly represented his native town in the Legislature, and was Speaker of of the House of Representatives in 1821 and 1822. At the earnest solicitation of his brothers who had largely invested in the mills here, he removed to Lowell, in 1831, and engaged in practice, first with Elisha Glidden, and afterward with Thomas Hopkinson. In 1838, he was elected Mayor, and re-elected in 1839. In sixteen days after his second inauguration, the accident occurred which deprived Lowell of one of the ablest and worthiest of her adopted sons. This shocking catastrophe filled the community with mourning; and preparations were made for a grand public funeral; but this, the family of Mr. Lawrence modestly declined. Appropriate resolutions were passed by the City Council, bearing testimony to his high-minded and honorable character,—his judicious administration of the city government,—his lively interest in the various public institutions with which he had been connected, —his unselfishness and liberality,—his efforts to promote the moral and religious interests of the place,—his amenity of behavior, and kindliness of feeling for all around him. His remains were interred in the cemetery of his native town.

Among the students who graduated from the law-office of Lawrence & Hopkinson, we must mention one, richly gifted and highly accomplished, who, with that loftiness of soul that marks the hero or the martyr, early turned his back on all the common prizes of life, and devoted himself to the suppression of intemperance, the enfranchisement of woman, and the emancipation of the slave—Wendell Phillips. The following interesting reminiscences of his sojourn in Lowell have been kindly furnished by Mr. Phillips himself:—

"Somewhere about October, 1833, I went (from the Cambridge Law School) to Lowell to finish the study of law and see practice in the office of Luther Lawrence. His partner had been Elisha Glidden, a most estimable man and a good lawyer. But at that time his partner was Thomas Hopkinson, afterward Judge of the Court of Common Pleas, and President of the Boston and Worcester Railroad. Mr. Hopkinson was one of the ablest men in the Commonwealth—thorough and exact in his knowledge of law, well read in general literature, and of the highest toned integrity. Mr. Lawrence was a gentlemanly, kind-hearted man, with the popular manners of his family, public spirited, and well fitted for county practice.

"I was admitted to the Bar at Concord in the fall of 1834,* and left Lowell immediately."

Carlyle tells us, "Genius is always lonely,—lonely as to its outward condition in its first years only,—lonely in its heart forever." But proofs are abundant, that Mr. Phillips, though unquestionably a man of high genius, entered *con amore* into society here, and engaged with zest in the amicable rivalry between the two leading social clubs of his time, one called "the Sociables," the other "the Agreeables." Two or three spirited articles were contributed to the *Journal* by him, touching the competition of these clubs for the palm of superiority in wit, culture and refinement. Of Lowell society in his time, Mr. Phillips presents us with the following graphic sketch:—

"Lowell was then crowded with able men—well read lawyers and successful with a jury; among them, scholarly, eloquent, deeply read in his profession, and a *genius*, was John P. Robinson. The city was rich in all that makes good society—amiable, beautiful and accomplished women,—hospitable and amply able to contribute their full share to interesting and suggestive conversation,—gentlemen of talent, energetic, well-informed, and giving a hearty welcome to the best thought of the day. The changes that thirty years have made in that circle would afford matter for a history deeply interesting and very largely sad."

In addition to the lawyers mentioned by Mr. Phillips, among Mr. Lawrence's contemporaries at the Bar, were Seth Ames, Isaac O. Barnes, Elisha and William Fuller, Samuel F. Haven,

---

*Horatio G. F. Corliss was admitted and sworn as an attorney at the same term,—on September 9th, 1834.

William T. Heydock, William and Francis Hilliard, Samuel H. Mann, Horatio C. Merriam, the Olcutts, Barzillai Streeter, Amos Spaulding and Nathaniel Wright, besides several who are still in practice here.

In 1839, the commodious edifice in which Kirk Boott and Luther Lawrence had successively resided, was purchased by the manufacturing companies, and devoted to the use of the sick in their employ. The Lowell Hospital Association was organized in 1840, for the purpose of managing it. The situation of the Lowell Hospital, near Pawtucket Falls, is beautiful, retired and commanding. The buildings are surrounded by trees, shrubbery and climbing vines. As that good man, Thomas H. Perkins,—the early patron and life-long friend of Daniel Webster,—gave his private residence as an asylum for the blind,—how well would Mr. Boott, were he now among the living, approve of this appropriation of his house as a hospital for the sick operatives of the mills! This Hospital was placed under the medical superintendance of Dr. Gilman Kimball, who retained charge of it until 1865, when Dr. George H. Whitmore succeeded him. The best accommodations are here provided for the sick and homeless operative,—at an expense but little exceeding the cost of board, to those who have means,—and gratuitously to those who have not.

From the same year dates the Lowell Horticultural Society.

In 1840, two public commons were laid out; the South Common covering about twenty acres of land, and the North Common about ten acres.

Several attempts had heretofore been made for the establishment of a theatre or museum in Lowell, but had failed. In 1840, this project was renewed with better success. The Museum was first started in the fourth story of Wyman's Exchange, by Moses Kimball, now of the Boston Museum. The first performance was on July 4th, 1840, and was an excellent substitute for the *blarny* usually indulged in on that day. The first collection of curiosities was procured from

Greenwood's old New England Museum in Boston. But the business did not pay. In 1845, Noah F. Gates purchased the Museum of Mr. Kimball; and the removal by him, in 1846, of the Museum into the building formerly owned by the First Freewill Baptist Church, provoked "strong indignation in Zion." The church was at once fitted up for dramatic entertainments; but so great was the opposition to it, that in 1847 the City Council refused to license any more exhibitions of this kind.

A petition, signed by twenty-two hundred legal voters, was hereupon presented to the City Council, praying for a renewal of the license. A prolix debate on the moral tendency of the drama ensued before the City Council. John P. Robinson and Thomas Hopkinson appeared in behalf of the petitioners; while Rev. Messrs. Thurston and True argued against the drama on "Bible grounds." The debate ended by the granting of the license as desired. The Museum was incorporated in 1850, with a capital of sixty thousand dollars; but it was shortly afterward destroyed by fire. Between 1845 and 1851 it flourished; but after 1851, it passed through various hands, and rapidly declined. In 1853, it was again burned. It was, however, subsequently reopened, and carried on till the thirtieth day of January, 1856, when not a vestige escaped the third attack of the devouring flames. During the period of its prosperity, it found employ for some thirty persons, and its salaries averaged over three hundred dollars per week. Some of the best plays of the ablest dramatists were successfully introduced. The stock companies were superior to those of most country theatres; and some of the brightest "stars" in the Thespian firmament appeared upon its boards.

In October, 1840, appeared the Lowell *Offering*, a monthly journal edited by Miss Harriet Farley, and Miss Hariot Curtiss, two factory girls. The pages of the *Offering* were filled exclusively by the contributions, in prose and verse, of women and girls employed in the mills.

"As the weaver plied the shuttle, wove she too the mystic rhyme."

Frederick the Great thought the Nibelungen Lied "not worth a charge of powder," and he could hardly regard the *Offering* as of higher merit than that immortal lay. Nevertheless, the singularity of its origin attracted great attention to the *Offering*, and for a time it had a wide circulation. It won the praise of John G. Whittier and Charles Dickens, and "praise from the praised" is honor indeed. "In its volumes," says Whittier, "may be found sprightly delineations of home scenes and characters, highly-wrought imaginative pieces, tales of genuine pathos and humor, and pleasing fairy stories and fables."*

On the eleventh of January, 1841, Benjamin F. Varnum, Sheriff of Middlesex County, died at his home in Centralville. He was born in Dracut, in 1795, and was the son of Gen. Joseph B. Varnum. He was a Representative in the State Legislature from 1824 to 1827, and a Senator from 1827 to 1831. When the Court of Sessions was abolished, and the Board of County Commissioners established, in 1828, he was appointed one of the Commissioners, and continued a member of the Board until his appointment as sheriff in 1831,—succeeding Gen. Nathaniel Austin. Like his father before him, he was continually employed in the public service, and his conduct commanded the approbation and respect of his constituents.

He was succeeded in the sheriffship by Gen. Samuel Chandler, of Lexington. Like Varnum, Sheriff Chandler continued in office ten years, and was succeeded in 1851, by Fisher A. Hildreth. John S. Keyes was appointed sheriff in 1853, and continued in office till 1860, when Charles Kimball succeeded him.

* Whittier's Miscellanies, p. 427.

On the seventh of April, 1841, all the bells in the city were draped in mourning, and tolled an hour, from twelve o'clock till one, in observance of the death of President Harrison. On Friday, the fourteenth of May,—that day having been designated by the President as a National Fast-day,—all business was suspended, and the obsequies of the deceased President appropriately solemnized. Many buildings, both public and private, were draped in sable. A long procession moved through the principal streets, composed of citizens, without distinction of party, in funereal garb. In the absence of Caleb Cushing, the appointed orator, Rev. Dr. Blanchard delivered an extemporaneous eulogy. A solemn torch-light procession in the evening closed the ceremonies of this National Fast-day.

It was during this year that the Cemetery was established. For this "garden of graves," covering about forty-five acres, Lowell is largely indebted to Oliver M. Whipple, who has been President of the Association ever since its organization. The Cemetery is situated on the east bank of Concord River, one mile from the centre of the city. The topographical survey was made under the direction of George P. Worcester. The grounds are laid out after the French style, combining therewith somewhat of the English mode of landscape gardening. Long, serpentine avenues, shaded by forest trees, intersect this sacred enclosure. In the central part of the Cemetery, in a group of young trees, stands a small, Gothic chapel, in imitation of Pere la Chaise, and other celebrated burial places in Europe. The consecration of this cemetery took place on Sunday, June 20th, 1841. Rev. Dr. Blanchard delivered the address, which, for "its appropriate extent of subjects, richness of thought, and felicity of expression," is said to have been rarely equaled on any similar occasion.

Until 1841, there had been no substantial bridge over Concord River, connecting Church and Andover streets. The first structure was a floating bridge for foot-passers. The next was a bridge set upon piles. But in the year above named, a double-arch stone bridge was constructed, which in 1858 was re-placed by the present single-arch structure.

In 1841, Benjamin F. Butler, Henry F. Durant, James M. Stone, Granville Parker and others, embarked in a sensational enterprise combining journalism, politics and reform. As the organ of the new movement, Augustus A. Cheever established a weekly newspaper called *Vox Populi.* It was not expected that the *Vox* would become a permanent journal: all that was contemplated was a temporary organ for those who felt like the Rev. Sidney Smith, that they *must write or burst!* A vigorous battle was waged against all the abuses that flourished under the Whig dynasty in Massachusetts, and especially against the illiberality then often exhibited in the management of our corporations. The *Vox* created a great sensation; and the aspiring attorneys at once acquired a notoriety which proved to some of them the stepping-stone to fame.

Josiah G. Abbott, then in the Senate from Lowell, having, in common with other Democrats, a bitter feud with Eliphalet Case, who controlled the *Advertiser,* was anxious to have a journal with which to fight Mr. Case. Upon his suggestion, Samuel J. Varney purchased the *Vox,* fought out the campaign against Case, and then continued the paper as a permanent journal. The *Vox* has never wholly forgotten its origin, but even now occasionally evinces a disposition to renew the struggle in which it first won its spurs. Among those who, at different times, have presided over the columns of the *Vox,* we may mention (besides Mr. Varney) A. B. Farr, J. F. C. Hayes, B. F. Johnson, Enoch Emery, J. T. Chesley, Thomas Bradley and Z. E. Stone, the present editor.

In January, 1842, Charles Dickens made "a flying visit" to Lowell from Boston. The chapter in his "American Notes," in which he presents the results of this trip, shows with what rapidity a man of genius can grasp all that is most characteristic in a community of which he has caught but a passing glimpse. An agreeable surprise was experienced by Mrs. Dickens, who found in the wife of Dr. Kimball, a lady who had once been her schoolmate at Edinburg. Neither of these ladies had known what ticket in the lottery of life had been drawn by the other.

On April 1st, 1843, died Dr. William Graves, one of the most prominent among the physicians and surgeons of the early days of Lowell. He commenced practice here in 1826. He had previously practiced at Deerfield in New Hampshire. He was a descendent of Oliver Cromwell, and was the father of Dr. John W. Graves, who for many years practiced his profession in Lowell, and who has long had charge of the United States Marine Hospital in Chelsea.

On the nineteenth of June, 1843, John Tyler, President of the United States, made a public visit to Lowell, accompanied by Abbott Lawrence, Isaac Hill, John Tyler, Junior, and others. The boys and girls of the High School, with their teachers,—together with the military companies, and a cavalcade of the citizens,—formed his escort; and the usual public greetings took place. Before leaving Lowell, the President and suite visited the works of the Middlesex, Lowell, Boott, and Merrimack companies, and expressed much gratification with the novel and marvellous scenes exhibited to them.

At the October Term of the Court of Common Pleas, held in Lowell, in 1843, the famous case of the Commonwealth *versus* Wyman* was tried. Daniel Webster, Rufus Choate and others appeared as counsel. An incident occurred in the course of the trial, which, perhaps, may deserve a place in this history, —being particularly illustrative of the tenacity with which Mr. Webster adhered to whatever position he might assume.

While engaged in some by-play with Mr. Choate, Mr. Webster wrote upon a slip of paper the following couplet from Pope, and then handed the slip to Mr. Choate:—

"Lo! where Meotis sleeps, and *softly* flows,
The freezing Tanais through a waste of snows."

*8Metcalf's Reports, pp. 247-297.

Mr. Choate at once took exception to the word "softly," which, he said, should read "hardly," and objected to this "rendering" of the poet. Mr. Webster stoutly affirmed that he had quoted the lines as Pope wrote them, and therefore needed no lecture on the duty of the correct citation of authors. A copy of Pope was procured, which settled the question adversely to Mr. Webster. He took up the book,—read the lines deliberately,—sat down,—turned to the fly-leaf of the volume,—and there wrote

"Spurious Edition of Pope.—DANIEL WEBSTER."

It was during this trial that Webster had his famous "passage" with Judge Charles Allen. In his closing argument for the defendant, Mr. Webster advanced certain propositions as principles of law, which were highly favorable to his client, and evinced a desire that the jury should accept them upon his personal authority. But the judge, in charging, cautioned the jury, that, however eminent the counsel, and however humble the Court, they must take the law, not from the counsel, but from the Court; and he observed that, in this case, the counsel had advocated propositions of law which they themselves knew to be erroneous. Mr. Webster dissented and attempted to explain. The judge said, rather sharply, "I don't wish to be interrupted." Mr. Webster promptly replied, "Neither do I wish to be misrepresented."

The judge resumed. Mr. Webster also resuming, the judge said in a peremptory tone, "The Court cannot be interrupted, sir." Mr. Webster, in a tone equally peremptory, rejoined, "Neither can I be misrepresented, your Honor."

The Court—"Sit down, Mr. Webster."

Mr. Webster—"I won't sit down, your Honor."

Thereupon the judge himself sat down, and Mr. Webster moved toward the door, but shortly returned, and gracefully apologized for his interruptions.*

---

*Law Reporter, January, 1844.

In 1844, was instituted the City Library, which now contains twelve thousand volumes. Its Board of Directors and its Librarian are chosen annually by the City Council.

In 1844, Elisha Fuller, who had practiced law here during twelve years, removed to Worcester, where, in March, 1855, he died. He was born in 1795, and was the youngest of five brothers, all of whom were lawyers,—namely: Timothy Fuller of Groton, father of Margaret Fuller Ossoli, and Representative in Congress; Abraham W. Fuller of Boston; Henry H. Fuller also of Boston, who came to Lowell in 1834 to advocate before the people the annexation of Belvidere, and to denounce Kirk Boott, who had thrown the weight of his great influence against the annexation of that fine faubourg to Lowell; and William W. Fuller, who practiced in this city about eight years, and then removed to Illinois, where he died in 1849. It was largely through the influence of Elisha Fuller that Edward Everett was elected Representative in Congress in 1826, in opposition to John Keyes of Concord. Mr. Fuller was then in practice in Concord, and would not submit to the domination of the old Concord *clique*, which so long controlled the politics of Middlesex County.

A few months subsequent to Mr. Fuller's departure, another Lowell lawyer, Henry F. Durant, removed to Boston. Few lawyers have practiced here, more noted for moral hardihood than Mr. Durant. Any man would have been deemed a lunatic, who should then have predicted—what has actually come to pass—that, twenty years later, "that felt-footed young man," as Choate once styled him, would return to Lowell, not to eliminate some scoundrel-client from the meshes of the law, but to stand in the pulpit of Dr. Blanchard, to exhort the assembled multitude to cease the mad pursuit of sin, and live for purer purposes, and lay hold on higher hopes!

In 1845, the Middlesex North District Medical Society was organized, being one of the auxiliaries of the Massachusetts Medical Society. The necessity of an institution to elevate the medical gentlemen of Lowell, in respect to personal character and professional attainments, had long been felt, and is still felt, by all who have the true dignity of the profession at heart. This necessity, however, has never been supplied. The Medical Society has wholly failed to meet it. Partly, doubtless, on account of the ever-changing character of her population, Lowell has always been an attractive field for quacks. Not to mention political quacks, who are common everywhere, we have had quacks of one class, who have flourished at the bar; we have had quacks of another class, not less numerous, who have flourished in the pulpit; but the faculty most prolific in quacks is the faculty of physic. Here the vender of every nostrum, the empiric, and the abortionist, have reaped a luxurious harvest. Not a year has passed during the last six lustrums, that has not witnessed the slaughter of more innocents in Lowell than Herod slew in Bethlehem.

In 1845, Rev. Dr. Miles published his "Lowell as it Was and as it Is." The reader of that book must not censure its author too harshly, for the *colour de rose* which he has so freely used in his pictures of the corporations. At the time he wrote and for several lustrums afterward, "it was a favorite belief with the American people, that corporations were the most efficient agents of production, even where the work was not so great as to be beyond individual enterprise. The older wisdom of the country turns more and more to the smaller establishments, which secure full, interested, personal supervision of labor. The English economy has always preferred this, except where the operations were beyond the reach of ordinary capital."* Moreover, some of the best thinkers that have lived in Lowell, including men of all parties, have entertained these riper views. Among these may be named Josiah G. Abbott, Benjamin F. Butler, Joshua W. Daniels, Henry F. Durant, Eliphalet Case, Fisher A. Hildreth, Thomas Hopkin-

*Walker's Science of Wealth, p. 69.

son, Paul R. George, William Livingston, Joshua Mather, John Nesmith, John D. Prince, Oliver M. Whipple and John Wright. Dr. J. C. Ayer contributed largely to revolutionize the common opinion by his pungent pamphlet on the "Uses and Abuses in the Management of our Manufacturing Corporations," in which he exposed, with just severity, the cliqueism, nepotism, and imbecility of certain corporation "rings."

In 1845, was found the first indictment against a Lowell journalist for libel. Samuel J. Varney, editor of *Vox Populi* was charged with a libel on Jacob Currier, a Lieutenant in the Army; but the case was never tried. In the year following, John C. Palmer, editor of *Life in Lowell,* was indicted for a libel on George D. Hodges, and tried, but found not guilty. A vitiated press is one of the worst of moral pests. For some years, the scurrility of all the local journals was disgraceful, not only to the editors, but to the people who tolerated and supported such organs. The Bar caught the infection, and about this time the grand jury seldom sat without plastering some of its members with criminal indictments —none but the most obscure being exempted.

In 1845, G. W. Boynton issued a map of Lowell, prepared from a survey ordered by the city.

In 1845, the Stony Brook Railroad Company was incorporated, with a capital of three hundred thousand dollars. On the first of July, 1848, this road, connecting Lowell with Groton Junction, was opened for travel, largely increasing our facilities for communication with other portions of New England, and with New York.

It was in 1845 that John G. Whittier took up his abode in Lowell as editor of the Middlesex *Standard.* He remained here less than a year, but during his sojourn prepared several admirable sketches of Lowell which are republished in his Miscellanies.

In 1845, the business of manufacturing was begun at Lawrence, nine miles below Lowell, by the Essex Company; and soon afterward the fisheries of Merrimack River became the subject of a controversy that has continued for twenty years.

One result of the building of the dam at Pawtucket Falls in 1822, was a diminution of the number of fish taken annually from the Merrimack. A still further diminution followed on the building of other dams, such as those at Amoskeag and Bow. Shad and salmon, however, were not entirely banished from the Merrimack, until after the erection of the dam at Lawrence in 1847.

This subject, however, never attracted the attention in Lowell which it deserves. What greater boon could be bestowed on the poor of Lowell, than a cheap and abundant supply of wholesome fish? As late as 1835, it is estimated that more than sixty-five thousand shad and over eight hundred salmon were taken from the Merrimack in Lowell alone.

In 1866, Messrs. Theodore Lyman and Alfred A. Reed, Commissioners on River Fisheries, made a report to the General Court, concerning the obstructions to the passage of fish up the Connecticut and Merrimack Rivers, suggesting the removal of these obstructions, and the re-stocking of these rivers with shad, salmon, and other fish, as in the olden time. The conclusions of the Commissioners were that "in order to re-stock the Connecticut and Merrimack rivers with shad and salmon, fish-ways must be built over the dams; the pollution of the waters must be prevented; New Hampshire should breed salmon; Connecticut should forbid the use of weirs and gill-nets; and stringent laws should be adopted for the regulation of fishing."

In compliance with the recommendations of these Commissioners, fishways have been erected around all the dams, and it can hardly be doubted that from year to year the salmon and the shad will resume their visits up the Merrimack, as in the olden time. The fishway at Pawtucket Falls is of the kind known as the "double stair," consisting of two parallel lines of tanks, each twelve feet square and a foot lower than the one next above. There are nine of these tanks, and at the bottom there is direct communication with the main channel of the river. The tanks are constructed of heavy masonry and timber, and are capable of resisting ice and freshets.

The fishway at Lawrence consists of a drawbridge reaching from the crest of the dam to a trough or pass. When the drawbridge is down it forms a sloping dam or trough twelve feet wide, with a fall of one foot in ten, with only a certain depth of water, up which the fish are to pass, aided only by resting tanks where they may pause in the ascent. In winter the drawbridge is raised and is thus secure from damage by ice.*

The year 1845 was a memorable one for our "brethren of the mystic tie." On the tenth of September in that year, the Charter of Pentucket Lodge,—originally granted March 9th, 1807, but surrendered in 1834, in consequence of the Anti-Masonic mania which then prevailed,—was restored, and a new impetus given to the growth of Masonry in Lowell. Since then, three other Lodges have been instituted here—Ancient York, in 1852; Kilwinning, in 1866; and William North, in 1867. Some months after the re-organization of Pentucket Lodge, Mount Horeb Royal Arch Chapter recovered the charter granted to it in 1826, and resumed its work. But Ahasuerus Council of Royal and Select Masters, chartered in the same year with Mount Horeb Royal Arch Chapter, was not re-organized until 1856. Since the Masonic Revival, signalized by the re-opening of Pentucket Lodge, five other organizations have been instituted in Lowell, viz.: Pilgrim Encampment of Knights Templars, in 1855; Lowell Grand Lodge of Perfection, 14°, in 1857; Lowell Council, Princes of Jerusalem, 16°, in 1857; Mount Calvary Chapter, Rose Croix, 18°, in 1858; Massachusetts Sov.·. Consistory, S.·. P.·. R.·. S.·., in 1859.

*Senate Document, No. 8, 1866; Storers' Report on the Fishes of Massachusetts; Westminster Review, July, 1861; Harper's Magazine, March, 1862; 13 Gray, p. 239; 4 Pickering, p. 145; 5 *Ibid*, p. 199.

In April, 1846, thirteen years from the day of his appointment, Joseph Locke resigned his office as Standing Justice of the Police Court; and Nathan Crosby was appointed in his place. Judge Locke continued to reside here until his death, which occurred November 10th, 1853, at the patriarchal age of eighty-two. He was born in Fitzwilliam, New Hampshire, April 8th, 1772, and graduated at Dartmouth College in 1797. His class furnished the Bar with several lawyers of more than ordinary calibre, and the pulpit with four clergymen of distinguished usefulness, besides two physicians, and two members of Congress. He studied law with Timothy Bigelow, and was admitted to the Bar in 1801, and the next year opened an office in Billerica. He was elected Representative from Billerica in 1806, and was re-elected seven times. He was eight years President of the Court of Sessions, and in 1816 was nominated a Justice of the Court of Common Pleas, but declined. He was a Presidential Elector the same year, and voted for Rufus King for President in opposition to James Monroe, who was elected. He sat in the Constitutional Convention of 1820, and was a member of the Governor's Council in 1822 and 1823. He removed to this city in 1833; and at once was appointed Justice of the Police Court. He was a Representative to the Legislature from Lowell in 1849. Judge Locke was a gentleman of the old school; an accomplished lawyer, thoroughly versed in that great body of reason, the gathered wisdom of a thousand years—the Common Law. This was his specialty, his *forte*. He also excelled in special pleading. His career of thirteen years as a police magistrate was marked by all the qualities that could confer dignity on the post, and develope in the Bar the best traits of the legal, and in himself the best traits of the judicial character. His decisions were comprehensive and logical, exhibiting a thorough knowledge of law, and vitalized with a true spirit of justice. Those who practiced before him concur in the attestation that he was a man of strong mind, clear and ready discernment, abundant learning and excellent skill in explaining and illustrating judicial problems. In dealing with criminals, especially the Celtic criminals, who were often before him, he exercised a broad and tender humanity that illustrated both ideal and practical justice.

Appropriate resolutions were passed, on the occasion of his decease, by the Lowell Bar, in which his personal integrity, professional ability and amiable manners were recognized and applauded.

Judge Crosby was born in Sandwich, New Hampshire, February 12th,* 1798, and graduated at Dartmouth College in 1820, in the same class with George P. Marsh, Judge Upton and Judge Nesmith. He commenced practice as a lawyer in his native state, but removed to Massachusetts in 1826, and practiced first at Amesbury, and afterward at Newburyport. He was early identified with the Anti-Slavery and other Reforms, and was one of the earliest and most active advocates of Railroads. The passage of the famous liquor law of 1838 brought him into the field as an advocate of that measure, and he lectured extensively under the auspices of the Massachusetts Temperance Union. He also edited the *Temperance Journal* and various documents that were issued during that interesting stage in the progress of the Temperance Reform. In 1843, he removed from Boston to Lowell, and was successfully employed in carrying out the excellent scheme for augmenting the water-power of the Merrimack River, by creating reservoirs more than a hundred square miles in extent, near the outlets of Winnepissawkee, Square and Newfound Lakes.

Since his elevation to our police bench, Judge Crosby has mitigated the asperities of law with the amenities of literature. An annual volume of obituary notices of eminent persons was projected by him; and two volumes were issued,—one in 1856, the other in 1857,—which will be a valuable legacy to future biographers and historians. A eulogy of Webster, a lecture

* Abraham Lincoln was born on the same day, nine years later.

on India, and other discourses delivered by him, have attested his possession of oratorical abilities of a high order.

In 1846, our population was twenty-nine thousand one hundred and twenty-seven. The city of Lawrence had just started; and to facilitate intercourse between the two places, the Lowell and Lawrence Railroad was incorporated during this year, with a capital of three hundred thousand dollars.

On the thirtieth of June, 1847, President Polk and his Secretary of State, James Buchanan, together with other distinguished gentlemen, visited Lowell, and were received by Mayor Bancroft at the Bleachery Depot, where congratulations were exchanged. He was escorted through the principal streets, with the usual ceremonies, by the City Guards, the Phalanx, and the Westford Rifle Company. The mills were closed, and all business suspended. The President and his party visited the Middlesex and Prescott Mills on the following day, and expressed much satisfaction with their visit.

On the twelfth of September, 1847, Patrick T. Jackson suddenly passed away at Beverly, in his sixty-eighth year. Twelve years previously, on the completion of the Boston and

Lowell Railroad, he felt that his longest day's task was done, and he was then disposed to retire from the active business of life. But a dark cloud settled down over this great and good man. While building up works for future generations, his property, which he had so hardly earned, passed from his hands. Speculation had made him, for the third time in his life, a poor man. But his powerful mind was not to be distracted even now; and he met his reverses with a dignified composure which would have done honor to a philosopher. He retrenched his expenses, which had previously been enormous and princely; resumed his harness with a cheerful spirit, and again went forth to the stern conflict of life. Under circumstances like these, ordinary life becomes a poem, and daily labor a triumph of heroism.

Mr. Boott died in 1837; and in consequence of his death the stock of the Locks and Canals Company seriously depreciated in value. The death of Mr. Boott had created a vacancy which only one man living could fill; and that man was Mr. Jackson. He accepted the agentship with the liberal salary of ten thousand dollars a year. His whole life had been one long school-term, eminently fitting him for this responsible post. How well he filled it, will be seen by the fact, that the stock of the company, when the reorganization in 1845 occurred, commanded sixteen hundred dollars a share, and that the same stock, after the death of Mr. Boott, sold for less than seven hundred dollars a share.

Before he closed his connection with the Locks and Canals Company, Mr. Jackson accepted the post of agent and treasurer of the Great Falls Manufacturing Company at Somersworth—a corporation which had encountered so many reverses, that a man of Mr. Jackson's stamp was absolutely necessary to their final success. He put their affairs in such admirable condition, that his share of their profits amounted to about twelve thousand dollars a year. This was in addition to the salary of ten thousand dollars a year, paid him by the Locks and Canals

Company. During a portion of the time he received other salaries besides. His aggregate income was truly enormous; —he was soon restored to competence;—but when we consider the extraordinary character of the man, and the *prestige* of success which attended him in all his undertakings, we shall find that he was actually the cheapest man that could be hired. No such salaries are now paid; no such men are to be found; and, indeed, none are in demand.

His abilities fitted him for the highest theatre of human action. He could have governed the vastest empire with unsurpassed splendor, had Providence called him to a throne. To unlimited grasp of mind, he united the capacity to master the most complicated details, together with spotless integrity, unconquerable self reliance, "honor enlightened by religion and guarded by conscience," independence in all his own opinions, and a catholic liberality toward the views of his opponents. The man never lived who more richly deserved to be sculptured in marble, or depicted on canvas, or whose praises could form a worthier theme for the orator or the poet.*

The wooden bridge over Concord River near the Cemetery was constructed in 1847, superceding the stone bridge below it.

In 1847, the great Northern Canal was completed,—being the greatest work of the kind in the United States. The object of the canal, as well as of the subterranean canal under Moody street, was, to keep constantly a fuller head of water than could previously be obtained, in the several canals that feed the water into the flumes of the various mills. The canal was constructed by the combined companies, in less than eighteen months, at a cost of five hundred thousand dollars. It was first filled with water on Thanksgiving-Day, in the year last mentioned. James B. Francis, the Agent and Chief Engineer of the Locks and Canals Company, was the architect of this stupendous work. Well may he say—

"*Exegi monumentum œre perennius.*"

* Lowell's Memoir of Jackson.

NORTHERN CANAL.

A great portion of the canal was excavated through the solid rock. Its length is nearly a mile; its breadth a hundred feet; and its depth eighteen feet. Its water-section is exactly fifteen hundred square feet. The banks are lined with a double colonnade of trees, tastefully laid out, with green plats, and beautiful summer prominades. Along these picturesque banks, will "future sons and daughters yet unborn," take sentimental walks by moon-light, while tales of love find tender audience, and visions of a matrimonial Elysium dance through their minds.

In 1847, the Appleton Bank was incorporated, with a capital of $100,000, since increased to $300,000.

In 1848, the Salem and Lowell Railroad Company was incorporated, with a capital of four hundred thousand dollars. The road was opened for travel, August 1st, 1850. The City Institution for Savings was also incorporated in 1848. Its design was to afford means to employ small sums of money to advantage, to those who desired to save a part of their earnings, but had not yet acquired a sufficient surplus to purchase a share in the banks, or in the public stocks. These little investments are made without that risk of loss, to which private loans are more or less exposed.

On the twentieth of February, 1848, at the suggestion of the City Council, all business was suspended, and the bells, draped in black, tolled an hour, from twelve o'clock till one, on the occasion of the death of John Quincy Adams.

On the sixteenth of September, 1848, Abraham Lincoln made a visit to Lowell, and addressed a Whig meeting in the evening, in the City Hall. An unfailing fund of strong common sense, a fine vein of mother wit and genial humor, a steady flow of clear and cogent argument, a frank and liberal partisanship, a broad and generous patriotism, "charity for all, malice for none"—these were the characteristics of his speech. He was listened to with close attention, and frequently loudly applauded. But with how much deeper interest would that audience have hung upon his words, had they foreseen that the genial countenance of their homely orator would one day be encircled with an aureole of glory—that, indeed, they were listening to a man who was to be enshrined forever in American history as second only to Washington, and hardly second to him!

The discovery of gold in Col. Sutter's mill-race in California, in August, 1848,—the greatest event, perhaps, since the discovery of America by Columbus,—wrought wonderful changes in the character of the operatives of the Lowell mills. The news of that event fell upon their ears with seductive thrill. From that day a change began to work itself out in the people here. The Americans started by scores for the land of gold. This Californian emigration, together with that to the great West, deprived Lowell of some of the best elements in her varied population.

In 1848, two fire insurance companies were incorporated in Lowell—the Howard, and the Traders and Mechanics'. The Lowell Mutual had been incorporated sixteen years previously.

On April 24th, 1849, the City Council invited President Taylor to visit Lowell. Public business compelled the President to decline. On July 13th, 1850, business was suspended, bells tolled, cannon boomed:—Zachary Taylor was no more.

On Sunday evening, September 11th, 1849, the fight between the Corkonians and the Far-Downers, commonly called "the Battle of Suffolk Bridge," was fought on Lowell street. One man was shot and several others injured by stones, of which ten cart-loads were used. Instead of the Militia, the Firemen were foolishly called out; the riot act was read, the aid of the Roman Catholic clergy obtained, and finally peace restored. Stephen Castles and twenty-four others were subsequently indicted as rioters, and some of them were afforded an opportunity to meditate on their folly within the walls of a prison. The controversy between the Corkonians and the Far-Downers was adjourned to the Greek Kalends, when it is hoped, it will be settled on its merits, without the intermeddling of Militia, Firemen, Priesthood or Police.

Two days subsequent to the riot, Father Mathew visited Lowell, and was honored with a public reception. While here, he administered the Temperance Pledge to about five thousand persons, and the beneficial fruits of his labors were long visible among his co-religionists. Among the results of his visit was the Mathew Institute, an Irish literary society, organized October 16th, 1849, and incorporated in 1855. It flourished till 1860, and then passed out of existence.

In 1849, the reservoir on Lynde's Hill was constructed by the Locks and Canals Company, under the direction of James B. Francis. Its capacity is two million gallons, and its elevation is about two hundred feet above the level of the mill-yards. It is supplied with water by force-pumps driven by water-power. A twelve-inch pipe connects the reservoir with the yards of all of the great corporations. From these pipes the water flows under a pressure of eighty pounds to the square inch, affording admirable means for extinguishing fires, not only on the corporations, but in the city generally."*

*Francis on the Means for Extinguishing Fire. Journal of Franklin Institute, April, 1865.

CHAPTER IX.

GENERAL HISTORY OF LOWELL. 1850–1860.

Gas—The Court House—Centralville—*Citizen and News*—Bloomer Ball—Mechanics' Fair—Reform School—H. S. Tremenheere—*Courier*-Butler Libels—George Wellman—Louis Kossuth—Temperance Court—Huntington Hall—Ten Hour Agitation—Samuel Appleton—Otto Club—Agricultural Society—Joseph Hiss—Elisha Bartlett—Abbott Lawrence—The Jail—Thomas Hopkinson—Thomas H. Benton—Mary Barnard—Mechanics' Fair—*Trumpet* Libels—Secret Societies—Robert Burns—Jane Ermina Locke—Trial for Perjury.

VIEW OF LOWELL.

On January 1st, 1850, Gas was first introduced by the Lowell Gas Light Company, which had been incorporated in 1849, with a capital of two hundred thousand dollars. The works of this company are capable of producing one hundred and fifty thousand cubic feet per day. Mertoun C. Bryant was their Agent till 1862, when Oliver E. Cushing succeeded him.

In 1850, the Prescott Bank was incorporated, with a capital of $100,000, now $300,000.

In the same year, the spacious Court-House on Gorham street was erected, costing about one hundred thousand dollars. This edifice is of brick, fire-proof throughout, and is one of the handsomest court-houses in the country.

In 1851, the area of the city was extended by the annexation of Centralville, previously a part of Dracut.

On June 4th, 1851, the *Daily News* made its first appearance; and three years later, Z. E. Stone established the *American Citizen*, daily and weekly. In 1856, these papers were united. Among the editors of these journals were Enoch Emery, Abram Keach, S. R. Streeter, Zina E. Stone, Frank Crosby, Leonard Brown, John A. Goodwin, and Chauncy L. Knapp.

On July 22nd, 1851, was held the famous "Bloomer Ball," the first practical attempt to introduce the costume originated by Mrs. Amelia Bloomer of Seneca, New York. The ball was a success, but the costume was not a success.

On September 16th, 1851, the Middlesex Mechanics' Association opened their first Fair, with Ithamar A. Beard as Superintendent. The Fair continued until October 16th, and the number of entrees on the catalogue of articles exhibited was 1483. The Committee of Arrangements consisted of Oliver M. Whipple, (Chairman,) Mertoun C. Bryant, (Secretary), Sewall G. Mack, Samuel W. Brown, William Fiske, D. A. G. Warner, Lucius A. Cutler, Josiah Gates. John W. Smith, Walter Wright, J. G. Peabody and David Dana.

In 1851, the Lowell Reform School was established for the reformation of juvenile offenders. There from twenty-five to forty boys have ever since been confined, under sentences imposed by the Police Court, and generally covering periods of six or twelve months. The offences for which boys are committed are truancy, larceny, disobedience to parents, defacing school-houses, fruit-stealing, etc. The institution has abundantly justified the hopes of Judge Locke, Dr. Huntington and others, who urged the utility of such an institution, years before this school was established. But the situation of the school in connection with the Alms House is decidedly objectionable. A truant boy is not necessarily vicious. His self-respect ought not to be wounded by assimilating him with paupers—much less with criminals. Moreover, the system is radically wrong, which puts wayward boys into the same dock, arraigns them at the same bar, and deals with them by the same forms, as drunkards, prostitutes and thieves.

It was in the fall of 1851, that the English writer, Hugh Seymour Tremenheere, visited Lowell. The results of his observation in America were published during the following year, in his "Notes on Public Subjects." His remarks on public education were enriched with a communication from the Rev. Dr. Edson, which provoked considerable hostile criticism, at the time, though substantially the same views had been presented by Dr. Edson, twenty years earlier, at a meeting of an association of the teachers of Middlesex County. He says:—

"Seeing that the system of public schools established by law was the only one possible under the circumstances of the country, I have applied myself with all the zeal in my power to make it efficient; and I have endeavored to cause the deficiency of religious instruction in the day-schools to supplied by encouraging Sunday Schools, . . seeing in them the only mode under our system to imprint on the minds of those who most require such teaching, the principles of Revealed Religion. My experience, however, has forced upon me the painful conviction that our public school system has undermined already among our population, to a great extent, the doctrines and principles of Christianity."

Of the young people who flow into Lowell from the neighboring states, he observes,—

"That they possess a knowledge of none, or nearly none, of the distinctive principles of the Christian faith, and that many are in a state of mind beyond that of mere indifference, though not precisely in that of those imbued with the principles of French and German Infidelity. I find in them a considerable indifference as to what sect they may belong to, thinking all religions alike, and generally showing a great ignorance of the Bible, which they profess to take as their guide.

"I find many not only unable to repeat any of the Ten Commandments, but entirely unaware of their being any Ten Commandments at all. I find them generally well grounded in the elements of what is called common education, and clever and acute as to all worldly matters that concern them, but very lax in their notions of moral obligation and duty, and indisposed to submit to any authority or control whatever, even from a very early age. . . . There is indeed a school of persons in this country, and a very numerous one, who think it wrong to influence a child in its adoption of any religious belief. Very commonly, also, no point of doctrine seems to have been effectually and thoroughly explained to them and taught as from authority. . . . From throwing off authority in regard to religious matters, and holding doctrines loosely, the step is easy to abandon them altogether, and accordingly . . . the great majority of those now growing up cannot be said to hold more than belongs to mere Natural Religion. I look upon this very prevalent condition of mind with very great apprehension, for all history shows that this is only the first downward step to complete irreligion and infidelity, and thence to the corruption of morals, such as was exhibited in the Heathen world. I much fear that we are making sure and not very slow strides in that direction, and while I deeply lament it, I am free to confess I see no present remedy for it in this country."

The children of the Irish population, the Doctor observes, "are well looked after by their priests." As to the rest, he says,—

"I believe that less than half of the whole number of children between the ages of five and sixteen attend any Sunday-school, or do so only most irregularly. It is easy to infer what sort of hold the Bible, its precepts and its doctrines, can be likely to have on minds thus loosely prepared for the temptations of life."

With those who mistake diffused superficiality for universal high culture, such views as these were not likely to be received with favor. But these views are not peculiar to Dr. Edson. Caleb Cushing, for example, holds that our public schools are inferior to those of many European countries, producing a much smaller proportion of pupils who thoroughly understand the four rudimentary arts—reading, spelling, writing and cyphering; while Ralph Waldo Emerson hails it as an auspicious sign, that the most advanced minds of the age have renounced Theology and fallen back on Morals.

In 1852, a personal political controversy of several years' duration, between Benjamin F. Butler and John H. Warland, editor of the *Courier*, reached its culminating point. This quarrel was begun originally by Mr. Butler, who, at a Democratic caucus, called attention to certain disfigurments on Mr. Warland's face, which he attributed to Warland's illicit dalliances with the fair, frail, black-eyed Creoles whom he had met while with Gen. Scott in Mexico. Such an insult was quite too much for Warland, who, with the "fine frenzy" of a poet, combined another frenzy of a far more savage kind. It was like waving a red flag before a fighting bull. Accordingly, the infuriated Warland proceeded to punish Butler by publishing in the *Courier* a series of the most galling personal invectives. Of course, Butler replied; and month after month the war of words waged—the *Courier* making daily discharges of printed filth on Butler, and Butler from the rostrum sending back a stream of foul abuse on Warland.

Butler and Warland were pretty evenly matched; but when Benjamin W. Ball came into the field as an ally of Warland, there was a preponderance of vituperation on the side of the *Courier*. Ball had previously distinguished himself by a volume of poems, and with the exception of John P. Robinson, he was probably the best Greek scholar that ever lived in Lowell. He wrote a caustic epitaph in rhyme, and several prose diatribes on Butler, some of which were not unworthy of Peter Porcupine or even Junius; though, for exquisite concentration of venom, the best of his squibs would hardly compare with the later effusions of "Brick Pomeroy," of the *La Crosse Democrat*.

Smarting under these blistering invectives, Butler appealed for protection to the Courts. Accordingly, at the February term of the Court of Common Pleas, the grand jury presented two indictments against Warland, and two against Samuel J. Varney, Warland's editorial associate, for libels on Butler in the *Courier*. Judge Hoar presided at the trials, the result of which shows how wide a gulf often separates law from justice. Varney, who was innocent, was convicted, and mulcted with a fifty-dollar fine. Warland, who was guilty, was acquitted; while Butler who began the fight, and Ball who joined it without provocation, were never called to account at all.*

Another event signalized the year 1852, of far more importance than any quarrels of politicians, journalists or lawyers. During that year, George Wellman completed his first working model of his self top card stripper—one of the most valuable

*Criminal Records of the Court of Common Pleas, Middlesex County, 1852, pp. 344–347 and 392–395; and 10 Cushing, 402.

The indictments are in Gen. Butler's hand-writing. Hereafter, as the solitary, curious student reads these cold, formal records, he will hardly realize what fierce and malignant passions burned themselves out in this intensely bitter quarrel.

inventions of the present century — which was patented in 1853. Two additional patents for improvements in this invention were obtained by Mr. Wellman — one in 1854, the other in 1857. Three patents for the same invention were also obtained by him in England — the last in 1860. The governments of France, Austria, Prussia, Saxony, Wurtemburg, Belgium, and Bavaria, have also granted patents for the self top card stripper.

Mr. Wellman was born in Boston, March 16th, 1810, and was the first-born son of his parents, a sound, healthy, productive couple, who subsequently had twelve other children; —a family such as would gladden the heart of Dr. Allen, if he could only find such an one, in these days of physical degeneracy and decay. About 1835, Mr. Wellman came to Lowell, and for many years had charge of a carding-room on the Merrimack Corporation. In 1845, he invented the stop motion, used on the dressing-frame and winder, but neglected to take out a patent for it. His mind, however, had been fixed on the invention of a self top card stripper while he was employed at North Chelmsford, long before the invention of this stop motion; and he continued thinking and working at it till he had realized his thought in a perfect working machine.

To show the value of this invention, it may be stated here that the average cost of stripping a card by hand was three hundred dollars per annum, all of which is saved by this invention, the application of which to each machine, involves an outlay of less than sixty-dollars altogether. This invention also saves from one-fourth to one-eighth of a cent per pound on the raw cotton.

In 1854, Mr. Wellman offered to sell to the corporations the exclusive right to use this invention in Lowell, for three thousand dollars. The agents of the companies met at the Merrimack Counting-Room, and after grave deliberation, stupidly declined the offer. Since then, more than twenty-five thousand dollars have been paid by these corporations for the use of the self top card stripper.

Mr. Wellman died, April 4th, 1864. His sun may be said to have gone down at noon, since he had not completed his fifty-fourth year. The pen of history can never be better employed than in recording the achievements of men of inventive genius, like Wellman. A late Commissioner of Patents has justly observed that—

> "All that is glorious in our past or hopeful in our future is indissolubly linked with that cause of human progress of which inventors are the *preux chevaliers*. It is no poetic translation of the abiding sentiment of the country to say that they are the true jewels of the nation to which they belong. . . The schemes of the politician and of the statesman may subserve the purposes of the hour, and the teachings of the moralist may remain with the generation to which they are addressed, but all this must pass away; while the fruits of the inventor's genius will endure as imperishable memorials, and, surviving the wreck of creeds and systems, alike of politics, religion and philosophy, will diffuse their blessings to all lands and throughout all ages." *

On May 6th, 1852, Louis Kossuth, the Hungarian patriot, then on a tour of triumph through the United States, by special invitation of the citizens, visited Lowell, and was received with the warmest enthusiasm. He was escorted by the military companies through the principal streets, attended by a procession of some thousands of citizens, amid the ringing of bells, the music of bands, the thunder of cannon, and the loudest demonstrations of joy. He visited several of the mills, and the Northern Canal. In the evening, in St. Paul's Church, he received an address of welcome from Mayor Huntington, and delivered a beautiful oration, characterized by what Mr. Choate would term "the sweetest, most melting, most awful of the tones that man may ever utter, or may ever hear,—the eloquence of an expiring nation!"

In 1852, the Legislature of Massachusetts enacted the first prohibitory liquor law. Early in the year following, under

---

* Holt's Decision on Goodyear's Patent, 1858.

the encouragement of certain zealous but imprudent friends of prohibition, Timothy Pearson undertook to enforce this law as a Justice of the Peace. The farce of a temperance court continued to be played by Pearson till the Supreme Court ousted him of his usurped jurisdiction.*

In 1853, the Merrimack Street Depot was erected, jointly by the City and the Boston and Lowell Railroad Corporation. Whether it was wise on the part of the city to engage in a joint enterprise of this kind, has been gravely questioned. Two spacious halls, were fitted up in the upper stories of this edifice:—one named Huntington Hall, in honor of Elisha Huntington; the other named Jackson Hall, in honor of Patrick T. Jackson.

Synchroniously with the building of this Depot, the City Hall Building was reconstructed, and the *hall* from which it took its name became a thing of the past. Many interesting memories are associated with that Hall. There had been witnessed the most tumultuous scenes in our early history. There had been fought the battle for the schools,—the battle for Belvidere,—the battle for the Charter,—the battle for the Market House,—the battle for Caleb Cushing as the "Representative Man." There the heart of young Lowell had throbbed under the passionate eloquence of Clay. There had spoken Abraham Lincoln, John Quincy Adams, Daniel Webster, Rufus Choate, Edward Everett, John M. Berrian, Lewis Cass, Levi Woodbury, Isaac Hill, and others of the great men of America, who have since passed out of time into history.

For some years prior to 1853, the policy of regulating by law the hours of labor in factories, had been one of the most prominent subjects of popular agitation. It had been a great source of power to the Coalition, enabling the Democrats and Free Soilers to overthrow the ascendency of the Whigs here, in spite of their protestations that they, too, were Ten Hour

---

* Commonwealth v. Emery, 11 Cushing, 406; Piper v. Pearson, 2 Gray, 120; Emery v. Hapgood, 7 Gray, 55.

Men.* On September 21st, 1853, the corporations reduced the hours of labor, of their own accord, to an average of eleven hours a day; and for a time the Ten Hour agitation subsided. Upon the revival of this agitation in 1855, when the Legislature seemed determined to enact a Ten Hour Law, the corporation managers in Boston adopted the policy of Walpole, and killed the Bill by secretly buying up some of the most influential of its advocates! The Legislature of 1855 has been the object of much opprobrium. It has often been compared to the Lack Learning Parliament which sat in England in the reign of Henry the Fourth. But the "Lobby" which controlled that Legislature, was more remarkable still. There the men who for years had clamored for a Ten Hour Law, and whose pockets had been lined with corporation gold, were seen "doing the heavy standing round," and suggesting to members that as the operatives were satisfied with the eleven-hour rule, it was not worth while to carry the matter further. Accordingly, the Bill failed.

On July 12th, 1853, died Samuel Appleton, (brother of Nathan, and cousin of William,) † aged eighty-eight years. He had been largely interested in Lowell Manufactures from the start.

In 1853, the Wamesit Bank was incorporated. Its capital is $200,000.

In 1854, the Merchants' Bank was incorporated, with a capital of $100,000, since increased to $300,000. The Five Cent Savings Bank was also incorporated during this year.

---

* In 1852, that drollest of local Whig politicians, Tappan Wentworth, actually induced all the Whig candidates for the Legislature to pledge themselves to vote for the Ten Hour Bill! This artful dodge assisted Wentworth into Congress; but, at the same time, all the Whig candidates for the Legislature were defeated.

† William Appleton died February 15th, 1862. He was chosen a member of Congress in 1850, and again in 1852. He was again elected in 1860, defeating Anson Burlingame.

In 1854, the Young Men's Catholic Library Association was incorporated; its object being literary and elocutionary culture.

In the same year, the Otto Club of vocalists was formed under the management of P. P. Haggerty. This club still lives. The Philharmonic Society, the Mozart Society and others, of older date, formed for the cultivation of instrumental music, have collapsed.

In 1855, the Middlesex North Agricultural Society was incorporated. Their Fair Grounds were purchased and their building erected in 1860.

On March 29th, 1855, Joseph Hiss and his associates on the famous Legislative "Smelling Committee" came to Lowell, and inspected the school of the Sisters of Notre Dame, established September 14th, 1853. While here, Hiss made the acquaintance of Mrs. Moody, *alias* "Mrs. Patterson," with whom he passed the night at the Washington House. The virtuous indignation of his colleagues was aroused at this, and the House of Representatives expelled him. The results of the visit were, to make Hiss notorious and the Legislature ridiculous, and to furnish some sensational cuts for the comic and pictorial newspapers.

On May 29th, 1855, the bicentennial anniversary of the incorporation of Billerica was appropriately commemorated by the people of that ancient town.

On July 16th, 1855, an act of the Legislature was submitted for the acceptance of the citizens of Lowell, providing for the abolition of the Police Court, and the establishment of a Municipal Court. It was rejected—yeas, 1330; nays, 1448.

On July 22nd, 1855, Dr. Elisha Bartlett died of paralysis at Smithfield, in Rhode Island. He was born in the same town, October 6th, 1804, and commenced practice in Lowell in 1827. He took an active part in local politics, and was Lowell's first Mayor. He subsequently held medical professorships in Pittsfield, Dartmouth, Baltimore, Transylvania,

Louisville and Woodstock. He also held a professorship for three years in the College of Physicians and Surgeons in the City of New York. He was the author of a variety of professional and miscellaneous works, and was one of the few who love to turn aside from the thorny road of professional practice, to tread the flowery paths of literature. His principal work was on the "Philosophy of Medical Science." A man of fine culture,—of incorruptible integrity,—with a clear head and a warm heart,—filling with distinguished credit some of the highest places of his profession,—and never playing the part of a demagogue; Lowell may cherish with peculiar pride the name and memory of her first Mayor.*

On the eighteenth of August, 1855, died Abbott Lawrence, who, though never a citizen of Lowell, had, for a quarter of a century, been closely identified with Lowell interests. Two of his brothers—Luther and Samuel—long resided here. He was born at Groton, December 16th, 1792, and educated in the public schools of his native town. He was assiduous in business, studious of books, and always prepared to take advantage of those chances which fortune now and then opens to every aspiring young man. He was first engaged with his brothers in the importing business, in Boston; and did not become interested in the Lowell companies till 1830. He rendered signal service in building up the cotton manufacture in America on an enduring basis, and gave his name to the city next below Lowell on the line of the Merrimack.

He was not by profession a statesman. But he was Commissioner in 1842 to adjust (with Lord Ashburton) the Northeastern boundary; he was also a prominent candidate for the Whig nomination for Vice President in 1848, and narrowly escaped the position which, on the death of Taylor, made Mr. Fillmore President of the United States. He was offered and declined the Secretaryship of the Navy, but accepted the post of Minister to England, in 1849, and honored both himself

* Huntington's Memoir of Bartlett, 1856.

and his country by the manner in which he discharged the duties of that highest office known to American diplomacy. He particularly distinguished himself in the negotiation for a ship canal between the Caribbean Sea and the Pacific, and would probably have succeeded had not Mr. Clayton, then Secretary of State, abruptly withdrawn the business from his hands. "On the whole," says Nathan Appleton, "it may be doubted, whether, since the mission of Dr. Franklin, any minister of the United States has accomplished a diplomatic success greater than must be awarded to Mr. Lawrence."*

On April 7th, 1856, on the resignation of S. P. P. Fay of Cambridge, (who had held the office thirty-five years), William A. Richardson of the Lowell Bar was appointed Judge of Probate. Shortly afterward, Luther J. Fletcher, another Lowell lawyer, was appointed Judge of Insolvency.

On May 13th, 1858, (the Courts of Insolvency having been reconstructed,) Judge Richardson was appointed Judge of Insolvency also. In these Courts of Probate and Insolvency, and also as one of the codifiers of the General Statutes, Judge Richardson has acquired a reputation seldom equaled in these departments of juridical labor.

In May, 1856, the case of Edward D. Clayes *versus* Louisa C. Clayes, a suit for a divorce, and a cross suit between the same parties, came on for trial in the Supreme Court here. Strange exposures were made which compromised several persons still living. Both parties were refused a decree.

On October 28th, 1856, while that great magician, Rufus Choate, was delivering one of his most powerful appeals for the Union, in Huntington Hall, the floor suddenly settled; and Lowell narrowly escaped a catastrophe ten fold more appalling than that which Lawrence afterward suffered by the fall of the Pemberton Mill. There were assembled, not only nearly all the Lowell politicians of all parties, (whose loss

*Memoir of Lawrence, 4th volume, 4th series of the Massachusetts Historical Society's Collections. pp. 495–507.

MIDDLESEX COUNTY JAIL, AT LOWELL.

would have been an infinite gain,) but more than three thousand people of either sex—as many as could stand in the hall when all the settees had been removed. The consequences of a fall of the building under such circumstances are too dreadful for contemplation.

On November 17th, 1856, Thomas Hopkinson, one of the ablest lawyers that ever practiced in Lowell, died at Cambridge, in his fifty-third year. He was born at New Sharon, Maine, August 25th, 1804; graduated at Harvard in 1830; studied law a part of the time here in the office of Lawrence & Glidden, and was admitted to the Bar in 1833. With him were associated as law-partners, first, Seth Ames, and afterward, Arthur P. Bonney. He was a Representative in the Legislature from Lowell in 1838 and 1845, and in 1846 was a member of the State Senate. In 1848 he was appointed a Justice of the Court of Common Pleas, but resigned his seat on the bench the following year to accept the Presidency of the Boston and Worcester Railroad, which position he held until his death. He sat in the Constitutional Convention of 1853 as a Delegate from Cambridge.

From 1856 dates the present Lowell Jail, constructed according to a design by James H. Rand. The architectural style of this edifice is semi-Gothic, differing in some respects from any other structure of the kind. The main body of the building is one hundred and twenty-three feet in length; and the width is ninety feet in front, and fifty-four feet in the rear. The entire frontage, including the wings, is one hundred and eighty-eight feet. It is four stories high, with an octagon tower on each of the front corners of the main body of the edifice. It was first occupied, March 20th, 1858. The male and female prisoners are kept entirely separate. One of the wings is devoted to female prisoners, and the other occupied as the residence of the Sheriff, who is also the Jailer. There are ninety cells for males, and twelve for females, two hospitals, four rooms for temporary confinement, with kitchens, wash-rooms, bath-rooms, and all the other accompaniments of a modern prison. The cost of this handsome edifice was about one hundred and fifty thousand dollars. The senseless manner in which the County Commissioners wasted the people's money on this jail, brought the "ring" which has so long controlled our county affairs into disrepute. But the power of this "ring" still remains unbroken.

On the sixteenth of January, 1857, the distinguished Thomas H. Benton visited the mills of Lowell, and spoke in the evening on the preservation of the Union, in Huntington Hall. Some of his observations were of a local character, and are too valuable to be omitted :—

"I have always loved to view the monuments of greatness. Lowell is one of those monuments herself. When I entered the Senate of the United States, in 1823, the Merrimack Company had just started their first mill. Now, Lowell has a population of nearly forty thousand, and a valuation of fifteen million dollars. During my first year in the Senate, I presented a statement that cotton would become a great staple of trade between the North and the South. But I was disregarded. Now, Lowell alone uses seventy or eighty thousand bales each year; yet this is but one of the many places where this article finds a market. The domestic consumption of cotton now exceeds in value the entire exports of the country in 1823.

"I have gone through your factories, from top to bottom, and have been astonished at the perfection of your machinery. But there was something which astonished me even more. It was the cleanliness which pervaded every department. It was the ample rooms, well ventilated in summer, and well warmed in winter. It was the neat and comely appearance of the operatives, both male and female. It was that which struck me. It was my business to converse with all. I conversed with the young women, and I found them attractive and comely, modest without being bashful, of easy confidence without assurance, ready in conversation without forwardness, and of great intelligence. I went into their boarding houses, and there all my ideas were reversed; for I had before me the picture of the operatives as they are (or were) in the old world,—living in small, narrow, confined, uncomfortable buildings, stinted for food and clothing. On the contrary, I found the operatives as comfortably and as handsomely situated as members of Congress in Washington. They live in large, stately, elegant houses, and you enter in the same manner as you enter a parlor in Washington. You are shown into the parlor, where you see the same kind of furniture as you will find in a Congressman's boarding-house in Washington. The tables are covered with better books and more of them, if we except public documents, than are usually found in a Congressman's parlor. It was near the dinner-hour when I went to one of these houses, and I carried my curiosity so far as to ask the mistress of the house to take me into the cooking department and show me how she cooked. She said she was taken unawares, and was not prepared for it. I said that that was exactly the thing I wanted; I wanted to see it as it was every day. Without more ado, she opened the door and led me in, and there was cooking going on in a room so neat that a lady might sit there and carry on her sewing or ornamental work. This was the condition in which I found the houses of the operatives; and to all these comforts they add the leisure to read and cultivate the mind. I was struck with this as a matter peculiarly interesting in those who are about to become wives of one generation and mothers of the next."

In 1857, James M. Harmon started a weekly paper of a highly sensational character—*The Trumpet.* His personalities cost him one severe physical castigation, and two indictments for libels, one on Judge Crosby, the other on a brother editor, Enoch Emery. For the former, he was tried, convicted and incarcerated for three months in the House of Correction.

In 1857, died Mary Barnard, a widow, and an operative in the Lowell mills. Upon the settlement of her estate, there remained about sixty dollars, which was paid by John A. Buttrick, her executor, to Oberlin College, her residuary legatee. He who valued the widow's mite above other more lavish gifts, will surely not forget Mary Barnard's charity. It was the first legacy to a strictly public object ever left by a citizen of Lowell.

On September 10th, 1857, was opened the second Fair of the Middlesex Mechanics' Association, with John W. Smith as Superintendent. It closed October 7th, and the number of exhibitors was 1225. The managing committee were Mertoun C. Bryant, (Chairman,) Alfred Gilman, (Secretary,) William Fiske, Josiah Gates, Josiah G. Peabody, Samuel W. Stickney, Erastus Boydon, Abiel Rolfe, James Cook, Sewall G. Mack, Andrew Moody, Hocum Hosford, John Simpson, Levi Sprague, Samuel K. Hutchinson, Samuel J. Varney, Amos Sanborn and Francis H. Nourse.

In 1858, two divisions of the Sons of Temperance were formed in Lowell—Wamesit and Pawtucket. Two others were afterward added—Passaconaway and Equality. Formed for one of the noblest purposes, they rapidly degenerated in character, and all of them collapsed. Other societies under different names, some of earlier, and some of later date, have had the same origin, and the same end.

In 1858, the late William Wyman projected an observatory, to be erected in Belvidere, to be one hundred feet high, and forty feet square. The foundations only were laid when Captain Wyman died; and the "Washington Observatory" exists only on paper. It was as much a work of folly as the Tower of Babel.

From the same year dates Washington Square.

On January 25th, 1859, the centennial anniversary of the birth of Robert Burns was celebrated under the auspices of the Burns Club, which has occasionally commemorated this day ever since 1832, by a supper, songs, speeches, etc.

It was about the same time that Howard Camp of the order of the Sons of Malta was organized. About seven hundred men paid five dollars a-piece to be initiated into the mysteries of Maltaism, which was probably the most elaborate humbug ever started.

On March 2nd, 1859, Plymouth Rock Lodge of the American Protestant Association was instituted. It was the first branch of this order in Massachusetts. Another Lodge of the same order was instituted May 27th, 1864, which took the name of Washington.

On March 8th, 1859, Jane Ermina Locke, wife of John G. Locke, died at Ashburnham. Much of her life was passed in Lowell. Mrs. Locke was well known in literary circles. A volume of poetical waifs, an essay on pauperism in Massachusetts, and numerous contributions, in prose and verse, to newspapers and periodicals, attested the fertility of her pen.

On September 22nd, 1859, the two hundred and fifth anniversary of the settlement of Chelmsford was signalized in that town by the dedication of a monument to the men of Chelmsford who served in the Revolutionary War.

About this time, there was no little agitation for a law correcting the abuse of proxy-voting in the meetings of stockholders of manufacturing companies, and for a law compelling these companies to hold their annual meetings where their works were carried on, etc. In the first years of the Merrimack Company, the annual meetings of the stockholders were held in Lowell. The dinners eaten on those occasions, at the Mansion House, and at the Stone House, were interesting incidents in the lives of those who had the great pleasure to be present. Such men as Daniel Webster and Jeremiah Mason attended, and treated the company to the richest feasts of post-prandial eloquence.

In December, 1859, Robert B. Caverly, Captain of the City Guards, caused Timothy Pearson, his Third Lieutenant, to be brought to trial at Salem for perjury. The indictment was supported by overwhelming evidence; and nothing seemed more certain than that Pearson would be compelled to exchange his uniform as a Lieutenant of the Guards for the less picturesque costume of the State Prison. But just in the nick of time, Benjamin F. Butler, the defendant's counsel, discovered a flaw in the record, and Pearson escaped. Nearly three years later, the irrepressible Caverly broke out again on his former Lieutenant, and petitioned the Supreme Court to expel Pearson from the Bar, for fraud, perjury, malpractice and extortion. The animosity of Caverly continued unappeased until Pearson paid him all his costs, and went away into the army. The victorious Captain then sat down, and tuning his triumphant song, produced his poem of the Merrimack.

CHAPTER X.

POLITICAL HISTORY OF LOWELL.

Whigism in the ascendant—Members of the General Court—Members of Congress—Edward Everett—Caleb Cushing—Degradation of local politics—A Lowell Caucus.

The principles of the old Whig party naturally took deep root in the minds of the Lowellians, whose industry was promised "protection" in the event of a Whig ascendency. "Two dollars a day and roast beef" was to be the pay of every mechanic in the promised Whig millenium. At the first State election in which Lowell participated, in April, 1826, she gave Levi Lincoln ninety-five votes, and James Lloyd fifty-three. From that time down to the Coalition triumph in 1851, Lowell faltered in her devotion to the Whig party only in 1836 and 1842, in each of which years she gave a majority for the Democratic gubernatorial nominee. In 1851, 1852 and 1853, she gave a plurality vote for the Whig candidates of those years, Robert C. Winthrop, John H. Clifford and Emory Washburn. In 1854, she lurched into Know Nothingism, and gave her vote for Henry J. Gardner, whom she also indorsed in 1855 and 1856. Since 1856 she has steadily supported the Republican candidates — Nathaniel P. Banks, John A. Andrew and Alexander H. Bullock.

No citizen of Lowell has ever been made Governor; though two have been elected Lieutenant Governors—Elisha Huntington in 1853, and John Nesmith in 1862. Three Executive Councillors have also been elected from Lowell—John Aiken in 1849, Homer Bartlett in 1854, and Josiah G. Peabody in 1856. Thomas Talbot of Lowell and Billerica was a member of the Executive Council in 1865, 1866, 1867 and 1868.

On May 8th, 1826, Lowell chose as her first Representative in the General Court, Nathaniel Wright.* Eight years later,

*For his successors in the House, see Appendix.

the same gentleman became the first State Senator from Lowell. John P. Robinson was Senator in 1835, William Livingston in 1836 and 1837, Joseph W. Mansur in 1840, Seth Ames in 1841, Josiah G. Abbott in 1842 and 1843, Royal Southwick in 1844 and 1845, Thomas Hopkinson in 1846, John A. Knowles in 1847, Tappan Wentworth in 1848 and 1849, John W. Graves in 1850 and 1851,* Ithamar W. Beard in 1852,† John A. Buttrick in 1855 and 1856, Arthur P. Bonney and Joseph White in 1857.

Prior to 1857, the State Senators were elected by the counties on general tickets. By an amendment to the Constitution, they have since been chosen by districts. The Senators from the Lowell District have been Arthur P. Bonney in 1858; Benjamin F. Butler, 1859; Ephraim B. Patch, 1860; Arthur P. Bonney, 1861; Daniel S. Richardson, 1862; Samuel A. Brown, 1863 and 1864; Tappan Wentworth, 1865 and 1866; Joshua N. Marshall, 1867; and Benjamin F. Clark, 1868. All of these gentlemen belonged to Lowell except the last, who is a Congregational clergyman in North Chelmsford.

On March 7th, 1853, Josiah G. Abbott, John W. Graves, Shubael P. Adams, Benjamin F. Butler, Andrew T. Nute, James M. Moore, Abraham Tilton, James K. Fellows, and Peter Powers, (being the whole of the Coalition ticket except James J. Maguire, who, on account of his Irish birth and Roman faith, was defeated,) were elected Delegates to the Constitutional Convention, in opposition to Elisha Huntington, Benjamin F. French, Daniel S. Richardson, George H. Carleton, Homer Bartlett, Benjamin C. Sargeant, Uzziah C. Burnap, William North, Stephen Mansur and James H. B. Ayer, Whigs.

On November 6th, 1826, Lowell participated for the first time in the election of a Representative in Congress. Twenty-

---

* Dr. Graves was the only Lowell member of the Legislature of 1851, who voted for Charles Sumner, for United States Senator.

† Benjamin Adams of Chelmsford was in the State Senate in 1853, and Peter Lawson of Dracut in 1854.

two votes—all that were cast—were then given for Edward Everett, who ran successfully as an independent Workingmen's candidate against John Keyes, the candidate of the old County "ring." At the next election, November 3rd, 1828, Mr. Everett, running as the Whig candidate, received two hundred and seventy-eight votes, and Leonard M. Parker ninety-five. At the election in 1830, Mr. Everett received two hundred votes, and his opponent, James Russell, fifty-one. Mr. Everett remained in the House of Representatives till 1836, but by the re-arrangement of Congressional Districts under the Census of 1830, Lowell was detached from his District, and ceased to be represented by him. The subsequent career of Everett as Governor, President of Harvard University, Minister to England, Secretary of State, and United States Senator, is a part of the history of the whole country.

The second Representative in Congress was Gayton P. Osgood, an able lawyer, an old bachelor, and a Democrat, who remained in Congress one term only—from 1833 to 1835. He was the only Democratic Representative Lowell ever had in Congress. He was of Andover.

In 1835, after a contest rarely equalled in the annals of party strife, Caleb Cushing was elected to Congress from the District including Lowell. The Lowell Whigs held a meeting at midnight to exchange congratulations over his election. There is abundant evidence that the Whigs of the District felt it a great honor to be represented by such a man as Mr. Cushing, who was recognized as the equal of any man in the House, and who was never tired of serving even the humblest of his constituents in every proper way. Mr. Cushing continued to represent the Lowell District till 1843. When the Whig State Convention, in 1842, under the dictation of Abbott Lawrence, passed their stupid resolution of "eternal separation" from the Administration of John Tyler, Mr. Cushing, following the lead of Mr. Webster, refused to concur. Thereupon, various hungry politicians, who were not worthy to black

Mr. Cushing's boots, combined to rob him of the confidence of his constituents by an active and unscrupulous use of the coward's favorite weapon—calumny. Weakened by these nefarious tactics, Mr. Cushing retired from Congress, and accepted the mission to China. It has been common to sneer at Mr. Cushing as one who *Tylerized.* But as between Mr. Cushing and his adversaries in the controversy of 1842, the calm verdict of history must clearly be given to him. His course throughout was in perfect harmony with his masterly address to his constituents, in September, 1841, in which he warned the Whigs against the folly into which they were then running under the Caucus-Dictatorship of Mr. Clay—the folly of committing "suicide, in order to avoid the danger of dying a natural death." Having elected Tyler, who was with them on most questions, though not wholly with them on all, he thought it the part of a practical Whig statesman to carry as many of his measures as he could under Tyler's Administration; and he was right. Mr. Cushing saw clearly and declared frankly that to follow the petulant policy dictated by Clay, was to waste life in a vain chase after bubbles. Considering with what blind persistence this fatal policy was pursued, and with what disastrous results, it cannot be wondered that Mr. Cushing, with his broader statesmanship and catholicity of feeling, held himself aloof until his *quondam* friends had achieved their ruin; and that afterward, when the old issues had become obsolete, and new issues had arisen, he sought a more congenial home in the Democratic party. Of his services as Colonel and Brigadier-General during the Mexican War, we shall not here speak. Nor is this the place to dwell on his subsequent career as Mayor of Newburyport, Representative in the Legislature,* Judge of the Supreme Court, Attorney

* During his long career in the Massachusetts Legislature, it is said, Mr. Cushing never received pay for a single day when he was not in actual attendance. His unselfishness in this contrasts strongly with the greediness of some Legislators of a later day.

General of the United States, President of the Charleston Convention of 1860, Commissioner to codify the United States Statutes, etc.

The successor of Mr. Cushing in Congress was Amos Abbott — a good, clever man, who had achieved distinguished success as keeper of a grocer's shop, at the cross-roads in Andover; but utterly insignificant in Congress. He retained his seat six years. In 1849, James H. Duncan of Haverhill, succeeded him and was re-elected for a second term.

In 1852, the Congressional election was closely contested between Henry Wilson, Coalitionist, and Tappan Wentworth of Lowell, Whig. The tactics used to defeat Gen. Wilson had better not be scrutinized too closely. His defeat, however, was one of the most fortunate events in a life remarkably full of vicissitudes. Had he been elected to the House in 1852, he would hardly have been a candidate for the Senate in 1855; and the chair then vacated by Edward Everett would probably have been filled by Marshall P. Wilder or Henry J. Gardner.

Mr. Wentworth's successors have been Chauncey L. Knapp, from 1855 to 1859; Charles R. Train, from 1859 to 1863; and George S. Boutwell, from 1863 to 1869.

It may here be mentioned that, in 1866, Benjamin F. Butler of Lowell and Gloucester was elected to Congress from the District including the last named town.

It must be confessed that Lowell has become a political Bœotia,—that her politics, her office-holders and her office-seekers are the opprobrium of the Commonwealth. She is cursed with miserable "bummers," of both parties, who, were they suddenly placed in the Common Council of New York, would have nothing to learn of political chicanery, but might be able to impart some valuable suggestions to Fernando Wood himself. There was a time when her position was quite otherwise,—when her citizens delighted in bringing into public life men of broad culture and of elevated character,—men who were not content with the small fame of mere place-holding, but who trained their minds assiduously to the study of the higher politics. That she may yet recover her former good name,—that a nobler set of men may hereafter arise,—a set worthy to stand in the place of Bartlett, of Hopkinson, of Lawrence, and of Robinson,—is a matter rather of brave hope, than of confident expectation.

The demoralization of our local politics began sometime prior to 1850, and was much accelerated by the Coalition of that time; but its grand impetus was derived from the Know Nothing movement of 1854, which suddenly changed all the loafers of the city, of native birth, into scheming politicians. To show how political meetings have been conducted in Lowell during the last dozen years, we present the following report—prepared at the time for another purpose—of the proceedings of a Republican caucus which met in Jackson Hall, September 29th, 1860, to choose delegates to the County, Councillor and Congressional District Conventions; the contest for the Congressional nomination being between Charles R. Train and George S. Boutwell:—

Promptly at the appointed hour, Hubbard Willson ascended the platform, and called for a nomination for the Chair. Several Train men instantly responded "H. G. Blaisdell," while about twenty Boutwell men shouted "Charles Cowley," who was almost unanimously chosen Chairman, with G. A. Gerry as Secretary. On motion of Timothy Pearson (Boutwell), it was voted that a committee of five from each ward be chosen by nomination from the floor, to nominate twenty-six delegates to the Congressional Convention. During the appointment of this committee, Theodore H. Sweetser moved that the meeting adjourn to the several ward rooms, and that the delegates be chosen there. The Chair decided that this motion was not then in order. Mr. Sweetser appealed from this decision to the meeting, and proceeded to discuss his appeal. Mr. Pearson rose to a point of order,—that the appeal was not debatable. The Chair overruled the point of order, and allowed Mr. Sweetser to proceed. Mr. Pearson then moved the previous question; but the Chair ruled that the previous question was not in order in a popular assembly. At the close of the debate, the Chair put the question, "Shall the decision of the Chair stand as the decision of the meeting," and appointed tellers to count the votes. The Chair was sustained—yeas 102; nays, 24. The committee was then filled—largely by Boutwell men.

Another committee was chosen in the same manner to nominate delegates to the County and Councillor Conventions. As there was no great contest over this part of the business, this committee was the first to report, and the report was adopted. Charles A. Stott offered a resolution endorsing the Congressional career of Mr. Train, which, being explained as not intended to instruct the delegates, was adopted. H. L. C. Newton stated that there were Democrats voting for the Train resolution, and inquired who was to decide whether a man was a Democrat or a Republican. The Chair answered that every man must decide for himself, subject to the control of the meeting.

The committee first chosen then reported, nominating John Wright, John Nesmith, C. L. Knapp, F. H. Nourse, J. G. Peabody, John W. Smith, and twenty others, mostly Boutwell men, as the delegates to the Congressional Convention. Mr. Pearson moved the adoption of this report. Mr. Sweetser moved an amendment,—that the names be voted on singly. The objection was made that the amendment was not in order; but this objection was overruled by the Chair. The amendment was lost—yeas, 97; nays, 113.

Enraged at the prospect of their defeat, the Train men now resolved to protract the meeting by an adroit course of parliamentary "filibustering" until enough of their opponents had gone home to leave them in the ascendant. Seeing this, at about eleven o'clock, the Boutwell men made and carried a motion to adjourn. Then ensued a "bolt" of the Train men—creating a division in the party which was not healed for seven years. Jonathan Ladd mounted the platform, and proposed that Linus Child be chosen Chairman. Mr. Child accordingly took the Chair, and twenty-six more delegates were chosen, all friends of Mr. Train.

Why so much importance was attached to the choice of the Lowell delegation, was, that the other delegates were so closely divided between Train and Boutwell that he who secured the Lowell delegation was sure of the nomination, which was equivalent to an election. Now that the seats of the Lowell delegates were contested, everything depended on getting a majority of the delegates from the towns. To aid them in this, the Train men subsidized several influential newspapers, and called a mass meeting in Huntington Hall, to denounce the Boutwell men for doing precisely what they had done themselves. Had a majority of the delegates outside of Lowell been friendly to Mr. Boutwell, the delegates of the bolters would have been excluded from the Convention. But the Train men having obtained a majority of the delegates outside of Lowell, they were enabled to secure the admission of the bolting delegates on the same footing as those regularly chosen.

Thus, it was largely through the Lowell caucus that Mr. Train secured his seat in Congress for his second term,—that George S. Boutwell became Commissioner of Internal Revenue, —that John S. Keyes obtained the United States Marshalship and a fortune,—that John A. Goodwin was made Postmaster of Lowell, and Jonathan Ladd Paymaster of Volunteers. Nor were these all or half the consequences, personal and political, of the meeting, the doings of which we have now recorded. No caucus ever held in Lowell,—not the Whig caucus of 1852, which was packed and controlled so skillfully by Tappan Wentworth,—nor the Union caucus of 1862, which had two Chairmen, and was about to choose a third, when the gas was turned off by the police,—has been more prolific of results than the Republican Congressional caucus of 1860.

CHAPTER XI.

MUNICIPAL HISTORY OF LOWELL.

Town—Selectmen—Clerks — Treasurers — City — Mayors—Treasurers— Marshals—Auditors—Chief Engineers—Physicians—Solicitors—Presidents of the Common Council—Election Troubles—Origin of Municipal Government.

Lowell is not a *municipality*, in the older and better sense of that word. Our population,—various in origin, heterogeneous in character, thrown together by chance, constantly distributing itself hither and thither, with nothing about it permanent except its changeability,—is, and always has been, grossly wanting in the municipal spirit. It would be easy to name many, of the living and of the dead, who were proud of Lowell, and who strove, with fond solicitude, to make her worthy of their pride. But the Lowellians generally have no such feeling. The *genius loci* is not in them.

This want of the municipal spirit has manifested itself in various ways—in business, in politics, and especially in the low character of too many of the men whom the caprices of the people, or the chance-medley of the caucus, has again and again invested with public functions. Under ordinary circumstances, time would gradually develop this minor form of patriotism. But it has not done so here. We have gone backward rather than forward. In the first years of Lowell, three-fourths of the men placed in public authority, were among the best men living here. But none will pretend that such has been the fact during the last twenty years.

John Stuart Mill observes that "the greatest imperfection of popular local institutions and the chief cause of the failure which so often attends them, is the low calibre of the men by whom they are carried on."

The municipal existence of Lowell began, March 1st, 1826, the date of Governor Lincoln's approval of the act incorporating her as a town. She continued a town during ten years. Her eleven boards of selectmen were as follows:

1826—Nathaniel Wright, Samuel Batchelder, O. M. Whipple.
1827—Nathaniel Wright, Joshua Swan, Henry Coburn, Jr.
1828—Nathaniel Wright, Joshua Swan, Artemas Young.
1829—Nathaniel Wright, Joshua Swan, Artemas Young,
1830—Joshua Swan, Artemas Young, James Tyler.
1831—Joshua Swan, Artemas Young, James Tyler.
1832—Joshua Swan, Matthias Parkhurst, Josiah Crosby, Benjamin Walker, S. C. Oliver.
1833—Joshua Swan, Matthias Parkhurst, Benjamin Walker, Elisha Huntington, S. C. Oliver.
1834—Joshua Swan, Elisha Huntington, William Livingston, Jesse Fox, Benjamin Walker.
1835—Benjamin Walker, James Russell, William Livingston, John Chase, William N. Owen.
1836—Benjamin Walker, James Russell, William Livingston, John Chase, William N. Owen.

Samuel A. Coburn was Town Clerk from the beginning, and continued in office two years after the adoption of the City Charter. He was succeeded in 1838 by Thomas Ordway, who held his office sixteen years. In 1854, William Lamson, Jr., became City Clerk; and in 1858 he was succeeded by John H. McAlvin, the present incumbent.

The office of Town Treasurer was filled by Artemas Holden from the incorporation of the town to the adoption of the City Charter.

The office of Town Tax Collector, created in 1828, was filled in 1828 by Luther Marshall; in 1829 by Josiah B. French; in

1830 by James Russell; in 1831 by William Lamb; in 1832 and 1833 by Isaac Bancroft; in 1834 by Joseph Tyler and Abner W. Buttrick, the last of whom was also Tax Collector in 1835.

The Act to establish the City of Lowell was approved by Governor Everett, April 1st, 1836. The canvass preceeding the first City election was an exciting one. The Whig and Democratic parties were nearly equally balanced, and party feeling was at fever heat. Each party was desirous of the honor of inaugurating the young municipality. Each party nominated its most available candidate. The Whigs concentrated their strength on Elisha Bartlett:—the Democracy nominated Eliphalet Case. The Whigs triumphed. Dr. Bartlett received nine hundred and fifty-eight votes; Mr. Case, eight hundred and sixty-eight; Oliver M. Whipple, seventeen; John Dummer, two. Dr. Bartlett was inaugurated as Mayor, and was re-elected in 1837. He was highly popular as Mayor; but on the expiration of his second term, he positively "declined all further service in this line."

The successor of Dr. Bartlett was Luther Lawrence, who was re-elected in 1839, and whose tragic death has already been recorded. The vacancy created by the death of Mr. Lawrence, was filled by the City Council by the election of Elisha Huntington, who was re-elected by the people in 1840 and 1841. Nathaniel Wright was elected Mayor in 1842, on the first "Citizens'" ticket that was run in Lowell. In 1843, he was re-elected on the Whig ticket. In 1844 and 1845, Dr. Huntington, who had been beaten by Mr. Wright in 1842, was again Mayor, and was succeeded in 1846 by Jefferson Bancroft. By an amendment to the City Charter, the time of the municipal election was now changed from the first Monday of March to the second Monday of December. annually. The commencement of the municipal year was also changed from the first Monday of April to the first Monday in January. Mr. Bancroft was re-elected Mayor in 1847 and 1848. In 1849 the

Whigs were again ousted, and Josiah B. French, Coalitionist, became Mayor. He was re-elected in 1850. During the next four years, the Whigs were successful, and elected J. H. B. Ayer in 1851, Dr. Huntington in 1852, and Sewall G. Mack in 1853 and 1854. The Know Nothing spasm of 1854 made Ambrose Lawrence Mayor in 1855. A Citizens' ticket restored Dr. Huntington to the chair that he loved so well in 1856, but broke down under him at the next election; and in 1857 Stephen Mansur became the first Republican Mayor. He was a good man, and made an honest effort to execute the laws for the suppression of the rum traffic, but was dropped at the next election, when, by a Citizens' movement, Dr. Huntington, for the eighth and last time, was re-elected to the executive chair. During the three following years the Republicans were successful: James Cook was Mayor in 1859, and Benjamin C. Sargeant in 1860 and 1861. Hocum Hosford succeeded in 1862* and 1863 on "Citizens'" tickets, and in 1864, without opposition, on a Republican ticket. Josiah G. Peabody became Mayor in 1865 and 1866, and was succeeded by George F. Richardson in 1867 and 1868.†

The first City Treasurer was William Davidson, and the first City Collector of Taxes, Bryan Morse, through whom the City lost $10,000 of its funds.‡ In 1837, the duties of Tax Collector were superadded to those of Treasurer. These offices have been filled by the following gentlemen—William Davidson from 1837 to 1842; John A. Buttrick from 1843 to 1846; Ithamar A. Beard from 1847 to 1850; John F. Kimball from 1851 to 1855; Isaac C. Eastman from 1856 to 1860; and George W. Bedlow from 1861 to 1864, when he resigned and was succeeded by Thomas G. Gerrish.

---

* At the election of Mayor in 1861, Dr. John W. Graves, Mr. Hosford's opponent, probably received a majority of the votes, but a fraud or mistake in counting the votes in Ward Five turned the scale against him.

† The Boards of Aldermen and Common Councilmen are republished annually in the Municipal Register, and are therefore omitted here.

‡ 7 Metcalf, p. 152.

The City Marshals have been—Zaccheus Shed in 1836 and 1837; Henry T. Mowatt in 1838; Joseph Butterfield in 1839; Zaccheus Shedd in 1840 and 1841; Charles J. Adams from 1842 to 1847; Zaccheus Shedd in 1848; George P. Waldron in 1849, and Zaccheus Shedd in 1850. Charles J. Adams came in again in 1851, but afterward resigned, and James H. Corrin succeeded him. From 1852 to 1854 Edwin L. Shed was City Marshal; in 1855, Samuel Miller; in 1856, William H. Clemence; in 1857, Eben H. Rand; in 1858, William H. Clemence; in 1859, Eben H. Rand; in 1860 and 1861, Frederick Lovejoy, to whom in 1862 succeeded Bickford Lang.

The City Auditors have been—John Nesmith, 1836; Joseph W. Mansur, 1837; Horatio G. F. Corliss, 1838; John G. Locke, from 1840 to 1848; George A. Butterfield in 1849 and 1850; William Lamson, Junior, from 1851 to 1853; Leonard Brown, 1854 and 1855; James J. Maguire, 1856; Henry A. Lord, 1857, and since 1857, George Gardner.

The Chief Engineers have been—Charles L. Tilden, 1836 and 1837; Jonathan M. Marston, 1838; William Fiske, 1839; Josiah B. French from 1840 to 1842; Jonathan M. Marston, 1843; Jefferson Bancroft, 1844 and 1845; Aaron H. Sherman from 1846 to 1849; Horace Howard from 1850 to 1852; Lewis A. Cutler, 1853; Weare Clifford, from 1854 to 1859; Asahel D. Puffer, from 1860 to 1862; Joseph Tilton, 1863 and 1864; Weare Clifford, 1865 and 1866; and George W. Waymoth, 1867 and 1868.

The sick poor of Lowell have had for their medical advisers the following City Physicians—Charles P. Coffin, from 1836 to 1839; Elisha Bartlett, 1840 and 1841; Abraham D. Dearborn, 1842 and 1843; David Wells, from 1844 to 1846; Abner H. Brown, from 1847 to 1850; Joel Spaulding, from 1851 to 1855; Luther B. Morse, 1856 and 1857; John W. Graves from 1858 to 1860; Moses W. Kidder, from 1861 to 1863; Nathan Allen, 1864 and 1865; and George E. Pinkham, 1866, 1867 and 1868.

The Law Department was not established till 1840, when Thomas Hopkinson was chosen City Solicitor. His successors have been—John A. Knowles, 1841; Richard G. Colby, 1842; Seth Ames from 1843 to 1849 ; Isaac S. Morse, from 1850 to 1852 ; Theodore H. Sweetser, 1853 and 1854 ; Arthur P. Bonney, 1855 ; Alpheus R. Brown, 1856 ; Robert B. Caverly, 1857 ; Alpheus R. Brown, 1858 ; Theodore H. Sweetser, from 1859 to 1861 ; Alpheus R. Brown, 1862 and 1863 ; Tappan Wentworth, from 1864 to 1866 ; and George Stevens, 1867 and 1868.

The following named gentlemen have been Presidents of the Common Council, most of them more than once—John Clark, Elisha Huntington, Thomas Hopkinson, Pelham W. Warren, Tappan Wentworth, Joseph W. Mansur, Oliver March, Daniel S. Richardson, Joel Adams, John Aiken, Ivers Taylor, George Gardner, Benjamin C. Sargeant, William A. Richardson, Alfred Gilman, Frederick Holton, William P. Webster, William F. Salmon, William L. North, George F. Richardson, George Ripley, Gustavus A. Gerry, and Alfred H. Chase.

In February, 1852, Mayor Ayer and his Aldermen were indicted by the Grand Jury "for a neglect of official duty." At the State election of 1851, the number of votes cast in Ward Four was 811 ; but, through a glaring blunder, the number returned was 8,038. But no fraud being intended, the defendants were not convicted.* The case was one of those, far too numerous, in which the inquisitorial powers of grand juries have been meanly used as the instruments of personal and political rivalry and rancor.

The incidents of our municipal history, that possess general interest, are few. Consequently this chapter is largely devoted to the successions of local officials. To some, such details will appear trivial. Nevertheless,

"These little things are great to little man."

Writers of a certain class speak continually of our modern forms of municipal government as having originated among

*Cushing's Contested Elections, pp. 639–674.

the Teutonic tribes of ancient central Europe. But those who have most carefully studied the history of republican and imperial Rome, know that these municipal institutions originated, not with the barbarous tribes of Germany, but with those masters of the ancient world—the Romans. For the purpose of promoting union and uniformity between the victors and the vanquished, and perhaps also from a love of methodicity, the Romans established in the cities of all the provinces which owned their sway, municipal institutions identical with those of the great mother-city, Rome. The forms thus established have continued in Europe until now; and it is a remarkable proof of the wisdom of the Romans, that when the great towns of the New World found it desirable to perfect their municipal institutions, they could devise no better forms than those instituted on the Tiber so many centuries ago.

In every city of that world-empire were two executive magistrates called *Duumviri*, answering to the Consuls at Rome. In lieu of the Senate, there was a body of *Decurions*, (so called because, originally, every tenth man belonged to it,) answering to our modern Aldermen, as the *Decuries* answered to Wards. The *Duumviri* were subsequently called Provosts or Bailiffs, and, at a still later day, Mayors; though some, perhaps, may say that the Mayor corresponds more nearly with the *Princeps Senatus*, or President of the Senate. Two changes —some may call them improvements—have been introduced: the executive functions have been vested in one officer, instead of two; while the legislative body has been divided into two branches, instead of sitting as one, as was the custom in Rome. Thus, the same municipal forms under which our ancestors lived in the times of the Cæsers, have outlived the dissolution of civilization in the ancient world, and, crossing the middle ages and the Atlantic, have come down to us.

CHAPTER XII.

LOWELL DURING THE REBELLION.

Gen. Whiting—F. G. Fontane—Gen. Butler—Capt. Fox—Fort Sumter—The Sixth—Riot in Baltimore—Ladd and Whitney—Hill Cadets—Richardson Infantry—Abbott Greys—Butler Rifles—Soldiers' Aid Association—The Twenty-Sixth, Thirtieth, and Thirty-Third—Lowell Officers Killed—The Conscription—Fifteenth Battery—Sanitary Fair—State Aid—Bounties—Summaries, etc.

In opening the record of the part borne by our people in the war for the suppression of the Rebellion, it is but fair to say, that some of the adherents of "the Lost Cause" were also, in early life, identified with Lowell. Several of these became quite famous: for the fame of a career is often wholly independent of its intrinsic merit.

> "The aspiring youth who fired the Ephesian dome,
> Outlives in fame the pious fool who raised it."

Major-General Robert E. K. Whiting, one of the most scientific, yet one of the most unfortunate of the Confederate chiefs, spent no inconsiderable portion of his boyhood in Lowell, and from 1845 to 1847 stood well as a pupil in the High School.

Mightier than the sword of Whiting was the pen of F. G. Fontane, one of the ablest of that junta of journalists whose passionate editorial appeals contributed so much to "fire the Southern heart," and precipitate the bloody struggle. He, too, passed much of his boyhood here, and wrote juvenile "compositions" in the High School, little dreaming how many spirited battle-scenes he would one day sketch over his famous *nome de guerre* of "Personne."*

The disruption of the Democratic National Convention of 1860, contributed directly and powerfully to that volume of influences the result of which was—War. Not the least among those who participated in that work of disruption was Ben-

* His father prepared "the Balm of a Thousand Flowers."

jamin F. Butler, who, born on Guy Fawkes' Day, has a congenital *penchant* for plots and conspiracies. What Dryden said of Shaftesbury, will apply to him:—

> "For close designs and crooked counsels fit,
> Sagacious, bold, and turbulent of wit. . . .
> A daring pilot in extremity,
> Pleased with the danger when the waves ran high."

He was born at Deerfield in New Hampshire, November 5th, 1818. In early infancy, he lost his father, a bold privateer, who scoured the Spanish main under the Columbian (or some other) flag. In 1828, his mother removed to Lowell, and placed Benjamin under that faithful "knight of the birch," Joshua Merrill, in what is now the Edson School. Graduating at Waterville in 1838, he made a short fishing voyage to the coast of Labrador. Cured of his boyish passion for the sea, he then returned to Lowell, studied law in the office of William Smith, and in September, 1840, was admitted to the Bar. His career as a Democratic politician began synchronously with his appearance in the Lowell Police Court, and culminated in the Charleston Convention, where, after a persistent struggle of twenty years, he first acquired national notoriety. He sat for one term in either branch of the State Legislature, and also in the Constitutional Convention of 1853. But his reputation was acquired chiefly in the courts of law, and in the caucuses of the Democracy.

Chosen a Delegate to the National Democratic Convention, in 1860, by a Douglas constituency, he set his constituents at defiance, and voted fifty-seven times for Jefferson Davis. When the Convention was rent in twain, he attached himself to the Southern wing of it, and flung out the banner of Breckenridge and Lane. On July 26th, 1860, at a Democratic meeting in Huntington Hall, he attempted to defend his conduct. No sooner had he been introduced than he was met by a storm of hisses, groans and yells, such as have seldom been heard outside of Pandemonium. At every pause in the tempest, Butler renewed his efforts to speak; but every such attempt was instantly balked by a renewal of the storm in all its pristine fury. Three-quarters of an hour were thus passed; but the sea of angry faces remained, and the tornado of hisses, groans and yells, continued unabated. Realizing the impossibility of getting a hearing at that time, and overcome by the violence of his own emotions, Butler beat an abrupt retreat to the ante-room, leaving his enemies to enjoy their triumph. Thus the Democrats snubbed their recreant chief. Thus Lowell disowned her foremost son.

Another meeting was afterward held, when Butler obtained a hearing; and never did the resources of his genius appear more inexhaustible than in the able and ingenius but specious and sophistical defence which he then put in. A man of such immense vitality as Butler can never be put down in this country without his own consent. The same man whom we have here seen "corked up" in Huntington Hall, and driven into the ante-room in a paroxysm of grief and mortification, will turn up again in this chapter, to be honored with a public reception after the style of Jackson, Kossuth and Sheridan.

On the ninth of January, 1861, the steamer Star of the West crossed the bar of Charleston with supplies for the Federal garrison at Fort Sumter. She was fired upon by the South Carolinians, and driven off. This was the true beginning of the war; though for three months afterward, the country slept on in the delusive belief that it was still at peace. During those three months, the great question was, How to relieve the garrison of Fort Sumter? To many minds the question presented insoluble difficulties. Lowell, however, had sent forth a man, to whose hard, practical mind this question presented no difficulty at all—Gustavus Vassa Fox.

He was born in Saugus, June 13th, 1821. In December, 1823, his father, Dr. Jesse Fox, removed to Lowell, and here Gustavus remained until June, 1838, when, through the influence of Caleb Cushing, he was appointed a Midshipman in the

Navy. Naval promotions in those days were slow, and it was not until 1852 that Fox rose to the rank of Lieutenant. He was one of the first of our naval officers who comprehended the great changes that were to follow the introduction of steam into the Navy, and obtained "leaves of absence" in order to gain experience in steam navigation. While "on leave" he served as mate to Captain Cumstock on board the Baltic. He was subsequently Captain, first of the Ohio, and afterward of the George Law, plying between New York and Panama. In 1855, he resigned his commission, and became Agent of the Bay State Mills at Lawrence.

Immediately after the return of the Star of the West to New York, in January, 1861, Captain Fox repaired to Washington, and submitted to General Scott, Secretary Holt and President Buchanan, a plan of his own for the relief of Fort Sumter. His plan was, to anchor three small men-of-war off the harbor of Charleston, four miles from the Fort, as his base of operations; and then to send three steam-tugs and a full complement of armed launches, manned by three hundred extra sailors, to carry the troops and stores to the Fort, running the batteries on Sullivan's and Morris's Islands. Scott and Holt approved the plan; but the vacillating counsels which prevailed at Washington during the last three months of Buchanan and the first six weeks of Lincoln, prevented its adoption until it was too late. It was not until the sixth of April that Captain Fox left New York with a part of the proposed expedition, the whole of which might have sailed as early as the preceeding January. Rough weather then came on, and he only arrived off Charleston in time to witness the bombardment of Fort Sumter, and to bring back with him Major Anderson and his command, after the surrender of the Fort to General Beauregard. The failure of this daring enterprize involved no loss of confidence in Captain Fox on the part of President Lincoln, who soon afterward made him Assistant Secretary of the Navy.

The fall of Fort Sumter produced a tremendous sensation in Lowell. The shock was common to the whole country. On the fifteenth of April, President Lincoln called upon Governor Andrew for two regiments of Militia. On the next day, he enlarged the call to a brigade of four regiments, which was assigned by the Governor to the command of Brigadier-General Butler. Immediately on the receipt of the first call, (April 15th,) Governor Andrew ordered Colonel Edward F. Jones, of the Sixth Regiment, to muster his command forthwith on Boston Common.

Four companies of this regiment belonged to Lowell, viz.:

Company C, (Mechanic Phalanx,) Captain Albert S. Follansbee.
Company D, (City Guards,) Captain James W. Hart.
Company H, (Watson Light Guard,) Captain John F. Noyes.
Company A, (originally Lawrence Cadets, subsequently National Greys,) Captain Josiah A. Sawtell, who, on his promotion to the Majority, May 18th, was succeeded by Captain George M. Dickerman*.

On the next morning, (April 16th,) these four companies, with two companies from Lawrence, one from Groton and one from Acton, of the same regiment, were mustered in Huntington Hall, where stimulating speeches were made to them, and prayers offered to the God of Battles for their success.

It was a cold, stormy and most dismal day, when, amid the prayers and cheers and tears of the people, the cars bore the Sixth Regiment toward Boston. In Faneuil Hall, they were joined by the other three companies attached to the Sixth, from Stoneham, Worcester and Boston.

After the departure of the Regiment, the City Council appropriated eight thousand dollars for the benefit of the families of these and other Lowell soldiers.

The progress of the Sixth through Worcester in the evening of the seventeenth, through New York City, through the State of New Jersey, and through Philadelphia, on the eighteenth, was a series of grand ovations, especially at Philadelphia.

---

*For the rosters of these companies, see Chaplain Hanson's History of the Old Sixth Regiment.

On the nineteenth, they reached Baltimore, and seven of the eleven companies crossed the city to the Washington Depot, unresisted. The track over which they had passed in cars drawn by horses, was then barricaded by the "roughs" of the city, leaving the regimental band and four companies behind, compelled to march on foot to the Washington Depot. The companies were C, of Lowell, Capt. Follansbee; D, of Lowell, Captain Hart; I, of Lawrence, Captain Pickering; and L, of Stoneham, Capt. Dike. Capt. Follansbee, as senior Captain, commanded the detachment, which numbered about two hundred and twenty men.

In their progress through Baltimore, these companies received all sorts of indignities from the mob, whose yells, oaths and execrations filled the air. In Pratt street, missiles were thrown and firearms discharged at the advancing column, and Capt. Follansbee ordered his men to fire at will. These demonstrations continued on both sides till the detachment rejoined their comrades at the Washington Depot, and the train started which bore them to the Capital.

How many of the rioters fell has never been ascertained. Some place the number at a hundred. The first man wounded on our side was George A. Wilson, of the regimental band. Fourteen others were also wounded during this riot, and four killed,—Addison O. Whitney, Luther C. Ladd, and Charles A. Taylor, all of the Lowell City Guards; and Sumner H. Needham, of the Lawrence Light Infantry. Whitney was twenty-two years of age, and a native of Maine; Ladd was a boy of seventeen summers, a native of New Hampshire; Needham belonged to Lawrence, and Taylor, probably, to Boston.

The news of this affair, often magnified into a battle, produced a profound sensation throughout the North. As the first bloody scene in the great tragedy of the Rebellion, the Baltimore riot of 1861 will not be forgotton as long as anything in American history is preserved.

The remains of Ladd and Whitney were brought to Lowell, on the sixth of May, 1861, and buried in the Lowell Cemetery with imposing ceremonies:—

> "Such honors as in Illium once were paid
> When peaceful slept the mighty Hector's shade."

Four years later, their bodies were removed to Monument Square. There, beneath the Monument which bears their names, they now rest; and there they shall remain "till a clarion louder than that which marshaled them to the combat shall awake their slumbers."

On reaching Washington, the Sixth was welcomed by the friends of the Union with inexpressible joy. The soldiers were quartered in the Senate Chamber, and remained there till the fifth of May, when they were removed to the Relay House, ten miles from Baltimore. There they formed a part of the command of Brigadier-General Butler, Department of Annapolis. They remained at the Relay House, protecting the Baltimore and Washington Railroad,—with the exception of two short visits to Baltimore,—until the close of their term of service. They returned to Lowell, August 2nd, and were honored with a public reception on the South Common.

On the day succeeding the affair at Baltimore, two new companies were formed in Lowell—the Hill Cadets, afterward Company D, of the Sixteenth Infantry, Captain Patrick S. Proctor; and the Richardson Light Infantry, afterward the Seventh Battery, Captain Phineas A. Davis. The Hill Cadets—the first company organized in Lowell during the Rebellion—were principally men who had belonged to the Jackson Musketeers,—who had been deprived of their arms by the Know Nothing Governor Gardner,—and who had been calumniated, even as late as the preceding January, as being ready to take part with South Carolina against their own adopted Commonwealth. It was not until they received the shock of a bloody civil war, that the native and the foreign born began alike to

"Nothing is here for grief, nothing for tears, nothing to wail
And knock the breast, no weakness, no contempt,
Dispraise or blame, but well and fair,
And what may quiet us in a death so noble."

feel that, in spite of all their little differences, they were all Americans at heart—loving their country with a warm and equal love, and ready to peril all in her defence.

On April 22nd, a third company was started by Edward Gardner Abbott. Men rushed to his recruiting office, and in three days his company was full—his father, Judge Abbott, pouring out money with an unsparing hand, to supply every real or imaginary want of the men. This company was organized April 25th, and took the name of the Abbott Greys. It was incorporated with the Second Infantry, and on May 24th, Abbott was commissioned as its Captain. Few, if any, volunteer officers were commissioned for three years' service earlier than Captain Abbott.

On May 1st, Eben James and Thomas O'Hare organized the Butler Rifles, afterward Company G, of the Sixteenth Infantry.

While the younger men of Lowell were filling the rosters of these and other companies for service in the field, the older men, together with the women, irrespective of age, were serving the common cause by contributions of money, clothing, provisions, books and everything else that could enhance the comfort of the soldier. With the view to systematize this patriotic and charitable ministry, Judge Crosby called a public meeting, April 20th, when the Soldier's Aid Association was formed—the first of the kind in the United States—germ of the Sanitary Commission, and germ of the Christian Commission. Judge Crosby was its President; M. C. Bryant, Secretary; and Samuel W. Stickney, Treasurer. The ladies and gentlemen who participated in this ministry represented every social circle and every religious society in Lowell.

It has been the standing reproach of Protestant communities, that they have no such sisterhoods as those through whose beneficent labors the Roman church is so much endeared even to the humblest of her children;—no societies of "the brides of God," who, for the love of Mary, renounce the world, and consecrate their lives to the divine ministry of charity. But great as is the debt due to orders like these, a ten-fold greater debt is due to the thousand soldier's aid societies that sprung up all over the North during the late War, to supply food for the hungry, clothing for the naked, instruction and amusement in health, tender care in sickness, litanies for the dying, requiems for the dead. And of all these societies this Lowell association was the precursor and pioneer.

In August, the Twenty-Sixth Regiment was organized and went into camp at Cambridge, whence, three weeks later, it was removed to Camp Chase, at Lowell. Here it remained till late in November, when it formed part of the expedition to Ship Island, in the Department of the Gulf. In the following December, the Thirtieth Regiment was organized at Camp Chase, under General Butler, who accompanied it to Ship Island. Three companies of the Twenty-Sixth, A, D, and H, and three of the Thirtieth, B, C and F, were composed of Lowell men. Nor were Lowell men confined to these companies alone, but were found, sometimes in considerable numbers, in many other organizations.

On September 5th, Gen. Butler returned to Lowell after the affair at Hatteras Inlet, and the people gave him a reception which contrasted strongly with that of the preceding summer. It was like the passage from the scaffold to the throne. Between these two receptions, the General had revised his political opinions, passing with characteristic agility from the extreme Southern to the extreme Northern side. The occupation of Hatteras Inlet was an event wholly insignificant in itself. But it served to relieve the gloom which filled the general mind after the defeats of Big Bethel and Bull Run. He was received at the Northern Depot by a committee of the citizens and escorted by the four companies of the Sixth Regiment, and an independent company—the Wamesit Rifles—together with a civic escort, to the Merrimack House, where he received an address of welcome from Mayor Sargeant, to which he replied at some length. The procession was then re-formed, and escorted him to his home by the bowlder-bottomed Merrimack.

Early in 1862, the Sixth and Seventh Batteries were organized. Both were composed chiefly of Lowell men.

On April 3rd, 1862, Surgeon Ebenezer K. Sanborn, of the Thirty-First Infantry, died of typhomania at Ship Island. Dr. Sanborn was born in Hill, New Hampshire, January 24th, 1828. His professional education was acquired with his uncle, Dr. Gilman Kimball, at Lowell, and with Dr. C. H. Stedman at Boston. He was a most successful surgeon, and an indefatigable student of his profession, in which he stood among the most eminent of his age. He achieved great success as a lecturer, and filled professorial chairs at Woodstock, Castleton, and Pittsfield. He left a widow, daughter of John Avery, and three children.*

On July 1st, 1862, President Lincoln issued a new call for 300,000 volunteers. Among the regiments organized in response to this call, was the Thirty-Third Infantry, of which companies A, F and G, with a portion of companies C and H, were from Lowell.

The President having on August 4th, 1862, issued a call for troops for nine months' service, the Sixth Regiment was among the first to respond. On September 9th, it left Lowell for Boston, and proceeded to Suffolk, Virginia. It remained in the vicinity of Suffolk during its entire period of service, performing necessary and useful duty, but taking part in no great battle—its only encounters with the enemy being some insignificant engagements on the Blackwater. Other nine-months' regiments drew on Lowell for recruits, especially the Forty-Eighth, which was stationed at Baton Rouge.

At the battle of Cedar Mountain, August 9th, 1862, fell Brevet Major Edward G. Abbott, Captain of Company A, of the Second Infantry, with seven of his men. He was born in Lowell, September 29th, 1840, and was less than twenty-one

* Memorial of Sanborn by Samuel Burnham; Communications of Mass. Medical Society, 1863.

years of age when, in the feverish rapture of battle, he passed to those "temples not made with hands." Graduating at Harvard in 1860, he entered the law office of Samuel A. Brown, where he remained until the fall of Sumter signalized the conflict, of which he was not to see the end. Passing at once from the profession of law to the profession of arms, his ardor and assiduity were only increased by the change.

In everything he sought thoroughness, and would not be content with half-knowing anything. Had he lived to complete the superstructure of which he had laid the foundations, he was sure to have attained the summits of his profession. To this he aspired with the ardent longing of a strong, whole-souled, generous nature. Nor did he dream of failure.

"In the bright Lexicon of youth,
There's no such word as fail."

He had a sense of honor worthy of the best days of chivalry. Perfect truthfulness characterized all his word and acts. "He dared to do right; he dared to be true;" he would not be such a coward as to lie. At the age of twenty, he had the intellectual maturity of a man of thirty. His native vigor of intellect was great, and his judgment remarkably sound. He was a born commander—cool, intrepid, self-reliant, indomitable—and took to the leadership of affairs as naturally as an eagle to the air.

The battle was drawing to a close when he fell; and during the fight, says General Andrews, (who was his colonel,) his conduct "was as brave and noble as any friend of his could desire." Just as the Union army began their retreat, Abbott was shot—the ball passing directly through the neck. One of his men, Lucius Page,* seeing him fall, ran to him, and asked, "Are you wounded?" Abbott with difficulty replied, "Yes." Page inquired, "Can I do anything for you?" But the dying captain was unable to reply. The blood gushed from his neck, and in a few moments, he was dead. Page brought away his sword, and said he could have lain down and died beside him.

His company, which was his pride, was always distinguished for its neat, soldierly appearance, and was, says General Andrews, "in every respect, fully equal to any that I have seen in the volunteer service." General Gordon says, "I saw him when he fell. I was proud that I had done something to educate him to the profession he so much, so peculiarly adorned."

The body of the lamented captain was buried with public honors on Sunday, August 17th. The same hand that suffused his infant face with the waters of baptism, also committed his body to the ground—"earth to earth, ashes to ashes, dust to dust." †

---

* Page was wounded and taken prisoner at Chancellorsville, and afterward died of his wounds.

† See Lowell *Courier*, August 21st and 26th, and September 11th, 1862. Also, Harvard Memorial Biographies, vol. ii, pp. 77–90.

Twenty days after Abbott's death, fell First Lieutenant James R. Darracott, of Company E, of the Sixteenth Regiment, who was instantly killed at the second battle of Bull Run. He was thirty-four years of age, and left a widow, daughter of Alexander Wright, and one child.

On October 5th, 1862, Captain Timothy A. Crowley, of Company A, Thirtieth Infantry, died at New Orleans, of intermittent fever. He was born in Lowell, February 14th, 1831, and after quitting school was long employed as a machinist in the Lowell Machine Shop. For several years, he was connected with the city police, and in 1858 was Deputy Marshal. He subsequently studied law, and was admitted to the bar in 1860. He was one of those over whom General Butler threw the magical spell of his peculiar genius; and no Scottish clansman of the medieval age ever followed his leader with more ardor and devotedness than Crowley.

> "No oath but by his chieftain's hat,
> No law but Roderick Dhu's command."

He was a corporal in the Watson Light Guard in their three months' campaign, and bore the colors of the Sixth Regiment during the Baltimore riot of 1861, with a steady courage that attracted the admiration of all. He then gathered the company of which he was captain at his death. He displayed fine abilities as an officer, and won the entire respect of all with whom he came in contact in the Department of the Gulf. He left a widow and two children. His remains were brought to Lowell, and buried with public honors, October 26th, 1862.

On December 13th, 1862, the Army of the Potomac under General Burnside advanced on the defences of Fredericksburg, but only to be driven back, after a sublime exhibition of its courage and a lavish outpouring of its blood, to its original lines. Among the killed in this engagement was Captain Thomas Claffey of Lowell. He was born in Cork, Ireland, and came to Lowell when a boy. Having secured such elementary education as a Lowell Grammer School affords, he became first an operative in the mills, afterward clerk to a shopkeeper, and finally a shopkeeper himself. He devoted all the time he could spare to the improvement of his mind. He made extensive forays into history, ancient and modern, sacred and secular. Entering the Twentieth Regiment as a private, he was soon promoted to a Lieutenancy for gallant conduct at Antietam.

At Fredericksburg, the command of his company devolved on him, and here his gallantry won him a commission as Brevet Captain. This honor, however, was conferred too late. Early in the engagement, he for whom it was intended, fell, shot through the mouth and neck; and so, amid the cloud and thunder of battle, the impetuous spirit of Captain Claffey took the everlasting flight. His body was not recovered. He was twenty-eight years old, and left a widow and two children.

On January 12th, 1863, General Butler, returning from New Orleans, was received by the people in Huntington Hall, where, in an elaborate speech, he defended his administration in the Department of the Gulf. He was accompanied by the gallant General Strong, who was mortally wounded, a few months later, in the last desperate storming of Fort Wagner.

On February 17th, 1863, the Fifteenth Battery, composed chiefly of Lowell men, was mustered for three years' service. Timothy Pearson was its Captain; but he being chiefly engaged in recruiting, the actual command of the Battery devolved largely on Lieutenant Albert Rowse.

On February 25th, 26th and 27th, 1863, the ladies of Lowell held their famous Soldiers' Fair, to replenish the funds of the Sanitary Commission. About five thousand dollars were realized by this fair, which was the second of the kind during the War—St. Louis, the Queen City of the West, having held the first. Five thousand dollars raised by this fair, —three thousand dollars collected through the Soldiers' Aid Association,—four thousand dollars contributed to the Boston Sailors' Fair of 1864,—numerous smaller sums collected and distributed through other channels, and innumerable contributions of clothing, shoes, etc.,—all combine to attest how faithfully and how efficiently the ladies of Lowell served their country in her most perilous hour.

It happened, by a strange contrast, that just as one portion of our people were exerting themselves so successfully for the benefit of our soldiers, others, (happily a much smaller number) were perfecting elaborate and ingenious schemes for stealing the large bounties which soldiers then received from City, State and Nation. This infamous business was carried on, not only by civilian-scoundrels, but also by several Lowell army officers; and if some of them were afterward punished for their peculations, their punishments were not half what they deserved. *Death,* by sentence of a drum-head court-martial, was the just penalty which Napoleon inflicted on officers who swindled *his* soldiers. But our soldiers were left to such redress as they could obtain from courts of law. The courts were right,* but they were altogether too slow. Private William Riley, for example, recovered judgment against Timothy Pearson for his local bounty of one hundred and fifty dollars; but before execution could issue, Pearson had

—— "folded his tent like the Arabs,
And silently stolen away."

On April 14th, 1863, the Andover Conference of Congregational Ministers met in Lowell. Upon adjourning, they called on General Butler in a body, thanked him for his recognition of the Higher Power, and pledged him their votes and their prayers! Imagine the Apostles calling on any Roman politician to thank him for recognizing his own Maker! Had we a painter among us, his easel could hardly be better employed than in portraying these reverend fathers, playing the game of mutual admiration with one in whose regards all the gods "from Jove to Jesus" stand alike indifferent,—but who has the good sense to see that rabbi, mufti, priest and parson

* Sullivan v. Fitzgerald, 12 Allen, 482.

are all useful as a higher order of constabulary, or moral police,—and who would copy the Broad Churchmanship of those philosophic Romans who "bowed with equal reverence to the Lybian, the Olympian or the Capitoline Jupiter."

Among the officers killed in General Hookers' advance on Chancellorsville, April 30th, 1863, was Captain George Bush, of Company B, Thirteenth Infantry. He was born in Middlesex Village, July 4th, 1834, and was the son of Francis Bush, of the well known firm of Bent & Bush, hatters. He entered the regiment as Second Lieutenant. He was engaged in nine battles, and in six of them he commanded his company. Two of his brothers were also in the army—Major Joseph Bush, and Lieutenant Francis Bush. He had a third brother, Edward Bush, who was accidentally drowned in Boston, in 1867.

On the following day, in the same battle, Captain Salem S. Marsh, acting Colonel of the Twenty-Second United States Infantry, and one of the finest officers in the regular army, was shot through the brain. He was born in Southbridge in 1836, and was the son of Sumner Marsh, long a citizen of Lowell. He graduated at West Point in 1858. When the War began he was stationed on the frontier, and with him were four other officers, his superiors in rank, natives of the South, who at once sent in their resignations, and without waiting for a reply, abandoned their posts, and went home. Undismayed by the difficulties of his position, the noble Marsh, then only a Second Lieutenant, at once assumed command, and, with the aid of the Surgeon and the non-commissioned staff, performed not only his own duties, but also the duties of the four officers who had deserted their flag. He was buried, May 17th, with the honors due to so gallant a career.

> "They that were true to their country and God
> Shall meet at the last reveille."

On June 3rd, 1863, an engagement took place at Clinton, Louisiana, in which Brevet Major Solon A. Perkins, of the Third Cavalry, was mortally wounded. He lived but two hours. He was born at Lancaster, New Hampshire, December 6th, 1836, and was the son of Apollos Perkins, who removed to Lowell with his family, in 1840. Having fitted for college in the High School, young Perkins entered the house of J. W. Paige & Co., in Boston, where he remained five years. From 1853 to 1856, he was attached to a mercantile house in Beunos Ayres, but ill health compelled his return home. In 1857, he became connected with a large mercantile firm in Valparaiso, and remained there two years; but in 1859, on account of civil war, all foreigners were ordered from Chili; and Perkins returned to Lowell. The knowledge of French and Spanish acquired in South America, was highly useful to him afterward in the Department of the Gulf, where, in 1862, he began his career under General Butler. Though only Second Lieutenant, the death of his superior, Captain Durivage, left him early in command, and he had abundant opportunities to develope his powers in numerous encounters with guerrillas.

"He had six horses killed under him in as many engagements, and when sent out on reconnoisances, was repeatedly cut off from his return route by a superior force, and obliged to bring off his command by strategem. On one occasion, he rode a hundred miles in twenty-four hours, and without leaving his saddle; and for the last six weeks of his life, he did not sleep in a tent at all, but upon the ground under an open sky, in the wind and rain."*

With fifty-five men, he once boldly engaged four hundred and fifty of the enemy, and routed them so badly that the leader of the Confederate force was put under arrest by his superior officer for his failure. By exploits like these he won a brilliant reputation, and was pointed out in New Orleans as the boldest and most successful cavalry officer in our army. In that beautiful picture-gallery in which, perhaps, Lowell will one day gather the portraits of her heroes, a high place will unquestionably be assigned to our most daring and dashing cavalry captain—*le beau sabre*—Solon A. Perkins.

"We will not deem his life was brief,
For noble death is length of days;
The sun that ripens Autumn's leaf
Has poured a summer's wealth of rays."

* Street's Funeral Sermon of Perkins, p. 14.

At the battle of Gettysburg, July 3rd, 1863, fell Captains John Murkland and David W. Roche. Captain Murkland was born in Paisley, Scotland, August 23rd, 1835, and in early boyhood came to Lowell. When the war began, he enlisted in Company B, of the Fifteenth Infantry. He first distinguished himself at the battle of Antietam, being then First Sergeant. For his gallantry there he was at once commissioned Captain. While in command of his company at Gettysburg, he was mortally wounded. He was buried July 14th, with military honors. He was married, but left no children. The other Lowell captain killed at Gettysburg, was David W. Roche, who went out as Second Lieutenant of the Hill Cadets, from which company he was subsequently transferred to Company A of the same regiment, and promoted to a captaincy. While at home on leave in the preceding March, he was married. The military career of Captain Roche was an honorable one, but it afforded him no opportunity for the acquisition of a specially brilliant fame. His remains were interred with public honors, August 3rd, 1863. He was thirty-three years of age, and a native of Cork, Ireland.

On October 6th, 1863, in a skirmish with a party of Quantrell's guerrillas, near Baxter's Springs, Kansas, Judge-Advócate Asa Walton Farr, of the staff of General Blunt, and seventy-seven others, were taken prisoners and shot. He was born in 1821, at Sharon, Vermont, (the native town of Joseph Smith, the Mormon prophet.) For seven years, he was a practicing lawyer in Lowell, and was District Attorney of Middlesex County in 1851 and 1852. For the last ten years of his life, he practiced in Wisconsin. He had also been a member of the Wisconsin Legislature. He left a widow and two children.

On July 15th, 1863, four hundred and nine names of Lowell men were drawn from the wheel at Concord, under the Conscription act, and the call based thereon;—but of these less than thirty were actually forced into the service. A lavish outpouring of money for National, State, City and private bounties saved Lowell from any extensive "draft" of her conscriptible men.

At the close of 1863 and early in 1864, the Fifty-Ninth Infantry and the Second Heavy Artillery were recruited. Both contained many Lowell men.

On April 2nd, 1864, Lieutenant Maurice Roche, brother of Captain D. W. Roche, died at Charlestown, of disease contracted in an unattached company of Heavy Artillery.

On April 14th, 1864, Lieutenant Charles B. Wilder, of the Steam Frigate Minnesota, was killed near Smithfield in Virginia. He was shot in the head by a party of the enemy's riflemen, who attacked a boat expedition, sent into Smithfield Creek, under command of Lieutenant Wilder, to dredge for torpedoes. He was thirty-four years of age, and left a wife and one child. He was buried in Lowell with naval honors, April 24th. His personal and professional qualifications were such, (said Admiral Lee,) as "to command the respect and esteem of all who were associated with him in the service."

Exactly three weeks after the funeral of Lieutenant Wilder, occurred the more imposing obsequies of General Henry Livermore Abbott. He was born in Lowell, January 21st, 1842. He and his brother, Major Abbott, fitted for college together in the Lowell High School, graduated together at Harvard in 1860, and together entered on the study of the law. When the war broke out, he joined the Fourth Battalion of Infantry as a private. On July 20th, 1861, he was commissioned Second Lieutenant in the Twentieth Infantry, and subsequently won successive promotions to First Lieutenant, Captain, Major and Brevet Brigadier-General. He took part in all the great battles of the Army of the Potomac preceding his death, and displayed such splendid qualities that every battle added to his renown.

It was once observed by Napoleon, that no army could bear the strain of the loss of more than one-third of its numbers. But, in the battle of Fredericksburg, December 11th, 1862, the company commanded by Abbott, lost thirty-five men out of sixty. The same company having been re-filled, afterward went into the battle of Gettysburg, Abbott still being Captain, and though full two-thirds of its members were killed or wounded, still preserved its *morale.*

A life so terribly exposed can never last long. While in command of his regiment, at the battle of the Wilderness, May 6th, 1864, and gallantly leading his faithful veterans to the charge, he was stricken down by a bullet and carried to the rear mortally wounded. "His devotion to his men was shown in his last suffering moments, by a direction that all the money he left should be used for the relief of widows and orphans of soldiers of his regiment." Truly, "the bravest are the tenderest." "Had he lived," said General Hancock, "he would have been one of our most distinguished commanders."

> "His growth in the last four years of his life was almost beyond belief. His career, short as it was, was long enough to show that his early death deprived his country of one of its most faithful and most precious champions, his State of one of its most worthy sons, his companions in arms of an associate beyond praise. No name holds such a place as his in the hearts of the surviving officers and soldiers of the regiment." *

In the summer of 1862, a wound received in the Seven Days' Battles brought him home "on sick leave." Before returning he made his last visit to Lowell—a visit of which bevies of Lowell *belles,* including some of the purest and fairest of earth or skies, still cherish tender recollections. As the youthful hero trod his native river-bank for the last time, and heard the plaintive murmurs of the Merrimack, which he was never to hear again,—perhaps the words of the poet were re-called to his mind, foreshadowing so sadly his own glorious but untimely end:

> "A thousand suns will stream on thee,
> A thousand moons will quiver,
> But not by thee my step shall be,
> Forever and forever."

On October 30th, 1863, Lieutenant George F. Critchett died at Lowell, of disease contracted in the Seventh Light Battery.

---

*Palfrey's Memoir of Abbott, Harvard Memorial Biographies, vol. ii, pp. 91—104.

He went out as a private, won promotion by merit, and had been offered the command of his Battery; but failing health brought him home to die, in his twenty-fifth year.

On May 31st, 1864, occurred the battle of Cold Harbor; (though a field where the number killed on the Union side was twenty times greater than the number killed of the enemy, might rather be called a *massacre* than a battle.) There two Lowell captains fell—Dudley C. Mumford, of Company G, Nineteenth Infantry, and John Rowe, of Company E, of the Sixteenth. The former was killed instantly; the latter was mortally wounded and taken prisoner, and died June 24th, 1864, in Libby Prison. Both entered their regiments as privates, and won their shoulder-straps by their valor alone.

On June 7th, 1864, about thirty men of the Second Infantry, who enlisted originally under the lamented Captain Abbott, returned to Lowell, having honorably completed their three years' service. Many of their comrades re-enlisted, and remained in the field until July, 1865. Returning in an unorganised manner, these war-worn veterans received no public reception whatever. This was much to be regretted; for no men "covered themselves with glory," more than these men of the gallant Second. The battles in which they took part were Jackson, Front Royal, Winchester, Cedar Mountain, Antietam, Fredericksburg, Chancellorsville, Gettysburg, Reseca, Kenesaw Mountain, Peach Tree Creek, Atlanta, Raleigh, Averysborough, etc. The Second and the Thirty-Third were the only regiments containing any considerable number of Lowell men, that accompanied the gallant Sherman in his grand march from Atlanta to the sea.

On July 21st, 1864, the Hill Cadets and the Butler Rifles, under Major Donovan and Captain O'Hare, were welcomed home on returning from their three year's service. In those tragic years, the Sixteenth took part in the battles of Fair Oaks, Glendale, Malvern Hill, Kettle Run, Chantilly, Fredericksburg, Chancellorsville, Gettysburg, Locust Grove, Wilderness, Spottsylvania, North Anna River, Cold Harbor and Petersburg—a record which their children and their children's children may look back upon with pride.

In July, 1864,—volunteers for one hundred days' service having been called for by the President,—the Sixth Regiment again responded, and was assigned guard duty at Fort Delaware.

Among the victims of the explosion of the Petersburg mine, July 30th, 1864, was Asa E. Hayward, then a private in the Fifty-First New York Infantry, but previously a First Lieutenant or Captain in the Massachusetts Twenty-First. He was wounded, captured and confined in Saulsbury prison. He succumbed under his sufferings, and died on being exchanged. He was forty years old, and left a widow (*neé* Fanny French) and three children.

On October 1st, 1864, Major Henry T. Lawson, of the Second Heavy Artillery, died at Newbern, North Carolina, of yellow fever. He had previously been Captain of Company I, of the Sixteenth Infantry. His remains were buried at Newton, where his family resided. He was the last commissioned officer that was identified with Lowell, who lost his life while in actual service.

Is the question asked, Why not mention those who were not of commissioned rank? The only answer is, that they are altogether too numerous, and with respect to many of them, no information is attainable. In mental and moral power, as well as in social rank, the privates were often superior to their officers. One Lowell boy, a private in the Forty-Fourth Infantry, son of Judge Hopkinson, had graduated at Harvard, studied law with Judge Gray, and contributed regularly to the *Atlantic Monthly.** Another Lowell private, Foster Wilson, has since served with credit in the City Council, and in the State Legislature. A third, Samuel M. Bell,

*He died of fever at Newbern, Feb. 13, 1863. Harvard Memorial Biographies, vol. 2, pp. 21–29.

has been chosen by his comrades, including officers as well as privates, President of the Army and Navy Union. A fourth, P. H. Welch, was head-salesman in a Broadway wholesale house, having a general under him as his clerk.

So with the Lowell sailors. John F. Devlin declined an appointment as Ensign, but served with credit as chief signal-quarter-master on Admiral Dahlgren's staff. Timothy Sullivan, too, refused the command of a clipper schooner, but became coxswain to Captain Meade, on board the San Jacinto, and, when stranded on No-Name Key, gallantly stood by, fighting desperately with the wreckers, as well as with the storm. But the roll of our "distinguished privates" would far outnumber that of our commissioned braves.

Among the civilians from Lowell who shared the fortunes of our armies in the field, was William Porter Ray, whose encyclopædic learning and affluent genius entitle him to a high place in the gallery of distinguished Lowellians. His natural gifts were altogether remarkable, and were improved by all the agencies that Harvard and Heidelburg employ to develop and discipline the minds of their sons. He was one of the brightest and best of the spoiled children of genius. He entered the ministry of the Protestant Episcopal Church, but became involved in a dispute with his Diocesan, (Bishop Upfold,) who temporarily suspended his functions. He was acting as one of the army correspondents of the New York *Times*, in Virginia, when his life was cut short by an attack of small-pox. His lyceum discourse on Rouseau, his article in the *Atlantic Monthly* on Dealings with the Dead, and several other productions of his pen, attracted great attention.

On October 28th, 1864, the Twenty-Sixth Infantry, received a public welcome home. The battles in which they were engaged were Winchester, Cedar Creek, and Fisher's Hill.

On January 28th, 1865, General Butler, made his famous speech in Huntington Hall, explaining the causes of his defeat at Fort Fisher. On the career of this remarkable man, it would be useless to pronounce judgment at present. All the judgments of history are subject to perpetual appeal;—those touching contemporaneous characters are seldom or never final. Parton's estimate of Butler will not be accepted finally; neither will that of "Brick Pomeroy." The former is surcharged with unreasoning panegyric; the latter with passionate vituperation. General Butler's reputation cannot be demolished; for it stands on a solid foundation—on his occupation of Annapolis and of Baltimore, and on his wholesome discipline at New Orleans. His coquettish dalliances with the Secessionists in 1860,—his first repulse at Big Bethel,—his later fizzle at Bermuda Hundreds,—and his grander *fiasco* at Fort Fisher,—will be viewed with leniency, in consideration of his prompt dash into Baltimore, and of the firm grip with which he held, as by the throat, the New Orleans "roughs." Said Cromwell to Lely, "Paint me as I am; if you leave out the scars and wrinkles, I'll never give you a shilling." General Butler has great faults; but he has many compensatory merits. He is no Cromwell; but he can afford to be painted as he is. Fully equal to many of "Plutarch's men," he is sure to live hereafter on the painters' burning canvass, and on the historian's pictured page. And when the throng of his calumniators are sleeping in unhonored and forgotten graves, his statue, in enduring bronze, will rise in some public square of our city, and be admired by millions that are now unborn.

On April 5th, 1865, the citizens flocked to Huntington Hall to express their joy over the fall of Richmond. Another meeting of patriotic jubilation was held, with more formal preparation, on the 10th.

On April 15th, 1865, the people of the whole country were shocked by the intelligence that, on the preceding night, the Patriot-President, Abraham Lincoln, had been shot by an assassin. On the day following, the grief of the people found appropriate expression in all the churches. On the 19th, a eulogy of Lincoln was delivered in Lowell, by George S. Boutwell, Representative in Congress.*

On June 13th, 1865, the Lowell men of the Thirty-Third Infantry, about ninety in all, returned to Lowell, their term of enlistment having expired. The Thirty-Third bore a gallant part in the battles of Fredericksburg, Chancellorsville, Beverly Ford, Gettysburg, Lookout Valley, Mission Ridge, Buzzard's Roost, Resaca, Cassville, Dallas, Golgotha, Culp's Farm, Kenesaw Mountain, Peach Tree Creek, Atlanta, Averysboro', Bentonville, and Goldsboro.'

On the seventeenth of June, 1865, the Ladd and Whitney Monument was dedicated with appropriate ceremonies. The lines inscribed upon this Monument, from the Samson Agonistes of Milton, were selected by the lamented Governor Andrew, who also delivered the dedicatory oration. His closing sentences expressed, in eloquent terms, the glowing hope that this shaft might stand for a thousand generations:

> "Henceforth shall the inhabitants of Lowell guard for Massachusetts, for patriotism, and for liberty, this sacred trust, as they of Acton, of Lexington, of Concord, protect the votive stones which commemorate the men of April, '75.
>
> "Let it stand, as long as the Merrimack runs from the mountains to the sea; while this busy stream of human life sweeps on by the banks of the river, bearing to eternity its freight of destiny and hope. It shall speak to your children not of Death, but of Immortality. It shall stand here a mute, expressive witness of the beauty and the dignity of youth and manly prime consecrated in unselfish obedience to Duty. It shall testify that gratitude will remember, and praise will wait on, the humblest who, by the intrinsic greatness of their souls, or the worth of their offerings, have risen to the sublime peerage of Virtue."

The procession previous to the dedication, though indifferently managed, was the most magnificent ever seen in Lowell. It presented an imposing array of National and State officials; the Staffs. of the Governors of Massachusetts and Maryland; officers and men who had served in the Army and Navy; members of the Lowell, Boston, Worcester and Lawrence City Governments; Selectmen of towns; Encampments of the

* Speeches relating to the Rebellion, pp. 356–371.

Knights Templar; Lodges of the Free Masons, the Odd Fellows, and the American Protestant Association; bodies of Infantry and Cavalry; Bands of Music, Firemen, Fenians, and miscellaneous organizations.

At the close of the War, the Mayor prepared the following abstract of the number of men furnished from Lowell under the several calls of the President, together with the amounts paid for City Bounties, and the sums expended by the city in recruiting:

1861, April 15th, call for 75,000 men for three months. Lowell furnished 223 men, at a cost of $596.08; average cost, $2.67 3-10.

1861, May 3rd, call for 50,000 men; July 1st, call for 600,000 men. Our quota under these calls was 2098 men for three years. The number recruited was 2390, at a cost of $65,681.78; average cost, $27.48.

1862, August 4th, call for 300,000 men, for nine months. Our quota was 235. We enlisted and furnished 557 men, at a cost of $22,162.25; average, $35.78 8-10.

1863, October 17th, call for 300,000 men. February 1, 1864, call for 500,000 men. Our quota was 288 men. We furnished 211 men, at a cost of $902.30; average cost, $4.27 6-10. The report of the Adjutant General, January 1, 1864, stated that we had at that time a surplus of 179 men.

1864, July 18th, call for 500,000 men; our quota, 627. We furnished (including 196 Navy recruits), 998 men, at a cost of $147,549.11; average cost, $147.94 1-2.

1864, December 19th, call for 300,000 men. No quota was ever assigned to Lowell under this call. I was informed by the Provost Marshal that our quota January 1st, 1865, was eight men short of all requirements. We continued our enlistments until the surrender of Richmond. The number enlisted subsequent to the call in December was 132 men at a cost of $17,039.55; average cost, $129.08.

Of the volunteers for 100 days, Lowell furnished 252 men, at a cost of $143.80—making the whole number standing to our credit 4763 men, and the whole cost of recruiting and bounties, $254,074.87. In addition to this we have expended for uniforms, equipments, interest on State aid paid, and other incidental expenses of the war, exclusive of the Ladd and Whitney Monument,* the sum of $39,141,02—making a grand total of $293,215.89. It should be stated that there were 450 men from our city who enlisted in the naval service, but in the apportionment which was made, only 196 were allowed to our credit. Had we received full credit for these men, our whole number furnished would have been 5022.†

The amounts of State Aid disbursed since the beginning of the War have been as follows:—1861, $21,912.30; 1862,

---

* This cost $4,500, of which the State paid $2,000.

† Peabody's Second Inaugural, pp. 6–7.

$87,439.78; 1863. $102,011.78; 1864, $90,135.40; 1865, $54,272.00; 1866, $35,760.00; 1867, $34,500.10.

At the close of July, 1865, the Lowell men of the Fifty-Ninth, a nine-months' regiment of infantry, returned, having been present in the battles of the Wilderness, Spottsylvania, North Anna River, Cold Harbor, Petersburg, Weldon Railroad, Poplar Spring, Fort Sedgwick, and Fort Mahone.

One regiment only, containing many Lowell men, continued in service later than the Fifty-Ninth. This was the Thirtieth, which was not mustered out until the following year. The battles in which the Thirtieth took part, were those of Vicksburg, Baton Rouge, Plain's Store, Port Hudson, Donaldsonville, Winchester, Cedar Creek and Fisher's Hill.

The Seventh and Fifteenth Batteries also remained in service some months longer. The Seventh was present in the engagements at Deserted House, South Quay, Somerton, Providence Church Road, Holland's House, Mansura, and Mobile. The Fifteenth was present only at the seige of Mobile.

With the mustering out of these men Lowell's part in the War of the Rebellion may be said to have closed. The last battle had been fought, the last army of the South disbanded. With a few exceptions, the soldiers and sailors of Lowell had returned to their homes, or to civil life elsewhere, or had lain down to the long sleep—the slumber that knows no waking.

Well, then, might Governor Bullock tender to the people of Lowell his generous tribute of eloquent congratulation :

"While the industry and wealth of other communities have been stimulated by the war, yours, I apprehend, have been checked and depressed. This, however, did not chill the ardor of your patriotism, which rose above every thought of private interest, and broke forth in great acts of generous and chivalrous devotion. Since the men of Chelmsford fought at Concord, Lexington and Bunker Hill, no record has borne prouder honors than those which cluster around the brow of the living, and over the graves of the dead soldiers of the Queen City of the Merrimack. In her honored son, Major-General Butler, she gave to the field one of the earliest and ablest general officers of the war, whose pen and sword have been alike devoted to the success of popular ideas throughout the contest, and who still serves his country with his efforts to crown victory with universal liberty. Lowell furnished at the first tap of the drum four companies, to the immortal Sixth, to protect the capital in the hour of gloom and almost of capture; she has filled every one of her quotas without a draft; she has left a surplus account of gallant men at the office of the Adjutant General from the beginning to the end; and she will ever appear, before the whole world, with the monumental renown of having contributed the first blood of the fifth epic of martyrs. Yes, the monument in yonder square shall transmit to distant generations your imperishable distinction as the patriot and martyr city! Garlands of mingled laurel and cypress, that shall neither fade nor decay, will surround the crest of your municipality so long as the noble river, in whose waters the infancy of this city was bathed, shall flow by and lave the seats of her industry and power! Hail therefore to-day, and welcome Lowell! that having no ancient annals or lengthened traditions, has passed into the classic sisterhood of chivalry, without a superior and with scarcely a rival!"

CHAPTER XIII.

GENERAL HISTORY OF LOWELL. 1860—1868.

Anna A. Dower—Bryant Moore—Prince Jerome—Nathan Appleton—Josiah G. Abbott—John Nesmith—Changes in Population—John P. Robinson—Shakespearean Festival—Elisha Huntington—Samuel A. Brown—Statue of Victory—Third Mechanics' Exhibition—General Sheridan—Manufacturers' Convention.

January 4th, 1860, was observed as a National Fast Day, by appointment of President Buchanan.

On January 10th, the Pemberton Mill at Lawrence fell, instantly killing or fatally injuring eighty-seven operatives, and wounding from fifty to seventy-five others. All the Lowell surgeons hastened at once to the assistance of the suffering victims.

On January 12th, Joseph Butterfield, for nearly fifty years a Deputy Sheriff, passed away, in his seventy-sixth year. He was born in Tyngsboro', and removed to Lowell about 1838. A man of the highest integrity and of great originality.

On March 30th, Mrs. Rhoda M. Wilkins died suddenly by poison. Suspicions were at once fastened on Anna A. Dower, who had been her attendant. She was arrested on an indictment for murder, was defended by Alpheus R. Brown and Edwin A. Alger. and after three trials was discharged.

On June 19th, Bryant Moore shot his third wife, Elizabeth A. Moore, through the head, at his house, No. 61 East Merrimack street. In the following December, Moore was brought to trial at East Cambridge, and was convicted of murder in the second degree. He was defended by J. G. Abbott, R. B. Caverly, and Charles Cowley who subsequently obtained a pardon for him from Governor Andrew.

On January 30th, 1861, a branch of the Carpenters' and Joiners' Union was established in Lowell. The Machinists and Blacksmiths were organized about two years earlier. Branches of the Painters', the Moulders', and the Coach Makers' Unions have since been formed, but the two former collapsed. These societies are all founded on the same basis, pursue the same objects, and encounter the same opposition, as the Trades Unions of Great Britain.

On July 14th, 1861, died Nathan Appleton—the last of the little band of enterprising men that founded Lowell. Though he went to Boston a poor boy, and rose to the highest affluence by his enterprize in manufactures and commerce, his life was by no means devoted to mere money-making. Elected repeatedly to the National and State Legislatures, he won eminent distinction as a statesman. His speeches on the Tariff were magazines of facts and arguments. He was an active member of several learned societies, and wrote with great vigor and ability on the Banking System, the Currency, Geology, Labor, Financial Panics, Slavery, the Union, Original Sin, the Trinity, etc. In a word, he stood among the foremost men of his times; and his death created a vacancy in manufacturing and commercial circles, which no living man could fill.*

* Robert C. Winthrop's Memoir of Appleton.

Only one member of his family ever resided in Lowell—Ebenezer Appleton, Treasurer of the corporation which bears his family name, who died here in 1834, at the age of forty-eight,—leaving a reputation for ability and integrity not inferior to that of Nathan.

On September 24th, Prince Jerome Napoleon, with his consort, the Princess Clotilde, daughter of Victor Emanuel, King of Italy, visited Lowell, having, doubtless, been recommended to do so by his friend, Michel Chevalier. More than a quarter of a century had elapsed since Chevalier's visit; the New England girls on whom he then gazed so admiringly, had passed away; and their places were now filled by a motley crowd of Americans, English, Scotch, Irish, Dutch and French Canadians, who were hardly likely to arouse that exquisite poetic sentiment which Chevalier felt for the factory-girls of 1834.

Two days after the Prince's visit, another National Fast Day was observed, by appointment of President Lincoln. National troubles were now thickening.

In 1861, the Mechanics' Savings Bank was incorporated—the last that has been started in Lowell.

In 1861, Lowell lost one of her ablest lawyers, and one of her most public-spirited citizens, by the removal of Josiah G. Abbott to Boston. He was born in Chelmsford, November 1st, 1815, and graduated at Harvard in 1832. After teaching for some months the Fitchburg Academy, he began the study of law in the office of Nathaniel Wright. In November, 1836, a few days after the completion of his twenty-first year, he was elected a member of the State Legislature, and in the following January, was admitted to the Bar. He formed a copartnership with Amos Spaulding, and the net earnings of the firm during the first year were five thousand dollars. He sat in the State Senate in 1842 and 1843, and in the Constitutional Convention of 1853. In 1855 he was appointed one of the Justices of the Superior Court for Suffolk County. Three years afterward, he resigned the Bench, and resumed his place in the front rank of the Bar. During the last fifteen years of his practice here, when he was associated with Samuel A. Brown, he probably tried more civil cases than any other lawyer in New England. His criminal practice was also large, though less extensive than that of B. F. Butler, who was so often his antagonist in the forum. Three sons of Judge Abbott won honorable distinction during the Rebellion, and two of them head the list of the noble army of Lowell's patriot-martyrs.

At the State election in 1861, John Nesmith was elected Lieutenant Governor by the Republicans—an appropriate though tardy acknowledgment of many years adherence, and of many important services, to the principles on which the Republican party came into power. Mr. Nesmith was born in Londonderry, New Hampshire, August 3rd, 1793, and removed to Lowell in January, 1832. He has been actively and conspicuously identified with the manufacturing interests of Lowell for more than a third of a century, and has contributed his full share to the development of the mechanic arts. A machine for the manufacture of wire fence, and another for the manufacture of shawl-fringe, have attested his inventive skill. The project for increasing the power of the Merrimack by creating great reservoirs near its sources, was originated by him. The utilization of the water-falls below Lowell,—in a word, the city of Lawrence,—was also first projected by him. Lawrence, indeed, existed in the brain of Mr. Nesmith more than ten years before she existed as a fact. Preparations for building mills where Lawrence now stands, were begun by him, in conjunction with Josiah G. Abbott and Daniel Saunders, as early as 1835, and were only postponed by the financial revulsion which then ensued. These preparations were finally carried out in a manner highly honorable to the projectors. Instead of buying up the lands of the farmers by stealth, (as was done at the origin of Lowell,) they frankly explained to the land owners that they designed to build a city, and proposed to pay them for their lands twenty-five per cent. more than they were actually worth. In 1863, Mr. Nesmith, resigned the Lieutenant-Governorship to accept the office of Collector of Internal Revenue for the Lowell District. In 1866, he published "Thoughts on the Currency, by an old Merchant," a pamphlet full of practical suggestions.

On October 14th, 1862, the steam boiler in the State Alms House at Tewksbury exploded, killing ten and wounding fifteen of the inmates.

On November 6th, died Ithamar W. Beard, in his forty-ninth year. He was a native of Littleton in this county, had practiced law in Lowell from 1842 to 1856, and had been Assistant Treasurer at Boston during the Administration of Franklin Pierce. In politics, he was always a Democrat.

On April 2nd, 1863, died Stephen Mansur, in his sixty-fourth year. He had been identified with Lowell for more than forty years, and had been a prominent trader from 1830 till the time of his death. He had filled various local offices, municipal and ecclesiastical, and what is much more, had always maintained a high character for honor and integrity.

On July 19th, died Rev. David O. Allen, D. D., at the age of sixty-three. From 1827 to 1853, he labored as a missionary in India. Compelled by failing health to return to the United States, he took up his abode in Lowell, and here wrote his "India, Ancient and Modern," a work containing more information on that country, than any single work yet published.

In 1863, the Lowell Horse Railroad Company was incorporated with $100,000 capital. Their road was opened March 1st, 1864. Four miles of road have been completed, costing, with equipments, $68,000.

The year 1863, was marked by an excess of deaths over births in Lowell. Dr. Nathan Allen, then City Physician, called public attention to the fact that, whereas, prior to 1863, the number of births had exceeded the number of deaths, in 1863, there were 695 deaths to 654 births—showing a loss of forty-one.

"Of the 654 births, he says, 427 were of foreign origin, leaving only 227 American; of the 695 deaths 322 were buried in the Roman Catholic grounds, with about 40 more foreigners who were Protestants and buried in other places, making 362 deaths of foreign origin. We then have 333 deaths to 227 births—a loss of over 100, in 1863, of the strictly American population. In 1862 of the 757 births, 510 were foreign, and only 242 American; if one-half the 641 deaths were American, (320), there is then a loss of 82 in 1862. The number of deaths in Lowell from 1856 to 1862 was 5,055, and the number of births for the same time 6,618. It is found by actual count that for several years, on an average, the deaths in Lowell are about equally divided between the foreign and the American, and the reports show that only one-third of the births belong to the latter class. By applying this rule, there is a loss from 1856 to 1862 of 308 persons by excess of deaths over births among the strictly American portion of our population. And there are good reasons to believe that this depopulating process will increase more rapidly hereafter than it has in past years."

While some have thus obstinately refused to propagate their species, others have exhibited a marvellous fecundity. Thomas Ducey has won distinction as the father of thirty-seven children, being twelve more than have been born to any other Lowell man. Elsewhere such services would be appreciated, Ducey would be sent to Congress or the General Court, or made Mayor. Here, he is without honor. He has not even been made a Justice of the Peace.

On January 8th, 1864, Dr. John C. Dalton, who had been for more than thirty years a practicing physician in Lowell. died in Boston in his sixty-ninth year. He was a gentleman of high culture and possessed many elegant accomplishments.*

On the twenty-third of April, 1864, through the instrumentality of Horatio G. F. Corliss, John F. McEvoy, William F. Salmon, John A. Goodwin and other admirers of Shakespeare, the ter-centennial anniversary of the birth of that immortal bard was celebrated in Lowell with observances that were admirably appropriate. Huntington Hall was splendidly decorated, and crowded, in the afternoon, to its utmost capacity. An opening address by Dr. Huntington, an oration by

* Green's Memoir of Dalton.

Rev. William S. Bartlett of Chelsea, choice readings from the great master by Miss Helen Eastman, and singing by the pupils in the public schools, formed the principal features of the celebration.* A Shakespearean dinner was eaten in the evening, followed by toasts, sentiments, songs, speeches, etc., in great abundance and variety. A Shakespeare Club was also formed, with a view to celebrating this anniversary as often as it returns.

On October 20th, 1864, died John P. Robinson, in his sixty-fifth year. He was born at Dover, in New Hampshire, was educated at Phillips Academy and Harvard University, studied law in the office of Daniel Webster, and commenced practice here in 1827. He soon rose to local eminence, and was counsel in some of the most important cases ever tried in this county. With him was associated Horatio G. F. Corliss, first as a student, and afterward as a partner. Robinson served one year in the State Senate, and five in the House of Representatives, and was one of the Committee on the Revised Statutes of 1836. He ran on the Whig ticket for Congress in 1842, but was defeated. The lovers of "sublime mediocrities," the blockheads who turned their backs on Caleb Cushing, could not be expected to bear true faith to Robinson;—they could be satisfied with nothing but "Deacon Abbott." Him they finally elected, leaving Robinson to smart under that keen sense of wrong which he could not but feel when he contemplated the unequal distribution of offices and opportunities. His opposition to Governor Briggs—one of the last events in his political career—suggested Lowell's song with the happy refrain,—

> "John P.
> Robinson, he
> Says he won't vote for Governor B."

Robinson was an able and accomplished lawyer, an eloquent and powerful orator, and a thorough classical scholar. Among the happiest days in his life, were those which he spent in

* See Lowell Shakespeare Memorial.

visiting Constantinople, Athens, Thebes, the plain of Troy, the field of Marathon, the pass of Thermopylæ, and other places of ancient renown.

Robinson was buried in the Lowell Cemetery. The mellow shades of evening were falling softly on an autumnal Sunday, when the remains of the scholar, the statesman, the orator, were laid away to rest "till the heavens be no more." The service was the burial office of the Episcopal Church, beginning with that lofty and sublime psalm—"the Funeral Hymn of the World"—in which the span-long life of man is contrasted so beautifully with the eternity of God. A feeling of subdued melancholy pervaded all present, such as that which Gray expresses in the immortal elegy which Robinson's friend, Webster, had read to him when dying:

> "The curfew tolls the knell of parting day;
> The lowing herd winds slowly o'er the lea;
> The ploughman homeward plods his weary way,
> And leaves the world to darkness and to me."

In 1864, the First National Bank was incorporated, with $250,000 capital.

On January 7th, 1865, died Isaac O. Barnes, Pension Agent at Boston. He was formerly a practicing lawyer in Lowell, and was noted as the most consummate wag that ever appeared at the Middlesex Bar. His whole life was a succession of jokes, not ending till his hands and feet had become cold with the torpor of death. He was sixty-seven years of age.

On July 25th, 1865, the Lowell Exchange was organized. But it proved a failure.

Two days later, the Erina Temperance Institute was formed, and proved a success. No agency has yet been introduced here, which has contributed so much to disseminate sound views, and to promote correct habits, touching the use of intoxicating beverages, as this Institute. It operates, too, where such an agency is most needed—among the Irish. and those of Irish extraction.

On December 11th, 1865, died Elisha Huntington, who had been identified with Lowell for more than forty years. He was born in Topsfield, April 9th, 1796, was educated at Dartmouth and at Yale, and commenced the practice of medicine here in 1824. As a medical practitioner, he realized a fair share of success; but he did not confine himself to his profession. He was, from the start, an active politician, and repeatedly filled all the little offices of Mayor, Alderman, Common Councilman, School Committeeman, etc. He was a candidate for both branches of the State Legislature, but was defeated; but in 1853, he was Lieutenant Governor. He was distinguished for kindness of heart, genial manners, fine literary tastes, and for natural gifts and mental attainments of a high order. He was sometimes thought too lavish in the expenditure of public funds; but his lavishness was economy itself, compared with the extravagance of some later administrations. If he had any fault at all as a public man, it was a want of continuity or consistency in his party relations. Thus he was run as a candidate, sometimes by the Whigs, sometimes by the Democrats, sometimes by the Republicans, sometimes by the Citizens; and he never allowed either personal or party obligations to stand between him and an office. His political latitudinarianism was largely atoned for by his many personal excellencies; but it contributed not a little to debauch politics, to lower the standards of public virtue, and to introduce that reign of low, vulgar, mean-spirited creatures, under which Lowell has suffered for many years. Aside from this greediness of office, Dr. Huntington was, in all his public relations, a model of a man, broad in his views, liberal in his sentiments, and not unfamiliar with the higher politics.

The revival of the cotton manufacture after the close of the War, attracted to Lowell hundreds of French Canadians. Though speaking another language, these new-comers soon caught the spirit of progress which characterizes other classes, and one of the first fruits of their immigration was a library society, called the *Association Franco-Canadienne de Lowell.*

About the same time, measures were adopted for importing operatives for our factories, from Continental Europe. No considerable number, however, has ever been imported, except from Great Britain. The prospect of having to receive from five to ten thousand Dutchmen, some fine morning, was by no means a pleasant subject for contemplation.

On March 22nd, 1866, the Sheridan Circle of the Fenian Brotherhood was organized. This society still lives, though the Lowell Circle, formed at an earlier day, has collapsed.

On March 23rd, St. Peter's School was established. It is under the direction of the Sisters of Charity, and is connected with St. Peter's Church. An orphan asylum has since been established in connection with this school.

June 1st was observed as a National Fast-Day, on account of the death of President Lincoln.

On June 8th, a delegation from the Boards of Trade of Chicago and other western cities visited Lowell. Young as Lowell is, in comparison with some of the cities from which these delegates came, she is old, if not *effete.*

On August 6th, the Music Hall was opened for theatrical performances, and the drama, after an interlude of ten years, recovered a permanent habitation in Lowell.

On October 10th, the Centennial of American Methodism was observed by a gathering of all the churches of that persuasion in Lowell at St. Paul's, and a generous contribution of funds to various denominational purposes.

On January 27th, 1867, died Samuel Appleton Brown, one of the most successful lawyers, and one of the most original characters that ever flourished at the Middlesex Bar. He was born at Ipswich, November 4th, 1810, and passed his boyhood in the same scenes with Rufus Choate, Judge Lord and N. J. Lord. He studied law with Nathan D. Appleton at Alfred, Maine, and was admitted to the Bar in 1840. Shortly afterward, he formed a copartnership with J. G. Abbott, and shared his extensive and lucrative practice for fifteen years.

Mr. Brown's ideal of a lawyer was a lofty one. Of the profession of the law, he thought, as did Bolingbroke, that it is, "in its nature, the noblest and most beneficial to mankind." He had none of those mean traits, none of the little arts of chicane, which often make the profession, (as the same writer declared), "in its abuse and debasement, the most sordid and most pernicious." His pure and elevated character, his spotless integrity, his scrupulous regard for truth and right, his ample learning, his untiring industry, his uniform courtesy and kindness, won him the highest honor and respect. He was especially beloved by the younger members of the Bar, who resorted to him and revered him as an infallible oracle of the law. His extreme caution and care touching all interests confided to him, combined with other qualities to mark him as one cast intellectually in an entirely original mould.

He served two years in the State Senate, where, if he made no brilliant record for himself, he made the fortunes of half a dozen other Senators who had the tact to utilize for themselves the elements of power which they found in him. But he took little pleasure in politics, having no affinity with such men as he too commonly found in public life. His own profession was his favorite field, and to it he sacrificed ease, comfort, health and even life itself. He ever felt that the duties of life are more than life, and that death is but an event in life.

"There is no Death! what seems so is transition;
This life of mortal breath
Is but the suburb of the life Elysian,
Whose portal we call Death."

On February 4th, 1867, the Young Men's Christian Association was organized, taking the place of a society of the same name, incorporated twelve years previously, which had collapsed.

On February 4th, 1867, was held the first fair for the benefit of the Old Ladies' Home, which was dedicated July 10th

1867. It is under the direction of a Committee representing all the Protestant Churches in Lowell, and is supported by charity, and the proceeds of fairs.

On April 29th, St. John's Hospital was incorporated under the auspices of the Sisters of Charity. The Livermore place in Belvidere, was purchased by them, and the hospital located temporarily in the dwelling-house where once Phillip Gedney, and at a later day Judge Livermore, resided. The cost of the estate was $12,000.

On April 1st, 1867, the Emperor, the Empress and the Prince Imperial, assisted in "the Coronation of Labor," by the formal opening of the Universal Exposition at Paris. On the same day, by a strange contrast, the mule-spinners of Lowell, in concert with those of other cities, struck for a reduction in their hours of toil. As suffering more than any other class of factory operatives by the eleven-hour rule, they felt it to be their mission to initiate the ten-hour system. Unfortunately, they did not understand the law of strikes, under the operation of which no strike can succeed when the places of the strikers can be filled with little delay, and with no very great detriment to the business of the employers. But few will have the hardihood to deny that the demand for the ten-hour rule was a just one,—that the factory operatives of New England ought not to be confined to daily toil longer than those of Old England.*

On Febuary 16th, a branch of the Ancient Order of Hibernians, a mutual benefit society, was established here.

On June 20th, 1867, died Abner W. Buttrick, for more than thirty years a prominent trader in Lowell. By his last will he bequeathed ten thousand dollars to Harvard University, to be used in assisting students for the Christian ministry.

The Anniversary of American Independence was signalized, in 1867, by the dedication of the Statue of Victory—Dr. Ayer's

* The first strike among factory operatives in the United States, occurred October 1st, 1836, when about three thousand Lowell factory girls left their work in the mills.

gift to Lowell. The figure is that of a draped woman, of heroic size, with wings, handing forth in her right hand the laurel wreath of victory, and holding in her left the harvest sheaf of peace. It stands in an appropriate spot, near the Monument which commemorates the first martyrs of the Rebellion.

Appropriate addresses were delivered by Mayor Richardson, Collector Russell, General Cogswell, General Underwood, and Postmaster Goodwin, and also by Dr. Ayer, who said:—

"While making the tour of Europe, I could not help contrasting the abundance of statues, columns, and other productions of art, which are there displayed for the public enjoyment, with the paucity of such objects in the United States; and I devoted some time to find a figure in marble or bronze, which I could present to our city as a commencement of this kind of ornamentation in Lowell. This figure was moulded by Rauch, the great Prussian sculptor, for the King of Bavaria. The originals, (for there is a pair of them,) in antique bronze, stand in front of the Royal Palace at Munich,—one on each side of the way; but I do not think they are either as appropriate or as effective as this is here. The monument in front of the Royal Palace at Berlin, erected to commemorate the triumph of the Prussians over Napoleon, was also executed by Rauch, both in marble and in bronze; and is considered the greatest work of its kind in the world."

In 1867, Benjamin F. Butler, John Nesmith, and Dewitt C. Farrington, their associates and successors, were incorporated as the Pentucket Navigation Company, for the purpose of freighting merchandise on the Merrimack River between its mouth and the line of the State.

On September 10th, 1867, the Middlesex Mechanics' Association opened their third Exhibition, under the Superintendency of Hocum Hosford. The Committtee of Arrangements were, Samuel K. Hutchinson, (Chairman,) Silas Tyler, Junior, (Secretary,) James B. Francis, T. F. Burgess, T. G. Gerrish, F. H. Nourse, N. G. Furnald, George F. Richardson, William D. Blanchard, J. G. Peabody, H. H. Wilder, Abiel Pevey, W. F. Salmon, Z. E. Stone, Jeremiah Clark, William Nichols, Cyrus H. Latham, O. E. Cushing, Charles Kimball and William O. Fiske. The Exhibition closed October 16th, having been visited by more than one hundred and twenty thousand persons. Over fifteen hundred persons, residents of twelve

STATUE OF VICTORY.

States, contributed to this exhibition, which was one of the best ever held in New England.*

On October 8th, Major-General Sheridan visited Lowell, and was honored with an enthusiastic reception in Monument Square. A battalion of veterans of the army and navy formed part of his escort. It consisted of five companies extemporized for the occasion, and contained many who had served under Sheridan in the field.

On December 18th, 1867, a National Convention of American Manufacturers assembled at Cleveland, Ohio, and recommended to Congress the abolition of all taxation on the necessary domestic industries of the country, and the imposition of taxation on the luxuries of life. These recommendations were cordially indorsed by a Convention of the New England Manufacturers, in Worcester, January 22nd, 1868. Until now, the manufacturers of the country had struggled to improve their prospects by crowding the lobbies of Congress and clamoring for protective tariffs. After fifty years of failure, they at last discovered that "that way no glory lies." Forgetting their former narrowness, and rising to higher and broader views, they now asked for such legislation only as would benefit all classes and not merely themselves. The adoption of these enlarged and enlightened views by these great representative bodies, marks an important epoch in the history of American Manufactures.

More than a third of a century has now elapsed since Chevalier wrote:—

"Lowell, with its steeple-crowned factories, resembles a Spanish town with its convents; but with this difference, that in Lowell you meet no rags nor Madonnas, and that the nuns of Lowell, instead of working sacred hearts, spin and weave cottons. Lowell is not amusing, but it is neat, decent, peaceable, and sage. Will it always be so? Will it be so long? It would be rash to affirm it; hitherto, the life of manufacturing operatives has proved little favorable to the preservation of severe morals. So it has been in France, as well as in England, Germany and Switzerland."

---

* A full report of it has been published.

It is probable that manufacturing pursuits are unfavorable to the preservation of severe morals; but, here, the process of deterioration has been kept in check, heretofore, by the ever changing character of our operatives. Now that our operative population has become less migratory, the dark forebodings of the amiable Frenchman may be realized. But we trust not. In view of the possibility of so direful a change, we would exclaim, in the emphatic words of good old Abraham Cowley:

"Come the eleventh plague rather than this should be,
Come rather sink us in the sea.
Come pestilence and mow us down,
Come God's sword rather than our own."

NECROLOGY OF LOWELL.

"Their name, their age, spelt by the unlettered muse,
The place of fame and elegy supply."

It is astonishing that any civilized commonwealth should continue, as Massachusetts did, generation after generation, with no public registry of deaths that was worthy of the name. Prior to 1833, our necrological records were meagre in the extreme. Few as were the men who lived and died within the present limits of Lowell, previous to that year, we have no record of half of them; and some, perhaps, are forgotten, who were more remarkable (as Sir Thomas Brown would say) "than any that stand remembered in the known account of time."

Captain Ford, the lumber manufacturer, died in 1822, at the age of 82; Joel Spaulding, the farmer, in 1823, at 81; Moses Hale, the pioneer manufacturer, in 1828, at 63; Benjamin Melvin, in 1830, at 77; Rev. Alfred V. Bassett, (sometime teacher) in 1831, at 25; Simon Parker, in 1832, at 74; Joel Lewis, the teacher, in 1834, at 34; Phineas Whiting, in 1835, at 68; and Jacob Hale, in 1836, at 70. In 1836, also died Reuben Hills, teacher, and Elisha Glidden, lawyer. And here we begin our more formal record of the deaths of some of those best known among Lowellians—excluding those whose deaths have already been mentioned in this history.

Date	Name	Age	Description
1837—Jan. 30	Nathaniel D Healey	24	Teacher
April 5	Artemas Young	52	Manufacturer
Aug. 8	Frances Ames	74	Widow of Fisher
Aug. 31	Benjamin Butterfield	78	Farmer
1838—March 2	Jeremiah Mason	68	Manufacturer
Aug. 5	John Kimball	40	Deputy Sheriff
1839—April 1	Benjamin Pierce	82	Politician*

*Governor of New Hampshire; father of President Pierce.

Date	Name	Age	Description
1839—June 7	Horatio Boyden	40	Manufacturer
	Samuel H. Mann	56	Lawyer
1840—Sept. 7	Benjamin Walker	39	Butcher
Sept. 26	Albert Locke	33	Lawyer
Nov. 1	Alvah Mansur	40	Trader
1841—April 2	Daniel Pearson	52	Operative
April 27	John Adams	45	Auctioneer
1842—May 5	Jane Atkinson	81	Widow of Benj.
Sept. 26	Robert Means	56	Agent
Dec. 5	Moses Shattuck	59	Superintendent
1843—May 5	William Paul	47	Designer
Sept. 17	Mark T Gilman	43	Paymaster
Dec. 10	Luther Marshall	62	Farmer
1844—Feb. 16	Zadock Rogers	70	Farmer
Oct. 14	James W Brady	55	Dyer
Nov. 11	George Pollock	52	Book Keeper
1845—May 18	E M Farrar	37	Trader
Oct. 15	Arza L Witt	35	Physician
Dec. 12	William Duesbury	57	Apothecary
1846—March 5	Nathan Wright	85	Farmer
March 18	Catherine L Patch *	34	Widow of William
June 23	John G Tuttle	44	Clergyman
1847—June 21	James Dugdale	65	Manufacturer
April 13	George Gillis	46	
Aug. 28	Roswell Douglass	43	Manufacturer
Sept. 24	William Cowley	25	Manufacturer
Sept. 30	Nathaniel Wright	27	Lawyer
	Jesse Phelps	47	Overseer
1848—June 22	Robert McKinley	44	Block Printer
Sept. 26	Peleg Bradley	56	Dracut Physician
Sept. 27	William Kitchen	69	Carpet Weaver
	John R Adams		Lawyer
Dec. 18	Jonathan Bowers	59	Lumber Trader
1849—June 7	Benjamin F Aiken	45	Merchant
Aug. 9	Ezra Sheldon	47	Contractor
Sept. 5	James Russell	63	Died of Cholera
Sept. 1	John Butterfield	32	Prof. of Medicine
Sept. 10	Nathaniel Goodwin	66	Clerk
Nov. 19	Edmund L LeBreton	45	Agent
1850—March 1	David C Scobey	35	Teacher
March 21	Samuel Farson	59	Farmer
April 4	James Stott	55	Manufacturer
May 17	Nathan Durant	46	Trader
June 11	George A Butterfield	31	Lawyer
June 26	William Johnson	47	Cabinet Maker
1851—March 4	Samuel Gibby	69	Block Cutter
March 4	David Robinson	75	
April 7	John Baron	50	Inn Keeper
April 21	Abner H Brown		Physician

* Missionary; died at Cape Palmas, West Africa.

Date	Name	Age	Description
1851—April 26	William Wade	69	Wood Measurer
June 12	Jacob Carlton	51	Machinist
Aug. 4	John T Dodge	26	Clerk
Aug. 20	James Fisher	70	Yeoman
Sept. 3	Charles H Barber	56	
Sept. 23	Christopher Baron	63	
Nov. 12	Edmund Hanscom	39	Trader
1852—April 2	Thomas S Hutchinson	35	Printer
June 8	Alexander Wright	52	Agent
June 9	Otis H Morrill	36	Teacher
July 3	Robert Hope	47	Dyer
Aug. 2	Emerson Melvin	57	Beer Maker
Aug. 7	Isaac Scripture	51	Baker
Sept. 3	Owen M Donahoe	43	Inn Keeper
Oct. 28	James Sharples	74	Manufacturer
Oct. 30	David Trull	80	Stone Layer
Nov. 4	Philip T White	44	Tailor
Dec. 5	Charles Bent	63	Hatter
Dec. 22	William H Sweetser	41	
1853—April 7	Jonas W Packard	40	Manufacturer
April 28	Robert Gardner	67	Trader
May 1	Henry J Baxter	50	Tailor
May 16	Benjamin F French	61	Banker
May 21	Moses Cheever	86	Farmer
May 30	Joseph Hutchins	36	Inn Keeper
May 30	Lawrence Hill	60	Blacksmith
July 9	J Davidson Tatom	52	Machinist
Sept. 23	Allen Haggett	45	Ticket Master
Oct. 6	Thomas P Goodhue	50	Post Master
Oct. 16	William Paul	63	Operative
Oct. 21	Prentice Cushing	66	Machinist
Oct. 24	Edward Everett	33	Designer
Nov. 6	Augustus M Wyman	42	
Nov. 20	Jonas Reed	69	
Nov. 22	Farwell Puffer	47	Card Manufacturer
Nov. 24	Nathan C Crafts	57	Operative
1854—Jan. 25	Daniel Billings	74	Carpenter
Jan. 27	William Gilmore	34	Overseer
Jan. 31	Alfred Whittle	44	Reed Maker
Feb. 7	Elisha Stratton	56	Shop Keeper
Feb. 21	Thomas D Smith	47	Engraver
March 11	Horatio N Hudson	37	Engineer
March 15	David W Grimes	54	Mechanic
March 20	Cummings Barr	59	Stone Layer
April 23	Dayton R Ball	29	Trader
May 9	Leonard H Coburn	26	Trader
June 3	Asa Farr	71	Trader
June 8	Samuel Garland	62	Woodturner
June 8	George U Stone	59	Physician

Date	Name	Age	Description
1854—June 22	Rodolphus W Sisson	45	Apothecary
June 26	James C Crombie	40	Operative
July 1	Timothy Weeks	53	
July 5	John Varley	70	Mechanic
July 30	Aaron H Sherman	55	Mechanic
Aug. 1	Jeremiah Taylor	55	Shop Keeper
Aug. 9	Isaac Guild	60	
Aug. 12	Uzziah C Burnap	60	Clergyman
Aug. 14	Addison Brastow	69	Watchmaker
Aug. 21	Edward Roper	44	Manufacturer
Sept. 4	Nathan Russ	75	
Sept. 7	Zaccheus Shed	60	Constable
Sept. 23	Perez O Richmond	69	Manufacturer
Oct. 12	Francis Hudson	84	
Oct. 14	Charles McDermott	70	Agent
Oct. 20	John McDonald	69	Manufacturer
Nov. 15	Elisha Adams	36	Butcher
Nov. 24	William Bell	54	Trader
Nov. 27	John O Benthal	51	Trader
Dec. 16	Windsor Howe	69	Manufacturer
1855—Jan. 3	Elmira W Bradley	25	Teacher
Feb. 17	John Mason	84	Yeoman
Feb. 28	Reuben Gale	80	Yeoman
March 2	Jacob Jenness	49	Trader
April 18	Francis Rogers		Lost in the Albany
May 5	Moses Kidder	66	Physician
May 23	Elisha Ford	77	Surveyor of Land
May 20	Thomas Bixby	80	Tanner
June 3	Jacob Matthews	75	Clergyman
June 21	Betsey Cox	83	
	Nancy H Green		Teacher
July 8	Daniel S Littlehale	31	Engineer
July 8	Benjamin F Holden	38	Assessor
July 25	William L Day	52	Wheelwright
Aug. 13	Simeon Spaulding	79	Farmer
Aug. 29	John G Pillsbury	37	Printer
Sept. 28	Jonathan Allen	40	Bookbinder
Oct. 8	Oliver G Whipple*	24	Manufacturer
Oct. 13	Timothy O'Brien	63	Clergyman
Oct. 24	Thomas Crossley	74	Trader
Nov. 1	Asahel Gilbert Jr	36	Trader
Dec. 21	John D Pillsbury		Physician
1856—Jan. 12	Thomas Scotchburn	67	Rope Maker
Jan. 26	John Bates	54	Calico Printer
Jan. 29	John Little	67	Manufacturer
Feb. 13	Simeon Moors	62	Farmer
Feb. 24	Benjamin Parker	53	Farmer
Feb. 29	Thomas Boynton	81	Farmer
March 2	Temperance Thomas	104	Widow

*Killed by a powder-mill explosion, at Gorham, Maine.

Date	Name	Age	Description
1856—March 7	John Trull	56	Stone Worker
April 8	William Cotter	38	Clerk
April 11	Ira Spalding	52	Housewright
May 11	Joseph Bradshaw	80	Straw Worker
May 30	Thomas Dodge	67	Machinist
July 26	David Dana	59	Plumber
Aug. 6	Ezra Adams	84	Farmer
Sept. 3	Benjamin H Shepard	35	Trader
Sept. 4	John Brierly	81	Laborer
Sept. 3	Catherine Mungan	108	Widow
Sept. 22	William H Gage	37	Shop Keeper
Oct. 26	Walker Lewis	58	Barber
Nov. 3	Joseph B Gage	30	
Nov. 9	Robert T Tremlett	32	Accountant
Nov. 21	Theodore Butterfield	62	Farmer
Nov. 21	Joseph Merrill	68	Clergyman
Nov. 26	Lewis Packard	67	Manufacturer
1857—Jan. 29	Frederick Parker	43	Lawyer
Jan. 26	Robert Anderson	50	Carpenter
Jan. 24	Lewis W Lawrence	40	Machinist
March 1	Nathaniel Critchett	46	Shoedealer
March 3	George H Carleton	52	Apothecary
March 17	Jonathan M Marston	50	Restorateur
May 18	Landon Adams	56	Manufacturer
June 19	Ira Frye	58	Clerk
June 22	Henry Whiting	35	Physician
July 6	Michael Roach	65	Undertaker
Sept. 6	Oliver March	48	Bookseller
Sept. 19	William L Ayling	41	Comedian
Oct. 7	Benjamin F Foster	45	Farmer
Nov. 22	John Allen	55	Physician
Nov. 26	Benjamin F Nealley	41	Grocer
1858—Jan. 23	Henry A Pierce	24	Journalist
Jan. 24	Eunice Green	86	Mother of Dr. J O.
March 2	Larkin Moors	85	Cordwainer
April 6	Israel Hildreth	68	Dracut Physician
April 14	Tisdale Lincoln	71	Trader
April 26	Joseph B Giles	52	Writing Master
May 7	Mary Burnet	98	Spinster
July 26	Stephen Weymouth	53	Watchman
Aug. 22	Ira B Pearsons	41	Lawyer
Sept. 20	Eldad Fox	49	Carpet Weaver
Sept. 23	Edward Winslow	62	
Oct. 5	Sarah C Livermore	81	Widow of Judge L.
Nov. 5	Nathaniel Wright*	75	Lawyer
Dec. 8	Moses M Tuxbury	66	Farmer

*Mr. Wright was the first member from Lowell in either branch of the State Legislature, and afterward Mayor. He was an able lawyer, and had an extensive practice at Pawtucket Falls before the building of Lowell.

Date	Name	Age	Description
1858—Dec. 24	Isaiah W Pelsue	53	Watchman
1859—Jan. 29	Timothy Frye	63	Clerk
March 10	Hazen Elliott	62	Assessor
March 17	John Adams	73	
April 6	Daniel Varnum	69	Farmer
April 12	Alanson J Richmond	39	Manufacturer
May 17	George Teel	73	City Crier
June 20	Patrick Manice	56	Fisherman
June 22	Varnum Balcom	66	Carpenter
June 23	Joseph M Dodge	67	Carpenter
June 24	Aaron Mansur	83	
July 18	William F Johnson		Comedian
July 22	William H Hobson	25	Engraver
Aug. 13	Amos Woodbury	59	Carpenter
Aug. 24	William R Barker	46	Shop Keeper
Aug. 30	William Atherton	51	Mechanic
Oct. 21	Daniel R Kimball	53	Stable-keeper
Oct. 22	Ebenezer O Fifield	78	Farmer
Oct. 31	Samuel W Brown	55	Superintendent
Nov. 7	Oliver C Prescott	32	Mason
Nov. 11	Samuel J Varney	46	Journalist
Nov. 14	Thomas Ordway	72	City Clerk
Dec. 19	Charles Maynard	49	Shop Keeper
1860—Jan. 31	Thomas Yeoman	82	Manufacturer
Feb. 19	Joseph Sweetser	73	Baker
Feb. 19	Richard Dennis	57	Machinist
April 10	Tristam Barnard	94	Farmer
May 29	Asa G Loomis	50	Collector
June 19	Joshua L Conant	59	Yeoman
July 6	Joshua Roberts	70	R. R. Agent
July 14	Nicholas G Norcross	54	Lumber Trader
Aug. 21	Joseph Hovey	76	Farmer
Aug. 26	Timothy McLaughlin	42	Trader
Oct. 17	Andrew Barr	61	Tailor
Oct. 23	Israel Cheney	72	Musician
Dec. 17	Sextus Sawtell	34	Musician
	Michael O'Brien	96	
1861—Jan. 5	Susan Webster	89	Widow
Jan. 10	Jemima Rogers	83	Widow of Zadoc
Jan. 10	Janet Wright	84	Mother of Alex'r
Feb. 28	Abraham Howe	72	Carpenter
Feb. 10	Leonard W Jaquith	45	Agent
March 16	Daniel West	54	Trader
March 16	Stephen C Moar	80	Farmer
March 22	Martha M Cox		Teacher
March 27	Royal Call	61	Physician
March 28	Susan Moody	80	Widow of Paul
March 30	Reuben Butterfield	78	Farmer
May 16	Otis Cutler	59	Cordwainer
May 16	Hiram Hersey	56	Victualer

Date	Name	Age	Description
1861—May 24	Moses Cheever	68	Teamster
May 30	William Goding	62	Manufacturer
May 31	Joseph Gray		Clergyman
June 21	Charles N Dolloff		Lost in the Levant
Aug. 1	Myron O Allen	30	Physician
Aug. 5	Thomas Hopkins	86	Clergyman
Aug. 27	Joseph Jenkinson	38	Barber
Sept. 27	Elhanan W Scott	36	Machinist
Oct. 10	Amos Merriam	68	Assessor
Oct. 17	Edward A Staniels	40	Apothecary
Nov. 12	Levi E Lincoln	46	Apothecary
Dec. 17	Thomas Brophy	65	Hatter
1862—Jan. 12	David Thissell	60	Farmer
Jan. 16	Harrison G Blaisdell	40	Lawyer
Feb. 2	James T McDermott	55	Clergyman
Feb. 9	John Bowers	69	Farmer
Feb. 17	Luther S Cheney	39	Victualer
Feb. 19	George W Bean	57	Insurance Agent
Feb. 22	James Patterson	67	Wool Buyer
March 9	John D Prince	48	Manufacturer
April 12	Benjamin Livingston	73	Farmer
April 20	William Bradley	69	Dyer
April 30	Patrick Lannan	85	Trader
May 1	Abram T Holbrook	57	Conductor
May 2	James P Appleton	51	Sign Painter
May 18	David Rogers	54	Stabler
May 24	Zachariah B Caverly	40	Minister to Lima
May 25	Horatio Bradley	57	Ticket Agent
May 25	Charles Smith	53	Overseer
June 11	Jesse Stiles	56	Overseer
Aug. 29	Otis L Allen	52	Trader
Aug. 4	Joseph Parker	80	Auctioneer
Sept. 2	Matthew F Worthen	57	Machinist
Sept. 14	Calvin Woodward	54	Trader
Sept. 20	Darwin Mott	39	Clergyman
Sept. 27	William Spencer	59	Agent
Sept. 30	John S Wyman	52	Mechanic
Oct. 28	William Greenhalgh	53	Engraver
Nov. 3	Thomas Lovett	82	Carpenter
Nov. 19	Mertoun C Bryant	39	Agent
Nov. 24	Charles L Tilden	55	Agent
1863—Jan. 10	David Grover	49	Operative
Jan. 10	Andrew Oates	82	British Soldier *
Jan. 26	Timothy G Tweed	54	Butcher
Feb. 16	Charles M Short	63	Grocer

* Fought at Corunna under Moore, and at Waterloo under Wellington, and was one of the twelve grenadiers who bore the remains of Napoleon to his grave at St. Helena. Several other Waterloo veterans closed their careers in Lowell.

Date	Name	Age	Description
1863—April 9	Charles A Davis		Physician
May 9	Amos Hyde	59	Machinist
June 19	Benjamin Mather	87	Surveyor
June 21	Leonard Woods	63	Machinist
July 7	Darwin D Baxter	52	Trader
July 20	William H Goding	40	Manufacturer *
July 20	Ira Bisbee	49	Machinist *
July 24	Hiram A Alger	37	Lawyer
Aug. 8	Catherine Wittie	101	
Aug. 8	Artemas Holden	87	Cooper
Aug. 25	Lizzie Emmons		Actress
Sept. 30	David R Kirby	51	Brakeman
Nov. 1	Frank C Huntington	33	N. Y. Merchant
Nov. 22	Otis Perham	51	Physician
Nov. 27	David Tapley	55	Trader
Dec. 30	Amos R Boynton	49	Physician
1864—Jan. 7	George Bingham	43	Trader
Jan. 8	Daniel Cass	76	Dentist
Jan. 14	Andrew J Butler	48	Trader
Jan. 18	Charles E Brazer	36	Clerk
Jan. 19	George Miller	42	Engraver
Jan. 22	Samuel Stone	72	Trader
Feb. 23	Abel Patten	59	Clergyman
Feb. 24	James S Olcott	62	Physician
March 15	James Duxbury	72	Engraver
April 4	Elijah L Cole	48	Physician
April 17	Jonathan Spalding	89	Farmer
April 17	Adin Holbrook	84	Manufacturer
April 17	Josiah F Evans	45	Tailor
April 21	Paul Hills	76	Farmer
May 6	Bryan Morse	81	Clergyman
May 9	Royal T Hazeltine	58	Carpenter
May 10	Zadoc Wilkins	82	Capt. in 1812 War
May 11	Dean Penniman	63	Trader
May 15	Cyril French	74	Trader
May 17	Samuel Abbott	52	Dentist
May 28	Daniel S Wait	49	Carpenter
May 29	J Wallace Thomas	29	Comedian
June 5	George Briggs	57	Mechanic
June 7	James H B Ayer	76	Clerk
June 23	A Waldo Fisher	70	Machinist
July 8	John Avery	64	Agent
July 8	Isaac Anthony	77	Machinist
July 9	Franklin Webster	49	Farmer
July 19	David M G Cutler	55	Mechanic
July 22	Nathan Hanson	86	Mechanic
Aug. 7	Benjamin Brown	82	Farmer
Aug. 14	John Buttrick	69	Carpenter

* Killed with three others by the explosion of a steam boiler.

Date	Name	Age	Description
1864—Aug. 15	William Wyman	82	Yeoman
Aug. 20	George Pierce	68	Physician
Aug. 24	Josephine S Pearson	20	Teacher
Sept. 4	Perley Parker	68	Yeoman
Sept. 24	Zadoc Rogers	59	Farmer
Oct. 12	William A Lamb	34	Clerk
Oct. 15	Isaac W Scribner	57	Physician
Oct. 18	Rufus Wilkins	57	Butcher
Oct. 18	Henry D C Griswold	46	Watchmaker
Oct. 30	Joshua Thissell	72	Farmer
Oct.	Jeremiah Kidder	48	Trader
Oct.	Lemuel Porter		Clergyman
Nov. 19	Aaron Cowley	65	Manufacturer
Nov. 21	Deliverance Woodward	79	Farmer
Nov. 6	Lizzie A Pinder	24	Teacher
Dec. 26	Dennis Crowley *	67	Mechanic
1865—Jan. 4	James W Boynton	39	Coal Dealer
Jan. 25	Joshua Melvin	72	Physician
Feb. 10	Jonathan Weeks	61	Clerk
March 12	James W Kershaw	36	Trader
March 12	Peter Powers	59	Mason
March 21	James Leavitt	60	
April 3	James Dennis	57	Machinist
April 10	Charles Walker	33	Physician
April 14	Alanson Crane	55	Manufacturer
April 19	William D Vinal	55	Dentist
April 23	Francis E Hicks	33	Clergyman
May 10	John Earle	83	Yeoman
May 22	William A Swan	63	Mason
June 20	Noah F Gates	48	Assessor
June 22	Joshua Mather	60	Manufacturer
July 3	Caleb Livingston	60	Trader
July 9	Joseph Manahan	67	Trader
Aug. 6	Joshua Bennett	72	Billerica Capitalist
Aug. 9	Charles Sherwin	61	Manufacturer
Aug. 13	William Wagner	93	Weaver
Aug. 26	Samuel P Buttrick	52	Carpenter
Sept. 2	Harvey Snow		Mechanic
Sept. 6	John Bennett	76	Surveyor
Oct. 9	Nathan Buttrick	55	Carpenter
Oct. 14	James K Dewhurst	69	Block Cutter
Oct. 30	Edwin L Shed	42	Deputy Sheriff
Nov. 1	J Wheelock Patch	27	Trader
Nov. 18	Patrick P Campbell	62	Physician
Dec. 25	Elmira B Stanton	28	Teacher
1866—Jan. 27	John Whitney	69	Manufacturer
Jan. 29	Daniel P Bradley	70	Farmer
Feb. 3	Benjamin O Paige	56	Manufacturer

* One of the first Irishmen that settled in Lowell; came in 1822.

Date	Name	Age	Description
1866—Feb. 3	Henry C Gray	30	Expressman *
Feb. 5	John McAlvin	66	Farmer
Feb. 5	Henry L C Newton	43	Printer
Feb. 7	Mahlon Snow	67	Farmer
Feb. 13	James Thompson	65	Physician
Feb. 24	Thomas Charnley	84	
March 20	Jonathan Knowles	86	Operative
May 9	Daniel H Dean	61	Trader
May 21	Benjamin P Rogers	52	Farmer
May 23	Lydia Wood	68	Shop Keeper
May 24	John Green	68	Gardener
June 23	Amos Hull	68	Undertaker
July 2	Horace Howard	64	Coal Dealer
July 17	Mehitable O Allen	93	Mother, Dr. N Allen
July 18	Richard P Mercer	66	Overseer
Aug. 6	Alonzo T Davis	55	Cap Maker
Sept. 3	Perez Fuller	69	Tailor
Oct. 12	George C Smith	59	Bolt Maker
Nov. 2	Charles Churchill	52	Trader
Nov. 7	Henry Smith	69	Trader
Nov. 11	David M Erskine	59	Trader
Nov. 18	Benjamin Dean	72	Engraver
Dec. 7	Asa Wetherbee	81	Carpenter
Dec. 18	James Winterbottom	80	Carpet Maker
Dec. 22	Zenas Crowell	62	Overseer
1867—Feb. 10	John Aiken	70	Agent
Feb. 28	John A Rogers	59	Manufacturer
March 2	William D Mason	74	Mechanic
March 2	Hananiah Whitney	75	Trader
March 23	Benjamin Skelton	84	Physician
March 27	Ransom Reed	64	Trader
April 1	Ivory Edwards	60	Mechanic
April 6	Jonathan M Allen	53	Prof. of Anatomy
April 10	Alfred E Nichols	37	Mechanic
April 21	Joshua Swan	79	Contractor
April 23	David Hyde	50	Broker
May 19	James O Patterson	63	Manufacturer
May 25	Charles W Dodge	41	Trader
June 15	Susan Prince	83	Widow of John D
June 24	Joel Stone	68	Trader
Sept. 1	Jeremiah Garland	77	Trader
Sept. 5	Caleb Crosby	61	Mason
Aug. 14	Jonas Balcom	84	Carpenter
Aug. 13	Thomas Midgley	50	Overseer
Oct. 6	Stephen S Seavy	53	Trader
Oct. 14	Henry B Stanton Jr	33	Post Office Clerk
Oct. 15	Charles A Babcock	52	Agent
Oct. 19	William Smith	77	Lawyer
Oct. 19	Thomas Slater	69	Chaplain at Jail

* Killed by steamboat explosion near Vicksburg.

Date	Name	Age	Description
1867—Nov. 6	Edward B Rawlings	62	Carpenter
Nov. 7	Josiah P Vickery	44	Painter
Nov. 27	Joseph Derbyshire	46	Farmer
Dec. 17	Elias P Marsh	58	Manufacturer
Dec. 15	Matthew F Worthen	21	Accidentally Shot
1868—Jan. 6	John Waugh	44	Trader
Jan. 19	Bethuel T Thompson,	50	Trader
Jan. 25	George Crosby	55	Trader
Jan. 27	James Adams	60	Overseer
Jan. 30	Maynard Bragg	71	Mechanic
Feb. 8	James O'Neil	102	Had 98 descendants
Feb. 18	Henry Smith	47	Machinist *
Feb. 19	Thomas Wright	45	Lawyer

LOWELL LEGISLATORS.

The State Senators from Lowell have been given on page 159. Our Representatives, too numerous to be named in the text, have been as follows:—

1826 and 1827—Nathaniel Wright.
1828—Nathaniel Wright and Elisha Ford.
1829—J. P. Robinson and J. S. C. Knowlton.
1830—Kirk Boott, Joshua Swan, and J. P. Robinson.
1831—Kirk Boott, Joshua Swan, J. P. Robinson, J. S. C. Knowlton and Eliphalet Case.†
1832—Ebenezer Appleton, Artemas Holden, O. M. Whipple, Seth Ames, Maynard Bragg, William Davidson and Willard Guild.
1833—S. A. Coburn, J. P. Robinson, Cyril French, Simon Adams, Jacob Robbins, J. L. Sheafe, Jesse Fox, Royal Southwick, Joseph Tyler and Jonathan Spalding.
1834—Samuel Howard, Kirk Boott, James Chandler, Osgood Dane, Jesse Phelps and O. M. Whipple. (Eleven vacancies, no others receiving a majority vote.)

---

* Killed with two others by the explosion of a locomotive.

† This was the last regular session of the Legislature that was held in May. The regular sessions have since commenced in January, annually—the members being elected in the preceding November.

1835—Kirk Boott, A. W. Buttrick, James Chandler, William Davidson, Artemas Holden, John Mixer, Matthias Parkhurst, Alpheus Smith, Joseph Tyler, O. M. Whipple, Benjamin Walker, William Wyman and J. A. Knowles.

1836—William Austin, A. W. Fisher, H. W. Hastings, Royal Southwick, Aaron Mansur, Sidney Spalding, W. W. Wyman, J. M. Marston, Stephen Mansur, Jonathan Tyler, J. L. Sheafe, Alexander Wright, Jesse Fox, J. B. French, S. H. Marvin, E. D. Leavitt and James Chandler.

1837—J. W. Mansur, Stephen Goodhue, James Wilson, J. K. Fellows, W. S Merrill, J. G. Peabody, Jesse Clement, J. G. Abbott, J. M. Doe, W. N. Owen, Charles Hastings, G. K. Eastman, Samuel Clark, Samuel Willard, John Mead, Loring Pickering, Richard Fowler.

1838—Jesse Fox, William North, Thomas Hopkinson, Jonathan Bowers, W. W. Wyman, J. M. Dodge, Perez Fuller, David Nourse, J. M. Marston.

1839—O. M. Whipple, Joshua Swan, Edward Winslow, Royal Southwick, William Davis, Hazen Elliott, David Nourse, H. J. Baxter, Jesse Phelps.

1840—Isaac Scripture, Jefferson Bancroft, Royal Southwick, Jesse Phelps, Nathaniel Wright, Alvah Mansur.

1841—Elisha Bartlett, Jefferson Bancroft, Samuel Burbank, William Colton, Franklin Farrar, R. G. Colby, Pearson Titcomb, G. W. Wendell, Benjamin Wilde.

1842—Jonathan Adams, Jonathan Tyler, E. F. Watson, Amos Hyde, Otis Allen, D. S. Richardson, J. L. Fitts, J. P. Robinson, Asa Hall.

1843—J. T. Hardy, Henry Smith, Samuel Lawrence, Jonathan Tyler, James Tower, Abram Howe, Roswell Douglass, D. S. Richardson, (one vacancy.)

1844—Joshua Swan, William Schouler, James Fenno, J. W. Holland, Daniel Balch, J. M. Dodge, J. A. Knowles, Franklin Farrar, J. L. Fitts.

1845—S. P. Adams, George Bragdon, Isaac Cooper, Joseph Griffin, Thomas Hopkinson, J. A. Knowles, John Mixer, Jesse Phelps, William Schouler.

1846—C. W. Blanchard, Leonard Huntress, G. N. Nichols, Sidney Spalding, Benjamin Wilde, G. A. Butterfield, (three vacancies.)

1847—D. S. Richardson, L. R. Winslow, Joshua Converse, Wm. Schouler, G. A. Butterfield, Ziba Abbott, Arnold Welch, J. L. Tripp.

1848—Ransom Reed, H. G. F. Corliss, James Fenno, Stephen Moar, S. W. Brown, Joel Powers, Sidney Spalding, Benjamin Green, Gilman Gale.

1849—Homer Bartlett, Joseph Locke, H. G. F. Corliss, Stephen Moar, Samuel Burbank, Ransom Reed, George Brownell, James Adams, Horace Parmenter.

1850—George Brownell, Francis Bush, Stephen Mansur, D. P. Brigham, Samuel Burbank, James Dinsmoor, J. M. Bullens, Jefferson Bancroft, William Ripley.

1851—Tappan Wentworth, Joseph Bedlow, James Dinsmoor, George Gardner, John Maynard, Hannibal Powers, Silas Tyler, Francis Bush, Jefferson Bancroft, William Ripley.

1852—W. S. Robinson, Erastus Douglass, J. E. Farnsworth, Luther Eames, Luther B. Morse, Otis H. Morrill, J. K. Fellows, A. R. Brown, Sidney Spalding, (one vacancy.)

1853—L. B. Morse, W. S. Robinson, John S. Fletcher, Jonathan Page, Caleb Crosby, J. M. Hadley, B. F. Butler, Luther Eames, William Roby, (one vacancy.)

1854—Ira Spalding, Daniel Ayer, Benjamin Poole, Solon Stevens, James Townsend, Daniel Holt, S. J. Tuttle, A. B. Wright, John Smith, William Brown.

1855—J. G. Peabody, J. P. Jewett, Henry Phelps, Jr., Horace Howard, S. A. Waters, S. W. Hanks, D. C. Eddy, Walter Burnham, Ransom Clifford, Weare Clifford.

1856—Weare Clifford, C. F. Hard, Jonathan Johnson, L. J. Fletcher, A. B. Roby, Asa Hildreth, Jonathan Weeks, Caleb Crosby, Henry Phelps, Jr., J. M. Burtt.

1857—S. P. Adams, Alfred Gilman, Joshua Merrill, J. A. Goodwin, I. L. Moore, Seth Pooler, J. S. Pollard, C. F. Hard, Ignatius Tyler, Noah Conant.

1858—William G. Wise, Sullivan Tay, H. G. F. Corliss, S. K. Fielding, John C. Jepson, George Stevens.

1859—M. A. Thomas, Sullivan Tay, John C. Woodward, T. Wentworth, Walter Burnham, John A. Goodwin.

1860—Stephen P. Sargent, David Nichols, Jeremiah Clark, Tappan Wentworth, Noah F. Gates, John A. Goodwin.

1861—Stephen P. Sargent, David Nichols, Jeremiah Clark, Hapgood Wright, Nathaniel B. Favor, John A. Goodwin.

1862—Paul Hill, Samuel W. Stickney, Sewall G. Mack, Hapgood Wright, Josiah B. French, Edward F. Sherman.

1863—Paul Hill, Lorenzo G. Howe, Frederic Holton, Tappan Wentworth, John A. Buttrick, Joshua N. Marshall.

1864—Jacob Rogers, Lorenzo G. Howe, Frederic Holton, Tappan Wentworth, George W. Partridge, Joshua N. Marshall.

1865—Jacob Rogers, William T. McNeill, Sullivan L. Ward, Horace J. Adams, John F. Manahan, Zina E. Stone.

1866—Foster Wilson, Lorenzo D. Cogswell,* Sullivan L. Ward, Hocum Hosford, John F. Manahan, Zina E. Stone.

1867—Andrew F. Jewett, Charles A. Stott, Oliver W. Smith, John F. Manahan, Edward F. Sherman.

1868—James B. Francis, Benjamin J. Williams, Oliver W. Smith, Josiah Gates, William McFarlin.

---

* William T. McNeill received the original certificate of election, but Mr. Cogswell successfully contested the seat.

LOWELL NAVAL OFFICERS IN SERVICE DURING THE REBELLION.

Ames, Pelham W., Paymaster of the Connecticut.
Bancroft, Kirk Henry, Surgeon of the Iosco; bombardments of Fort Fisher.
Birtwhistle, James, Master of the Madawaska.
Boynton, James A., Engineer of the Cornubia.
Brown, William S., Engineer of the Canonicus; bombardments of Fort Fisher; occupation of Charleston.
Colby, Edward P., Surgeon of the William G. Anderson.
Cowley, Charles, Paymaster of the Lehigh; Fleet-Judge-Advocate, Staff of Admiral Dahlgren; two days' bombardment of Fort Sumter; eight days' bombardment of Fort Pemberton and the batteries on the Stono; battles of Honey Hill and Gregory's Landing; occupation of Savannah and Charleston; * blown up in Santee River by a torpedo, which destroyed Dahlgren's Flagship, Harvest Moon; reconnoitering expedition to Cuba.
De Arville, Louis, Engineer of the Fort Donelson.
Dennis, William H., Assistant, Coast Survey.
Eaton, Joseph G., Midshipman.
Fuller, Darius A., Engineer of the Iuka.
Francis, George E., Surgeon of the Ouichita.
Fox, Gustavus V., Lieutenant; Assistant Secretary; expeditions to Fort Sumter and Russia.
Garabedian, Hetchadore P., Engineer of the Geranium.
Garrigan, Michael, Engineer of the Malvern; bombardments of Fort Fisher.
Guild, Charles F., Ensign; Secretary to Admiral Porter; all Porter's engagements on the Mississippi and at Fort Fisher; now Paymaster in the regular Navy.
Guild, Charles M., Paymaster of the Shenandoah; bombardments of Fort Fisher; still in the service, in the Asiatic Squadron.
Gilmore, John D., Engineer of the Cherokee.
Lawrence, Alvin, Engineer of the Glaucus.

* Had the attack on Fort Johnson, Sunday morning, July 4th, 1864, been directed by a competent officer, Charleston would have been occupied eight months earlier. Two regiments of infantry and two sections of artillery were carried to James Island in boats, which were to have left Morris Island at two o'clock in the morning, but were delayed till four o'clock. The delay was fatal. The attacking column was repulsed, and the number killed, wounded or captured exceeded the entire garrison of the fort. Among the Naval officers accompanying the storming column was the author of this work, who was there wounded.

Lawrence, George, Paymaster of the Pawnee; eight days' bombardment of Fort Pemberton and the batteries on Stono River, near Charleston.

Lawrence, George W., Engineer of the Malvern.

Lawson, Frederick B., Surgeon of the Huntsville.

Leavitt, Erasmus D., Jr., Engineer of the Sagamore; capture of Appalachicola; bombardments of Tampa, Christabel River Batteries, and St. Andrews.

Leavitt, William A., Engineer of the Nita; engagement with batteries on the Suwannee River.

Long, James, Ensign.

Marthon, Joseph, Master of the Hartford; battle of Mobile Bay; still in the service.

McCracken, William, Mate.

Mason, William, Engineer of the Quaker City.

Maxfield, James G., Apothecary of the Osceola.

McDaniels, Thomas J., Engineer of the Louisiana.

O'Brien, James, Master of the Albatross.

O'Hare, John, Mate; killed at Fort Fisher.

Osgood, George C., Surgeon of the Chillicothe.

Oates, John H., Mate of the Congress; engagement with the Confederate ram Merrimac.

Racao, Frederick W., Engineer of the Harvest Moon; occupation of Charleston; blown up by a torpedo in the Santee.

Reenstjerna, Lars M., Engineer of the Aroostook.

Riley, James, Engineer of the Tallahatchie.

Scribner, James E., Engineer.

Slocum, John P., Engineer.

Snell, Alfred T., now Lieutenant Commander of the Ticonderoga; bombardments of Sumter, Wagner and Fisher; battles of Balls' Bluff and Mayport Mills; capture of Machias Point, Port Royal, Jacksonville and Fernandina; wrecked in the Glaucus.

Vaile, John Henry, Engineer of the Lehigh.

Wilder, Charles B., Lieutenant; killed in his boat by sharpshooters, April 11, 1864.

Wright, Emory, Paymaster of the R. R. Cuyler; bombardments of Fort Fisher.*

---

*In the absence of authentic data, I have found it impossible to make this record perfect or complete. Almost every officer served on several different vessels in the course of the War; but the ship in which his most important service was rendered is the only one herein named. There were several naval officers concerning whom I could find no information at all.

Of the many Lowell sailors who lost their lives in the Naval service, I have only been able to recover the names of Harvey S. Adams, James Brayton, Joseph Cheatham, Francis Corey, George Derbyshire, Michael Dohany, Thomas Faulkner, David Marren, Jeremiah McCarty, Thomas McKenna, Thomas Moore, George F. Parks, Albert Paul, John Roach, David B. Tilton, Harrison A. Tweed, John Driscoll, John Chandler and Edward Garrity.

LOWELL ARMY OFFICERS.

THREE YEARS' MEN.

Abbott, Edward G., Capt. and Brev. Maj., A, 2; killed at Cedar Mountain, August 9th, 1862.
Abbott, Fletcher M., Capt., Staff of Gen. William Dwight.
Abbott, Henry L., Maj. and Brev. Brig. Gen., 20; killed at the Wilderness, May 6th, 1864.
Allen, Edwin, 1st Lt., 78 U. S. Col. I.
Ames, John W., Col., 6 U. S. C. T., and Brev. Brig. Gen.
Ayling, Augustus D., 1st Lt., D, 29.
Bailey, Walter S., Capt. 28.
Bean, James W., 1st Lt., 7 Batt.
Blanchard, C. F., Capt., B, 30; died January 20, 1864, aged 58.
Blood, Andrew, Capt., H, 26.
Bonney, Seth, Maj., 26; now 1st Lt. 27th U. S. Infantry.
Boyd, Hugh, 1st Lt., I, 16.
Brady, James W., Capt., 9 Md.
Brady, Allen G., Col., and Brev. Brig. Gen., 17 Conn.
Bradley, William H., Surg., 7 Batt.
Bradt, James G., Surg., 26; died January 22, 1868, aged 30.
Burgess, Charles W., Capt., I, 30.
Burnham, Walter, 1st Lt., and Brev. Maj., Engineers.
Bush, Francis, 1st Lt., Q. M., 44.
Bush, George, Capt., B, 13; killed at Chancellorsville, April 30, 1863.
Bush, Joseph, Capt., 1 Vt.; now Brev Major 22 U. S. Infantry.
Butler, Benjamin F., Maj. Gen.
Caldwell, John A. L., 1st Lt., 4 Cav.
Carey, Paten M., 2nd Lt., 3 Cav.
Carll, Alonzo W., Staff, 2 Ind.
Carney, George J., Major, Staff of Gen. Butler.
Carney, James, 2nd Lt., H, 30.
Cassidy, Patrick R., Capt., 40.
Cassidy, Thomas, D, 28.
Claffy, Thomas, 2nd Lt. and Brev. Capt., G, 19; killed at Fredericksburg, Dec. 13, 1862, aged 28.
Clark, Charles F., 1st Lt., Corps de Afrique.
Clark, Edwin R., Capt., B, 30; now 2nd Lt., 26 U. S. I.
Cleaveland, John P., Chaplain, 30.
Coburn, Charles H., 1st Lt., 1 U. S. Col. Cav.
Colton, Charles C., 1st Lt., 2 Corps de Afrique.
Comerford, John A., Maj., 3 Cav.
Condon, John P., Capt., 19.
Cooke, Homer A., Assist. Q. M.
Critchett, George F., Capt., 7 Batt; died, October 30, 1863.
Croft, Frederick, 2nd Lt., B, 19.
Crosby, William D., Capt., 21.
Crowley, Patrick E., 1st Lt., 20.
Crowley, Timothy A., Capt., F, 30; died at New Orleans, Oct. 5, 1862.
Crowley, Timothy B., Capt., and Brev. Maj., B, 10 N. H.
Currier, Charles M., 1st Lt., 4 N. H.
Curry, Patrick, 2nd Lt., 3 Cav.
Dana, J. J., Brev Brig. Gen.
Danforth, Henry, Capt., 40.
Dame, Lorin L., Lt., 15 Batt.
Darracott, James R., 1st Lt., E, 16; killed at Manassas, August 29, 1862.
Davis, George E., Adj., 26.
Davis, Phineas A., Capt., 7 Batt., and Asst. Adj. Gen., Staff of Gen. R. S. Foster.
Deming, John F, Adjutant, 109 Penn.
Devoll, Andrew J., 2nd Lt., 7 Batt; dismissed.
Dickerman, George M., Capt., A, 26.
Dickerman, Orlando W., 1st Lt., A, 26.
Donovan, Matthew, Maj., D, 16.
Donahoe, Joseph J., Adj., 10 N. H.
Donahoe, Michael T., Brig. Gen.
Dudley, John G., Capt., 30.
Eastman, Ezekiel W., 1st Lt., H, 26.
Eayrs, Charles G. A., Surg., 17.
Elliott, Richard A., Capt., 2 La.
Emerson, Charles F., 2nd Lt., 26
Emerson, Moses C., Lt., Corps de Afrique.
England, Thomas, 1st Lt., 30
Farr, Alpha B., Col., 26.
Farr, Asa W., Judge-Advocate, Staff of Gen. Blunt; killed by guerrillas, Oct. 6, 1863.
Farrar, William E., 1st Lt., 7 Batt.
Farson, James, Capt., B, 30.

Ferris, Eugene W., Capt., D, 30.
Ferris, Marsh A., Capt., D, 30.
Field, David C. G., 1st Lt, Gen. Butler's Staff.
Field, George W., Capt., 59.
Fifield, William A., 1st Lt., 59.
Fish, Obed M., Capt., 2 Art.
Fiske, Edward A., Maj., 30.
Fiske, William O., Brev. Brig. Gen.
Follansbee, George, Capt., 1 H. A.
Foster, Enoch 1st Lt., A, 6; died July 21, 1863.
Foster, John D., 1st Lt., C, 30.
Fox, Lorenzo S., Asst. Surg., 26.
Francis, George E., Asst. Surg.
Francis, James, Lt. Col., 2, and Div. Inspector, Staff of Gen. Williams.
Frost, Benjamin W., Capt., H, 26
Fuller, Henry A., 2nd Lt., F, 30.
Fuller, Lucius O., 2nd Lt., F, 26.
Gage, Daniel P., Asst. Surg, 33.
Gelray, Joseph, Col., 57, and Brev. Brig. Gen.
George, Albert, 1st Lt., 14 Batt.
George, John F., Capt., G, 2.
George, Paul R., Assistant Quartermaster; rejected by the Senate; died Feb. 29, 1864, aged 56.
Gilman, John H., Asst. Surg., 10.
Greenwood, Frank W., Capt, La.
Grimes, David E., Capt., 46; died Oct. 30, 1865, aged 39.
Grush, Joseph S., 2nd Lt., 15 Batt.
Haggerty, Peter, Major and Assis't Adj. Gen., Staff of Gen. Butler; died at New Orleans, July 8, 1866, aged 36.
Hall, James, Lt, N. Y.; killed in battle.
Hull, Winthrop H., Adj., 23 Me.
Harwood, John, Asst. Surg., 10 N. H; died March 16, 1863.
Hastings, Charles, 2nd Lt., 2.
Hayward, Asa E., 1st Lt., 21; killed at Petersburg, July 30, 1864.
Hill, James E.
Hill, John B., 1st Lt., 17.
Hinckley, Wallace, Adj., 2 H. Art.; died at Beaufort, Sept. 4, '65, ag. 21.
Hixon, Lloyd W., Asst. Surg, 13.
Homer, Charles W., Chaplain, 16.
Hopkins, Charles S., Assist. Q. M.,
Hopkins, James A., Capt., 17 U. S. Infantry.
Howe, Pliny R., 2nd Lt., H, 26.
Howe, H. Warren, Capt., 30.
Hubbard, William E., Lt., 8 N. H.
Huntington, James F., Capt., 15 Ohio Batt.
Hutchinson, Edward J., Capt., 48 N. Y.; died July 3, 1865, aged 36.
Johnson, Andrew J., 1st Lt., A, 26.
Johnston, Brent, Jr., Major, F, 30.
Johnston, Thomas B., Capt., B, 30.
Jones, Charles E, Capt., 33.
Kelsey, Jeremiah, A, 2.
Kelley, Thomas, 1st Lt., 30.
Kelty, Eugene, Capt., I, 30.
Knapp, Charles M., Q. M., C. T.
Ladd, Jonathan, Paym'r; dismissed.
Lamson, Henry P., Lt., F, 30.
Lamson, William H., Major, 33; died June 25, 1865, aged 35.
Lawrence, George P., Paymaster.
Lawson, Henry T., Major, 2 H. A.; died Oct. 1, 1864, at Newbern.
Lawson, John, Capt., 2 Art.
Leach, Ivory, 2nd Lt., 2 Sharp Shoot.
Leighton, Walter H., Asst. Surg., 188 Penn.
Lord, Charles P, 1st Lt., F, 8 Me.
Louger, William F., 1st Lt., C, 2 Art.
Loverin, William F., 1st Lt., C, 30.
Lundy, Francis H., 1st Lt., K, 2; served in the British Army, in the Crimea.
Madden, James, Captain, 10 N. H.; killed at Petersburg, June 3, 1864.
Magee, D. A., Capt., 2 Cav.
Maguire, Michael T. H., 1st Lt., 10 N. H.
Mansfield, Francis, Chaplain, N. Y.
Marsh, Salem S., Capt., 2 U. S. Infantry; killed at Chancellorsville, May 1, 1863.
Marston, William W., Capt., 12 La.
Maxfield, Jared P., 2nd Lt., 3 Cav.
McAlpine, Thomas D., 1st Lt., V. R. C.
McAlpine, William T., 1st Lt., C, 2.
McAnulty, Peter, 1st Lt., G, 19.
McClafferty, Matthew J., Maj.
McCurdy, William G., 1st Lt, 7 Batt.
McGee, James, Major, 3 Cav.
McLaughlin, James, 2nd Lt., 10 N H.
McQuade, Frank, Major, 11.
Mead, Samuel H., Lt., 69; died July 26, 1864.
Merserve, Henry, 2nd Lt., 33.
Miles, William H., 1st Lt., 2.
Minassian, Simon G., Asst. Surg.
Mitchell, John, 11 U. S. Infantry.
Morrill, Edmund D., 2nd Lt., 15 Batt.
Mower, Joseph A., Col. and Brev. Maj. Gen.

Mumford, Dudley C., G, 19; killed at Cold Harbor, May 31, 1864.
Munsey, Alfred T., Capt., 1 La.
Murkland, John, Capt., B, 15; killed at Gettysburg, July 3, 1863.
Murphy, Daniel J., 2nd Lt., I, 19.
Needham, Herbert A., 2nd Lt., H, 33.
Norcross, Frederick M., Asst. Q. M.
Norcross, Nicholas W., Paymaster.
Noyes, Edward J., Maj., 1 Tex. Cav.
O'Hare, Thomas, Capt., G, 16.
Paine, Patrick, 2nd Lt., 10 N. H.
Parker, John M. G., Q. M., 30.
Parsons, Benjamin W., 1st Lt., 3 Cav.
Peabody, Baldwin T., 1st Lt., G, 33.
Pearson, Timothy, Capt., 15 Batt.
Pendergast, Richard, 1st Lt., B, 2.
Perkins, Solon A., 1st Lt. and Brev Maj., 3 Cavalry; killed at Clinton, June 3, 1863.
Philbrick, Caleb, Capt., G, 33.
Pickering, George A., 1st Lt., 33.
Pinder, Albert, 1st Lt., 59.
Poor, Charles E., 1st Lt., 38 Col. U. S.
Prescott, D. Moody, Capt., F, 33.
Prescott, Frank O., 1st Lieut., F, 33.
Proctor, Patrick S., Capt., D, 16; died March 1, 1867.
Pulcifer, Alfred H., Capt., 2 H. A.
Pulcifer, John C., 2nd Lt., 2 Art.
Reed, George E., 2nd Lt., C, 30.
Reed, Nathaniel K., 1st Lt., 30.
Reed, Phillip, 2nd Lt., U. S. A.
Richards, William H. H., 1st Lt., 30.
Ricker, William G. A., 1st Lt., Col. Cav.
Richardson, Charles H., 2nd Lt., 26.
Robinson, Charles S., 2 Lt., 7 Batt.
Robinson, J. A. A., 2nd Lt., 1 Col. U. S. Infantry.
Roby, George W., 1st Lt., B, 22.
Roche, David W., Capt., K, 16; killed at Gettysburg, July 3, 1863.
Roche, Maurice, 1st Lt., H. A.; died April 2, 1864.
Rose, George W., 2nd Lt., A, 33.
Rowe, John, Capt., E, 16; died June 24, 1864, in Libby Prison.
Rowse, Albert, 1st Lt., 15 Batt.
Russell, Daniel W., Capt., B, 10 N. H.; killed at Cold Harbor.
Russell, Daniel, Lt., N. Y.; died in the service.
Sanborn, E. K., Surgeon, 31; died at at Ship Island, April 3, 1863.
Sawtell, Josiah A., Lt. Col., 26.
Skinner, Theodore R., 1st Lt.
Sawyer, Nathan D. A., Capt. A, 2.
Sinclair, Henry A., 2nd Lt., 33.
Smith, Stephen B., Adjutant, 26.
Shaw, Daniel W., 1st Lt., 26.
Shipley, Samuel D., Lt. Col., 30.
Short, Richard H., 1st Lt., 10 N. H.
Sladen, Joseph A., 1st Lt., and Brev. Capt., 26 U. S. A.
Smith, Walter N., Capt., B, 11.
Snow, William H., Adj., 2 Art.
Sperry, H. Austin, Capt., 30.
Sperry, Charles, 1st Lt.
Stevens, George W., Adjutant, 23 O.
Storer, Newman W., Capt., 7 Batt.
Sullivan, Francis, 1st Lt., 15 N. Y.
Thompson, James B., 2nd Lt., G, 16.
Thompson, Joseph P., 1st Lt, G, 33.
Tierney, Peter, 2nd Lt., 30.
Tilton, Warren W., 2nd Lt., 19.
Vaile, Edward, 1st Lt., 30.
Vance, William G., Lt., V. R. C.
Varnum, John, Capt., U. S. C. T.
Warren, Benjamin, Capt., D, 26.
Warren, Thomas A., 1st Lt., F, 30.
Waugh, Archibald, 1st Lt., A, 33.
Webster, Peter L., 2, H. A.
Webster, William P., Provost Judge, Eastern Virginia.
Weymouth, Harrison G. O., Maj., U.S. Southern Volunteers.
Wheldon, Charles M., Lt. Col., C. T.
Whiting, Joseph B., 2nd Lt., D, 26.
Wiley, William I., Capt., Col. La.
Willey, William H., 2nd Lt., A, 26.
Williams, Charles H., 2nd Lt, 7 Batt.
Williamson, David H., Adj., 11.
Winn, George B., Capt., 3 La. Col.
Yeaton, Reuben F., Capt., 1 La. Cav.
Young, William, 2nd Lt., B, 11.

LOWELL SOLDIERS WHO DIED IN SERVICE DURING THE REBELLION.*

> " On Fame's eternal camping ground
> Their silent tents are spread;
> And Glory guards with solemn round
> The bivouac of the dead."

Abbott, Samuel D., 1 Sharpshooters
Adams, Charles A., Sergt., F, 33
Allen, George S., 1 Sharpshooters
Ansart, Atis E., I, 16
Auld, James T., 12 Batt
Austin, Seth J., A, 33
Babcock, Alonzo J., Sergt., H, 2
Badger, Willard F., F, 33
Baker, Daniel W., G, 3 N H
Baker, S. C., Sergt., A, 10 N Y
Baldwin, Clark G., C, 30
Ball, Henry C., A, 2
Barry, Edward, G, 20
Barry, John, D, 16
Barrett, John, H, 30
Bartlett, Ebenezer H., 7 Batt
Bartlett, Reuben A., 7 Batt
Bascom, Wallace, A, 2
Bassett, Joseph C., Sergt., A, 2
Bean, Lyman W., 1 N H Batt
Bean, William H., B, 19
Bickford, Charles H., B, 2
Bickford, William H., Sergt., D, 2[illegible]
Blessington, Bernard, C, 1
Blessington, Hugh, B, 30
Blodgett, John F., C, 30
Bohonan, George W., Corp., F, 33
Bowden, Ernest, G, 33
Bowles, Ira, H, 6
Bradford, William, B, 11
Bradt, Charles A., C, 44
Breen, Thomas, K, 32
Briggs, John, Jr., A, 2
Bright, Henry C., A, 2
Brown, Frederick H., C, 2
Brown, John, 7 Batt
Brown, Robert, 7 Batt
Brown, Joseph M., 30
Bullard, William T., A, 2
Bumpus, B. F., A, 2
Bumpus, Ephraim, C., 2
Burbank, Augustus F., Sergt., B, 30
Burbank, George W., 5 U S Cav
Burns, Frank, B, 40
Burns, John A., Corp., F, 30
Burns, John, I, 1 H A
Burns, Thomas, I, 16
Bush, James M., 2 N. H.
Butterfield, Frank S., D, 26
Butterworth, John, Ellsworth's Zouaves.
Buxton, George W., Corp., A, 2
Cadwell, Charles D., 7 Batt
Cain, George W., Corp., B, 19
Caldwell, Charles, G, 16
Carnes, Thomas, I, 32
Carpenter, Henry A., 1 Batt
Carroll, Peter, K, 48
Carroll, Martin, G, 30
Cassidy, Francis, G, 19
Caulfield, Alfred J., 7 Batt
Chase, Volney P., A, 19
Chase, Wilson, 7 Batt
Cheever, William B., A, 30
Christie, Robert, B, 2
Cobb, Andrew J., D, 33
Connor, Timothy, G, 33
Connor, James, D, 2 H A
Coonery, John, I, 9 Conn
Clark, Francis W., D, 26
Clark, Henry A., C, 24.
Cleaveland, Harmon, 7 Batt
Clements, Abraham, B, 11
Clink, Richard W., Corp., B, 11
Cocklin, John, B, 30
Cole, Albert G., H, 5
Cole, David W., H, 30
Collins, Timothy, B, 19
Comerford, William H., A, 26
Conahy, James, 142 N Y
Conlan, James, G, 32
Conlan, John, G, 32
Conley, James E., 2 H Art
Cook, Barnabas, B, 26
Cook, William P., F, 33
Cooper, George, K, 45

* This list gives the surname and Christian name of the soldier, the letter of his company, and the number of his regiment or battery. When not other wise designated, the organizations belonged to Massachusetts.

Costello, Michael, G, 3 Cav
Coughlin, James, 1st Sergt., D, 16
Cox, Philip, B, 30
Coy, Eliab W., K, 2 H A
Craig, Harrison J., 7 Batt
Crane, Patrick
Creamer, Matthew, I, 3 U S I
Crehore, Charles W., A, 30
Crosby, Frederick A., Corp., C, 30
Cross, Ira M., G, 16
Cross, William B., A, 6 Mass.
Crowley, Bartholomew, G, 19
Cunningham, John, H, 48
Curley, Michael, 15 Batt
Curry, Peter, D, 16
Custy, Michael, I, 16
Cutts, Charles A., D, 6
Daggett, Andrew J., A, 2
Daly, William, 7 Batt
Davenport, Elijah, 7 Batt
Davis, Gustavus J , G, 30
Dean, Cameron, H, 26
Dearden, John, A, 30
Deary, Patrick, B, 11
Deering, William, B, 2
Dempsey, Christopher E., Corp., G, 32
Dempsey, John, I, 16
Devlin, Michael, B, 30
Dohany, Patrick, E, 26
Dolanary, John, F, 30
Donahoe, Cornelius, G, 16
Donovan, John, A, 30
Drach, Emil, K, 31
Dresser, Charles, 2
Duffy, John, 7 Batt
Duffy, Thomas, 6 Batt
Duncan, John H., F, 8 Maine
Durgin, Charles P., G, 8 N H
Durgin, Leavitt C., Sergt., A, 2
Dustin, Eben S., A, 2
Dyar, Looman H., A, 2
Eacott, Henry, G, 19
Eastman, Albert D., 2
Eastman, Daniel E., C, 30
Edds, John H , B or E, 30
Enright, James, 48
Ewan, Thomas K, 48
Ewing, Samuel, F, 33
Ewing, William. H, 30
Farnsworth, David W., C, 30
Farrell, Richard, F, 13 U. S. Infantry
Finton, Peter, I, 9 Conn
Finnegan, William, A, 11
Fisher, George W., B, 30
Fisher, Thomas, D, 59
Fiske, John L., 7 Batt
Fiske, John S., 13
Fleming, James, A, 2
Flood, Thomas, D, 16
Ford, Robert H., A, 26
Foss, John C., E, 2
Foster, Henry C., Sergt., A, 26
Foster, James L., A, 2
Foster, Silas P., A, 2
Foster Willard, A, 2
Fox, George I., C, 6
Frawley, John, G, 33
Freeman, Isaac S. D., F, 16
Frost, John, D, 30
Gale, John A., 33 U. S. Infantry
Gallagher, Edward, H, 48
Gallagher, James, G, 3 Cav
Gallagher, John, D, 16
Galvin, John, G, 16
Gannon, Thomas, B, 1 Cav
Garland, Owen, E, 9
Gardner, George, Jr., D, 6
Garrity, Hugh J., I, 16
Gates, Horatio N., Corp., G, 16
Gay, Edward, F, 13 U. S. Infantry
Gillon, Hugh, B, 11
Gilman, Aaron W., 15 Batt
Gilman, Newall G., A, 2
Gilmore, Isaac E., A, 26
Gilson, Albert, B, 2
Gilson, John, B, 26
Gilson, Warren W., C, 30
Gilpatrick, John, A, 26
Golden, Barney, G, 33
Golden, Dennis, F, 26
Golden, Owen, B, 30
Goodhue, David H., C, 6
Goodhue, John, A, 26
Goodwin, Alonzo, G, 16
Goodwin, Thomas J., A, 26
Gordon, John, 2
Goulding, Owen, D, 16
Granville, John, G, 3 Cav
Gray, Timothy, A, 2
Gray, James, I. 41
Gray, James, A, 3 Cav
Greeley, John E., B, 11
Greenleaf, Ruel W., Corp., C, 30
Griffin, Patrick, 6 Batt
Hall, James N., N Y
Hall, Jeremiah S., Corp., A, 2
Halleran, Michael, H, 26
Hamblett, Alpheus, A, 30
Hamilton Edward, F, 13 U. S. Infantry.
Handly, Frank, E, 26
Harmon, Elbridge, 2
Harriman, Alonzo D., B, 30
Harriman, Charles L., A, 33
Harriman, John, G, 16
Harrington, Daniel, D, 59
Harrington, Daniel, H, 1 U S Art
Haselton, Henry T., A, 2
Haskell, Charles W., 7 Batt
Hassett, Martin, B, 30
Hayes, Patrick, 1 N Y Chasseurs
Heald, Joel M., C, 30
Heath, Martin V. B., C, 30
Herrick, Andrew J., A, 6
Heslan, Bernard, F, 30
Hibbard, Thaddeus A., A, 2
Hilton, Moses M., G, 6
Hodge, John A., G, 59
Hoffron, Michael, I, 59
Hollihan, Patrick, 2 Cav
Holmes, Silas S., Sergt., L, 1 Cav
Honeybun, Thomas, 6 Batt
Hopkinson, Francis, 44

Horn, Charles C., A, 26
Hosmer. Edwin, 59
Hosmer, Nathan D., I, 30
Howard, Edwin F., K, 31
Howard, James, A, 26
Howe, Orin S., G, 16
Hoye, Patrick, A, 2
Hudson, John P., 7 Batt
Hudson, Jonas F., D, 26
Hughes, John, Sergt., I, 16
Huntington, John P., 7 Batt
Huntington, John H., A, 26
Hurd, Frank G., Sergt., G, 26
Hurley, James J., B, 17
Hutchins, Everett E., F, 33
Hutchins, Warren E., 7 Batt
Jacobs, Andrew G., G, 19
James, Edwin S., A, 33
Jeffers, Matthew D., G, 3 Cav
Jones, Charles H., G, 16
Jones, Edward, Corp., G, 16
Jordan, John, H, 26
Judge, James, F, 33
Kain, Edward, D, 16
Kanna, John, G, 16
Kavanagh, James A., G, 16
Kearns, Peter, G, 33
Kearns, Patrick, F, 30
Keefe, John, G, 28
Keenan, John G., 11 U S Infantry
Keith, John H., C, 6
Kelley, Hiram, A, 26
Kelley, Michael, B, 30
Kelley, Thomas, K, 15
Kempton, Frank J., D, 26
Kempton, Orin, Jr., D, 26
Kennedy, John, Sergt., I, 16
Kenney, Charles, Corp., 15 Batt
Kenney, John, Jr., Corp., G, 3 Cav
Kerrigan, Phillip, E, 11 U S I
Keyes, Patrick, 51 N Y
Kirk, James, G, 30
Kittredge, Charles E., I, 2
Kittredge, George H., U S Cav
Knapp, Freeman, Corp., F, 33
Ladd, Luther C., D, 6
Lahiff, Michael, I, 16
Lahiff, Timothy, H, 48
LaMountain, George A., A, 11 U S Infantry
Lamphear, George B., B, 30
Lane, Joseph H., Musician, G, 33
Lapont, Edwin, H, 11
Leeman, William A., F, 7 Conn
Legro, Herman A., D, 6
Linsky, Dennis, E, 28
Livingston, Nelson S., A, 2
Lockling, Leonard A., F, 33
Lockling, Joel M., E, 1 Cav
Lone, Francis, W., I, 30
Louger, John, F, 33
Loughran, Bernard, 3 Cav.
Loverin, Luke W., D, 6
Lynch, William, B, 11
Maguire, Edward, N H
Mahan, Michael, H, 30
Mahoney, Frank, C, 9
Malone, John, E, 4 N H
Manchester, Delos W., H, 26
Manning, John, B, 2
Manuel, William L. G., F, 54
Mansur, James M., Corp., G, 33
Marble, Charles H., A, 26
Marden, James P. P., 2 Cav
Martin, James, B, 30
Martin, Michael, G, 16
Martin, Thomas, 15 Batt
Maskell, Henry H., H, 26
Mathews, Oren E., 7 Batt
Maxwell, Charles L., K, 12
Maxwell, Thomas, G, 30
Maynard, Beriah, F, 5 Vt
Maynard, Dennis, 96 N Y
McAllister, Samuel, G, 16
McAnulty, Thomas, G, 33
McCabe, John T., D, 30
McCabe, Hugh, G, 30
McCahey, Thomas, Scott's 900 Cav
McCanna, John, B, 30
McCarthy, Jeremiah, F, 30
McCarty, John, B, 30
McCormick, Nathaniel, B, 63 N Y
McCorry, Peter, G, 31
McCrea, Terrence, D, 9
McCutcheon, William, C, 30
McDermott, Owen, M, 1 H A
McDonald, Edward, G, 30
McDonald, Hugh, 7 Batt
McDonald, James, 15 Batt
McElliott, Michael, 64 Ill
McEvoy, Joseph, Corp., I, 16
McGinley, John, G, 16
McGoon, John B., A, 33
McGuire, Hugh, F, 30
McKenzie, Angus C., Corp., F, 33
McKernan, John, B, 30
McKinley, Robert, H, 30
McKissock, Robert, Jr., 4 N H
McLaughlin, Edward
McLaughlin, William, A, 1 H Art
McMahon, Patrick, D, 16
McManus, John, F, 30
McMorrow, John, G, 19
McNabb, John, B, 30
McNamara, Peter, F, 9
McNulty, Neal, H, 30
McNulty, Thomas, G, 33
McQuaid, Thomas, G, 16
Mercer, James P., A, 32
Merrill, Benjamin, F, 33
Miles, Newell W., D, 11 U S I
Milnor Thomas R., 39
Mitchell, James F, 11 U S Infantry
Molloy, Pat, A, 11
Monahan, James, D, 16
Montague, Thomas, D, 16
Moody, Edwin A., Corp., C,
Moore, Ira W., Serg., B, 30 24
Moran, Hugh D., 16
Moran, James, E, 30
Moran, John, F, 30
Morgan, Henry, 7 Batt
Mulcahy, William, G, 16
Mullen, James, B, 30

Mullen, Michael J., A, 30
Mulligan, Charles, Serg., G, 3 Cav
Murphy, Dennis, 3 U S Art
Murphy, John, A, 11 U S I
Murtagh, James, F, 30
Murtle, John, L, 1 H A
Nason, Royal T., A, 26
Nelson, Andrew, A, 2
Nelson, Robert, G, 16
Nelson, Samuel, G, 16
Newman, Charles H., C, 2
Noonan, Michael, E, 26
Norris, William, C, 3 Vt
Norton, Bradford S., Sergt., A, 26
Nudd, John H., H, 4 N H
Nutter, Luther P., A, 2
Oakes, James, B, 2
Oates, Andrew, F, 30
O'Brien, James, I, 26
O'Brien, John J., B, 29
O'Connell, James, G, 19
O'Conners, Timothy, V R C
O'Grady, Michael, F, 19
O'Grady, Thomas, G, 16
O'Donnell, John, D, 14 U S I
O'Hare, Charles M., 1st Serg., G, 16
O'Neil, Dennis, F, 30
O'Neil, John, G, 16
Ordway, John H., D, 11 N H
O'Reiley, Patrick, A, 30
O'Rourke, Patrick, H, 30
Page, Lorenzo F., D, 26
Page, Lucius, Corp., A, 2
Page, Rinaldo, 7 Batt
Paine, William W., Serg., G, 33
Palmer, William, F., C, 2 H A
Park, Orin R., Corp., A, 6
Parmalee, Alfred S., Corp., C, 30
Peabody, Hiram, C, 30
Pearson, Edwin P., C, 1 H A
Penn, Charles H., Corp., E, 11
Peterson, William, 48 Pa
Pettes, Andrew J., Sergt., D, 59
Phelps, Elias A., G, 19
Philbrick, Charles W., B, 2 N H
Pike, Charles O., B, 30
Pike, Dominicus S., E, 30
Plimpton, Samuel, E, 30
Plumado, Oliver, 2 Cav
Pollock, Thomas C., N Y S M
Polson, Frank B., D, 17
Pomfret, Michael, B, 30
Prescott, Evander A., 15 Batt
Proctor, Alvin L., G, 16
Prouty, Sidney S., A, 2
Purcell, John, K, 67 N Y
Putnam, Alonzo, 15 Batt
Quinn, Patrick, A, 30
Rafferty, John, B, 2 H Art
Ramsey, Nehemiah S., C, 30
Randall, George P., E, 30
Ray, Norman J., A, 33
Read, John H., Musician, C, 16
Ready, John C., A, 1
Reed, George E., C, 30
Reilly, Patrick, K, 1 N Y
Reynolds, John, A, 26
Reynolds, Michael, H, 26
Reynolds, Patrick, D, 16
Richardson, Luther L., A, 26
Richardson, Hudson M., 7 Batt
Riley, Patrick, G, 56
Riley, Patrick, K, 69 N Y
Ritchie, Robert, H, 2 Del
Rourke, Dennis, E, 9
Rushworth, John B., F, 33
Russell, Albert M., E, 22
Ryerson, Horace, A, 2
Sanborn, Levi C., C, 2
Sargent, Charles D., D, 26
Sawtell, Luther, Jr., I, 26
Sawyer, Bernard H., A, 26
Scannell, Ambrose P., I, 1 N H Cav
Scully, John, Wagoner, A, 29
Scully, John, F, 30
Searles, Henry D., A, 26
Shannon, Charles, F, 30
Shaughnessey, James, F, 30
Shaw, Chase S., Sergt., A, 26
Shea, John, G, 19
Sheppard, James W., B, 29
Sherwell, Walter, F, 33
Short, William, A, 10
Simons, Timothy, C, 12
Sleeper, George, Corp., G, 16
Smith, Charles D., E, 9
Smith, Edward, I, 30
Smith, Henry L., C, 30
Smith, John, D, 59
Smith, William B., C, 30
Smith, William F., A, 33
Smith, Michael, B, 30
Smith, Peter, E, 30
Smithson, George, A, 9 Vt
Snell, David, D, 26
Spalding, E. O., A, 2.
Spaulding, George W., 7 Batt
Spaulding, Oscar A., A, 2
Stanford, Freeman S., B, 6 Vt
Stephens, Alexander, B, 2
Stephens, John, B. 2
Stevens, Warren H., U S Sharpsh'ters
Stevenson, Cushman S., B, 2 Cav
Stewart, William, I, 16
Stickney, Henry, G, 33
Strong, Martin V. B., 1 Sharpshooters
Sullivan, Eugene, B, 30
Sullivan, Jeremiah, 4 U S Batt
Sutherland, George, C, 30
Swain, George W., Corp., C, 6
Taylor, John, Z., F, 17
Tenney, John, F, 30
Tetreau, Jeremiah, F, 33
Thissell, Joseph W., G, 33
Thomas, Richard E., Corp., A, 26
Thompson, Lafayette F., Hospt. Stew.
Thompson, James, G., A, 26
Thompson, John, F, 13 U S Infantry
Thompson, Richard A., A, 30
Thompson, William, D, 26
Thurston, Anson G., C, 6
Tighe, James
Tighe, Matthew, I. 19
Tighe, Patrick, Corp., F, 30
Tilton, James G., H, 48

Tracy, Thomas, K, 20
Trull, Zenas B., 2 Sharpshooters
Tully, James, M, 1 H A
Tye, Henry, K, 2
Unsworth, Richard, 26
Waddle, James, G, 16
Wallace, John A., B, 2
Ward, James F., F, 58
Webster, William M., B, 30
Wedgewood, Edwin S., A, 26
Welden, Thomas, D, 16
Whalan, Philip, D, 59
Wheat, Josiah C., A, 26
Wheeler, John P., 7 Batt
Whipple, Calvin, 1 Batt H A
Whipple, Woodman, D, 3 Vt
Whitcomb, Valentine, A, 30
White, Harvey, C, 74 Ohio
Whitney, Addison O., D, 6
Whitney, James M., 1 H A
Whitten, Eben B., Sergt., A, 2
Whittier, Ruel, Corp., B, 2
Williams, Anson W., 3 Cav
Wilson, Joseph H., A, 26
Wilson, Lafayette, A, 33
Winsor, George W., 4 Batt
Withee, Thompson H., A, 26
Woods, John, I, 16
Woodward, George E., D, 26
Worth, Charles H., B, 2 N H
Wright, Lewis C., A, 2
Wright, Charles H., 11 Ohio
Young, Albert C., H, 26
Young, James, F, 30

CORRECTIONS.

The chapter of Manufacturing History was sent to press before J. H. Sawyer had succeeded George Motley as Agent of the Appleton Company's Mills.

The chapter of Church History was printed before the ordination of Rev. F. R. Morse as pastor of the Worthen Street Baptist Church, and before the author had seen Dorchester's History of St. Paul's Church, which contains many interesting details touching the growth of Methodism here.

On page 35, for "President," read "a member."
" " 35, for "presided at," read "participated in."
" " 89, for "Lambert," read "Lambord."
" " 124, for "A. B. Farr," read "Asa W. Farr."
" " 223, to the necrological record, add "March 3, Henry M. Hooke, 53, Physician."

www.ingramcontent.com/pod-product-compliance
Lightning Source LLC
LaVergne TN
LVHW020057110826
845151LV00005B/1498

* 9 7 8 1 4 2 5 5 2 2 0 1 8 *